John Stuart

The Book of Deer

John Stuart

The Book of Deer

ISBN/EAN: 9783743407619

Manufactured in Europe, USA, Canada, Australia, Japa

Cover: Foto ©ninafisch / pixelio.de

Manufactured and distributed by brebook publishing software (www.brebook.com)

John Stuart

The Book of Deer

THE BOOK OF DEER

Edited for the Spalding Club

By JOHN STUART, LL.D., Secretary

EDINBURGH

PRINTED FOR THE CLUB BY ROBERT CLARK

MDCCCLXIX

The Spalding Club.

DECEMBER MDCCCLXIX.

President.

THE DUKE OF RICHMOND.

Vice-Presidents.

THE EARL OF KINTORE.
THE EARL OF SEAFIELD.
THE EARL OF ABERDEEN.
THE LORD LINDSAY
THE LORD SALTOUN.

The Council.

John Angus, City Clerk, Aberdeen.
Sir James H. Burnett, Baronet.
John Hill Burton, LL.D., Advocate, Edinburgh.
Charles Chalmers of Monkshill.
James T. Gibson-Craig, W.S.
Archibald Davidson, Sheriff of Midlothian.
Charles Elphinstone Dalrymple of Kinellar Lodge.
M. E. Grant Duff of Eden, M.P.
The Right Rev. A. Penrose Forbes, D.C.L., Dundee.
Sir James D. H. Elphinstone, Baronet.
The Earl of Errol.
A. W. Franks, British Museum.
James Giles, R.S.A., Aberdeen.
William Cosmo Gordon of Fyvie.
George Grub, LL.D., Advocate, Aberdeen.
Cosmo Innes, Advocate, Edinburgh.
Alex. F. Irvine of Drum.
The Right Rev. James Kyle, D.D., Preshome [deceased].
D. Laing, Esq., LL.D., Signet Library.
Alexander Morrison of Bognie.
Colonel Forbes Leslie of Rothie.
Wm. Leslie of Warthill.
Cluny Macpherson of Cluny.
Lord Neaves.
John Ramsay of Barra.
Professor Scott, Aberdeen University.
Professor Sir J. Y. Simpson, Bart., Edinburgh.
The Earl of Southesk.
The Rev. Alex. Taylor, D.D., Leochel-Cushnie.
George Tulloch, LL.D., Aberdeen.
John Webster, Advocate, Aberdeen.

Secretary.

JOHN STUART, LL.D., General Register House, Edinburgh.

Treasurer.

JOHN LIGERTWOOD, Advocate, Aberdeen.

TABLE OF CONTENTS.

PLATES IN THE BOOK OF DEER.

The Plates are numbered in the order of their occurrence in the Manuscript, but a few of them are arranged to suit the letterpress.

Preface.

I.

INTRODUCTORY—MONASTERIES OF ST. COLUMBA—ONE OF THEM AT DEER—CHURCHES FOUNDED BY NATIVE SAINTS—ST. FERGUS, ST. DROSTAN—THE BOOK OF DEER: ITS HISTORICAL VALUE—THE LATER CISTERCIAN ABBEY OF DEER.

AMID the darkness which enshrouds those missionaries who imparted to the heathen tribes of Alba the blessings of the Christian faith, the form of St. Columba stands out with exceptional clearness of outline; and the popular instinct has not erred which ascribes to him the largest share in the great work, and traces to his mission the most enduring results.

The almost contemporary pages of his biographer, St. Adamnan, enable us to realise to ourselves the system adopted by the great missionary in his enterprise. When he first took possession for Christ of the little island of Hy, which, under the name of Iona, was to become illustrious for all time from its association with him, he founded upon it a monastery, in conformity with the system which then prevailed, not only in the country of the Scots from which he came, but throughout Europe.

Every fresh settlement which the saint effected as he pushed his Christian conquests, whether in the islands of the Hebrides or in the mainland country of the northern Picts, consisted of a monastery for a body of clerics, from which they might disperse themselves in circuits among the surrounding tribes, returning to their home for shelter and mutual support.[1]

One of these monastic settlements was that of Deer, in Buchan, a district of Aberdeenshire, which, projecting into the German Ocean, forms the most easterly point of Scotland ; and the legend in the Book of the Gospels of this house preserves in traditional detail the circumstances which marked the infancy of the establishment.

It represents the arrival at Aberdour, a sheltered bay on the rocky shores of Buchan, of St. Columba, accompanied by his pupil Drostan ; but we are left to conjecture whether the strangers arrived by sea in one of the frail coracles so much in use with the saint and his followers, or were on a landward circuit through the northern districts.

The mormaer or ruler of the district of Buchan, who seems to have been on the spot, made an offering to the clerics of the "city" of Aberdour with freedom from mormaer and toisech.

There are reasons for believing that a considerable population was gathered in the country around the rocky coast of Aberdour[2]

[1] The same course was followed in the Northumbrian monasteries. Of St. Cuthbert we are told that, leaving Mailros, he would spend sometimes several weeks together among the people settled in the glens and hillsides of the Cheviots and the Lammermoor, returning afterwards to his monastery for repose and the refreshment of society, as the bird to the ark ; and of St. Aidan's wanderings we also hear in the pages of Venerable Bede (B. iii. c. 17), who elsewhere describes the practice of the time, "Erat quippe moris eo tempore populis Anglorum, ut veniente in villam clerico vel presbytero cuncti ad ejus imperium verbum audituri confluerunt."—(B. iv. cap. 27.)

[2] In the country, about a mile inland from the bay, numerous hut-foundations have been discovered, some of them under a great depth of moss. In some parts of the moss, trees and roots have frequently been turned up, apparently the remains of an early forest. Similar hut-foundations have been found along the coast in the country southwards.

and the red Dun[1] which overlooked its southern side; and as we are frequently able to trace the progress of the Roman armies through places of dense population, where their "ways" were led amid the raths and abodes of the Britons, so we may infer from the numerous churches dedicated to Celtic saints, throughout Scotland,[2] in sites of early settlement, that the missionaries

[1] The colour of the rocks at Dundarg is of a dark red, and the neck of the Dun was cut off from the land by transverse earthworks, of which portions still remain.

[2] Of these there are two classes—first, the churches actually founded by the saints themselves in the course of their missions; and next, the foundations of later date dedicated to the memory of the saints by their spiritual successors. The names of St. Ninian, St. Kentigern, and St. Columba, were held in reverence throughout the kingdom, and churches were dedicated to them in all parts of Scotland. In other cases, the dedications are more restricted in their range, and suggest their origin in the circuit of the patron saint himself.

Of this character are the churches dedicated to St. Fergus, which seem all traceable as original foundations by himself in the course of his labours, as they are related in the Breviary of Aberdeen (Part. Estiv. fol. clxii.) According to this authority, St. Fergus, after having performed the office of a bishop for many years in Ireland, came on a mission to the western parts of Scotland, in company with a body of presbyters or clerics. Arriving in the neighbourhood of Strogeath, he and his friends settled there for a time, leading a somewhat solitary life; but seeing the country good and suitable for settlement, St. Fergus put his hands to the work, and erected three churches. From thence he pursued his course to Caithness, where he preached to the rude people of the country, and drew them to the faith, not more by the truth of his doctrine than by the greatness of his virtues. Again, leaving Caithness he arrived in Buchan, in the place which came commonly to be called Lungley, and where the church which he built is dedicated to his memory. Forsaking Buchan for the country of Angus, he settled at Glammis, where he erected fresh *cenobia* to God, choosing this as the place of his rest. Here accordingly he died, and here, after his death, many miracles were wrought by his relics. So great were these, that in course of time an abbot of Scone, with much devotion, removed his head from his tomb, and placed it in his own monastery at Scone, where, in like manner, miracles were wrought through the merits of St. Fergus.

This is the legendary account of the saint, and many circumstances concur to prove its substantial accuracy.

were attracted in their Christian warfare to these by the denseness of the neighbouring population. St. Columba, on his first mission to Pictland, sought out at once the royal seat of Brude, near Inverness, and he may have been led to the verge of Buchan by the presence of the chief and his followers at one of his residences.

It is probable that the clerics tarried at Aberdour for a time, and founded a monastery on the land which had been granted to them.

In later times the parish church of Aberdour was dedicated to St. Drostan.[1] It was placed by the brink of a gorge, on a ledge or table-land overlooking the burn of the Dour, at a spot about 150

Beginning with his first supposed settlement, we find that the three neighbouring churches of Strogeath, Blackford, and Dolpatrick, in Perthshire, were all dedicated to St. Patrick, according well with the idea that the founder was a missionary fresh from the influence of the Irish church.

The church of Wick in Caithness was dedicated to St. Fergus himself—a fact which may be held to support the legendary statement of his visit to that country.

The parish church of Lungley, or, as it has long been called, St. Fergus, is dedicated to him, and preserves the memory of his labours in Buchan, while the parish of Glammis, where he finished his course, also owns him as its patron saint. Here his memory is associated with a holy well, which still freshens the glen in which the hermitage of the saint is said to have been placed.

And, finally, the alleged removal of the saint's head to Scone may be held to be established by the following entry in the accounts of the Lord High Treasurer of Scotland, recording one of the many like offerings made by King James IV. at the shrines of saints :

xi October 1503. To the kingis offerand to Sanct Fergus heide in Scone xiiii. s.

[1] According to the legend of St. Drostan in the Breviary of Aberdeen, he was descended of the royal family of the Scots. His parents, in consequence of his devotion to religion, sent him to his uncle, St. Columba, in Ireland, to be perfected in his studies. Afterwards he became a monk at Dalquhongale or Holywood, of which place he came to be abbot. Desirous of a stricter life, he retired to Glenesk, in Angus, where he led an eremitical life, and founded a church or monastery by the side of lonely Lochlee, where his memory still survives in such names as "Droustie's Well" and "Droustie's Meadow," after all other trace of his foundation has long vanished.—(Land of the Lindsays, p. 61.)

The parish of Edzell, in Glenesk, is said to be dedicated to St. Drostan. The parish

yards distant from the shore of the Moray Firth. In the beginning of the sixteenth century, the bones of the saint were here preserved in a stone chest, and many cures were effected by means of them.[1] In the face of the rock, near where the stream falls into the sea, is a clear and powerful spring of water, known as St. Drostan's Well.

The legend states that thereafter they came to another of the mormaer's "cities," which being pleasing to Columcille, as full of God's grace, he asked it in gift. This the ruler declined. Thereafter his son became sick, and was all but dead, when the mormaer besought the prayers of the clerics for his recovery, and gave them an offering of the "town" which he had formerly refused. They complied with his request, and their prayers were heard in the recovery of the son.

On the land thus granted the clerics founded a monastery, which came to be known as that of Deer.

But this having been done, the island saint must hasten to other districts to diffuse the precious seed entrusted to him, and establish other colonies of missionaries. Before doing so, however, he transferred to Drostan all his authority over the newly-founded church: in the words of the legend, "After that, Columcille gave to Drostan that town, and blessed it, and left as his word, that 'whosoever should come against it, let him not be many-yeared

of Skir-durstan, on the banks of the Spey (now united to Aberlour), had St. Drostan for its patron. He was also patron of the parish of Alvie, higher up the river; and a chapel at Dunaughton, in that parish, was dedicated to him.—(A Survey of the Province of Moray, pp. 261, 286; Elgin, 1798. Shaw's Hist. of the Province of Moray, p. 371; Elgin, 1827.) The churches of Insch in the Garioch, and of Rothiemay on the Deveron, belonged to St. Drostan, besides those of Deer and Aberdour. In Caithness his name was had in reverence, as we find a church dedicated to him in the parish of Halkirk, and Cannisbay was also one of his churches.—(Origines Parochiales Scotiæ, vol. ii. pp. 758, 792.)

[1] Breviar. Aberd. Part. Hyemal. fol. xx

[or] victorious.' Drostan's tears came on parting with Columcille. Said Columcille, Let Dear be its name henceforward."[1]

This "town" was about twelve miles inland from the first settlement of the clerics at Aberdour. It was placed on the fertile banks of the river Ugie, sheltered by wooded heights, on one of which it is probable that another rath of the mormaer was placed;[2] while the district seems to have been the seat of an abundant population, of which many traces yet remain.

The Book of Deer is a memorial of the monastery thus founded by St. Columba and his disciple. It contains the Gospel of St. John complete, and portions of the other three Evangelists, in writing probably of the ninth century, besides a collection of Memoranda of grants by the Celtic chiefs of Buchan, written in Gaelic at a later time.

In subsequent chapters of the Preface translations of the latter will be found, together with notices of the condition and polity of Celtic Scotland, designed to illustrate the bearings of the Book of Deer on an early and obscure period of our national history. I need, therefore, only here advert to the great interest and value of these *memoranda*. On various points connected with our early history, regarding which the historical student has hitherto had to grope his way, amid faint

[1] As to the name of Deer, see p. xlviii. *post*. The spelling of the word has varied at different times. In its first form it is Déar, "tear," in harmony with the traditional belief of its origin. In the charter of David I. it is Dér. It afterwards appears as Deir, Dere, and Deer. The last has been the ordinary spelling for a long time, and I have retained it, in the belief that, as the word is commonly pronounced, this is nearest to the earliest form of it.

[2] On the hill of Biffie (the Bidben of the grants), and on the opposite hill of Bruxie (of old Altrie—the Alterin of the records), circular foundations are still traceable, and others have been obliterated in recent times. In the district there was formerly a great number of stone circles; and many cists, flint weapons, and other indications of early settlement, have at various times been discovered within its bounds.

light and doubtful analogies, these entries supply new and solid standing-ground. They enable us to discover the condition of the Celtic population of Alba, separated into clans, under the rule of the mormaer, with their chiefs or toisechs, and their brehons or judges.

We discover the division of the country into town-lands, with fixed boundaries, and can trace the different and co-existing rights in them of the ardrigh, the mormaer, and the toisech. We are likewise furnished with notices of various kinds of burdens[1] to which they were subject.

The period embraced in these entries is towards the conclusion of the Celtic period, while the patriarchal polity had not yet given way to the feudal kingdom; the monastic system—at least in the northern districts—was yet flourishing, and the parish and territorial diocese were unknown.

Of what great interest is it, then, to have preserved to us in the Gaelic notices of the Book of Deer such authentic glimpses of the departing economy, which they enable us to understand, while they at the same time throw light on the origin of some of the institutions which superseded it!

I have attempted to sketch the progress of events which, shortly after the period of these memoranda, led to the development of the monastic into the parochial system, and to the substitution of the church of the parish, in the room, and often on the site of, the earlier church of the monastery (chapter v. p. cvii.)

At an early period, the possessions of some of the chief monas-

[1] The amount of some of these was determined by the number of davochs comprised in the territory, affording the earliest instance in our records of a system, which at a later period formed the basis for apportioning the national taxes.

teries in Alba—foundations of Culdees, such as St. Andrews, Dunkeld, and Abernethy—had been secularised, and when our earliest records enable us to understand their position, they appear in the hands of laymen.

It was not so in the case of Deer, the clerics of which, down to the middle of the twelfth century, were still receiving, from the bounty of the Gaelic chiefs of the district, additions to their monastic inheritance, in the whole of which they were secured by King David I., with full immunity from all secular exactions. It is plain, however, from the terms of the royal charter, that attempts had been made to "enslave" the monks, probably in the same way as the chiefs of Ireland usurped the rights of the monasteries of that country, and that they were able to maintain their "freedom" in virtue of the grants recorded in their "Book," being the venerable volume now printed for the Members of the Spalding Club.

There seems little reason indeed to doubt that we may trace the occurrence of these memoranda to the attempts made by laymen to usurp the property of the clerics, and to the changed circumstances which demanded *written* evidence to maintain them in possession.[1]

But this was only for a time. The parochial arrangements which had been spreading in the southern parts of the kingdom, very soon after came to supersede in the north as well, the earlier condition of things. One result of the change was the conversion of the churches of the smaller monasteries into parish churches.

[1] The forged charters, which are of such frequent occurrence among the records of religious houses, seem to have been in many cases attempts to give a legal form to grants which had originally been made by unwritten symbolical gift; and in others to replace some written grant which had been lost.

The monastery of Mortlach, a house of early foundation, with its dependent monastery of Cloveth or Clova,[1] continued to flourish till the time of David I., when both re-appear in record as churches of districts.

The monastery of St. Congan at Turreff became the church of the parish of that name,[2] and the House of St. Drostan at Deer now disappeared in like manner in the parochial arrangement of the country; while in both cases the lands of these monasteries seem to have been resumed by the Earls of Buchan, the representatives of the earlier mormaers.

If, however, the monastic possessions of Deer and Turreff fell into the hands of the Lords of Buchan, it is certain that they were not long retained by them, and (in the expressive language of an early Irish record) that they did not continue "dead" in their hands.[3]

[1] Mortlach was probably founded by St. Moloc or Mo-luag, to whom the church was dedicated. This saint, according to our early writers, was the pupil of St. Brandan. He was the founder and patron of Lismore in Argyll, a country throughout which he laboured, as well as in that of Mar. Becoming associated with St. Boniface, he shared the labours of that saint in the northern regions, and dying in extreme age was buried in the church of St. Boniface at Rosmarkie. It is probable that Mortlach was one of the "chief" monasteries of Alba, while Cloveth was one of secondary importance and subject to Mortlach (*post*, pp. xxvii. lxxvii.) There may yet be seen the remains of a ruined church at Cloveth (now Clova), and close to it a well called in the district *Simmerluak* (St. Moluak), a name which preserves the connection of Cloveth with the mother church of Mortlach.—(Breviar. Aberd. Part. Estiv. fol. vi. Boece, Scotor. Hist. fol. clxxviii. ed. 1526.)

[2] For the history of the Celtic monastery at Turreff, see p. cxxiv.

[3] In an account of the officers of the Kings of Connaught, translated from the Irish by Dr. O'Donovan, it is stated, "Forty-eight town-lands constituted the patrimony of his four royal chiefs—namely, O'Flanagan, O'Maelbreanainn, Mac-Oireachty, and O'Feenaghty, together *with all dead church-lands*, which are described as "lands taken

At the period of King David's confirmation to the clerics of Deer (p. 95) of their rights and immunities, Colban was the mormaer, through his marriage with Eva, the daughter and heiress of Gartnat, the former mormaer.

Their grandson Fergus, who came to be styled *Earl* of Buchan, left a daughter, Marjory, who by marriage with William Cumyn carried the earldom to him.[1]

In the year 1219, William, Earl of Buchan, founded the Cistercian Abbey of Deer at a spot about two miles westward of the church of the parish which came in place of St. Drostan's monastery.[2]

at an early period from the church by the oppressive conduct of the laity, and not claimed by the church afterwards.—(Trans. Kilkenny Arch. Soc. vol. ii. p. 346.)

[1] Both Colban and Fergus had natural sons, who witness charters of William Cumyn in favour of the house of Deer. They are styled "Magnus, son of Earl Colban," and "Adam, son of Fergus, Earl." An earlier Adam appears as a witness to a charter of Earl Fergus, where he is designated "frater comitis."—(Illustrations of the Antiquities of the Shires of Aberdeen and Banff, vol. ii. pp. 427-8. Collections on the Antiquities of these Shires, vol. i. p. 406.)

[2] The site of the parish church, and, as I believe, of the Celtic monastery, resembles that selected for other early religious establishments in Scotland. It was erected on a knoll or rising ground called Tap Tillery, on the bank of the Ugie, the waters of which almost surround it. The ancient church of St. Boniface at Invergowrie was built on a spot on the north bank of the Tay, almost insulated by the river. The early foundation of St. Fechin, at St. Vigeans, near Arbroath, occupies the top of a steep hillock rising from the banks of the Brothock, and at all these early churches have been found sculptured stones of the class peculiar to the Pictish Country. An early description of the parish of Deer preserves the following tradition connected with the building of the old church of the parish:—"The founders, intending to build the church on a neighbouring hill called Biffie, south-west of Deer about a quarter of a mile, as they were digging for a foundation, heard a voice saying,

It is not here
Ye'll big the kirk of Deer,
But on Top Tillery
Where mony corps man lye."

—(Collections, *ut supra*, p. 401.)

Of the foundation-charter no trace has been discovered, but it seems to have conveyed, among other possessions, the church of the parish of Deer, with the lands which had been the property of St. Drostan's monastery; and we can recognise in the rentals of the new foundation, down to its dissolution in the sixteenth century, some of the town-lands which had been granted by the Gaelic mormaers and toisechs.[1]

The munificent spirit of the founder led him to add to his first gift the lands of Barry in Strathisla, and Fochyl on the Ythan, and it manifested itself in his grandson, the last earl of his race, who bestowed on them the church of Kynedwart.

Under these circumstances, the change from the primitive monastic system to the parochial one, was beneficial in every point of view. The place of the clan-monastery was now occupied by the *church of the district*, endowed with ample tithes, while in its neighbourhood arose the stately Cistercian abbey, enriched with the same lands which had been dedicated to a religious use in earlier times.

It is not necessary for our purpose to follow in detail the history of the later monastery, but it may be permitted to notice the less propitious and curiously different circumstances attending its concluding days, when a second ecclesiastical change occurred.

The turn of affairs which set King Robert Bruce on the throne of the Scots, was fatal to the fortunes of the Cumyns, who, having espoused the opposite side, were so utterly overthrown that, according to a chronicle of the time,[2] of a name which numbered at one

[1] See Celtic Entries in Book of Deer, *post*, p. xvii.

[2] Extracta e variis Cronicis Scocie, p. 103.

time the three Earls of Buchan, Marr, and Menteith, and more than thirty belted knights, there remained no memorial in the land save the orisons of the monks of Deer.

Sir Robert de Keith, the great Marischal of Scotland, espoused the fortunes of Bruce, and, among other rewards of his faithful service, he received a grant from that monarch of the pleasant lands of Alden on the banks of the Ugie, which adjoined the townland granted to St. Drostan's house by the toisech of Clan Canan (p. xxvii.)

From that time the strength of the house of Marischal in the province of Buchan, especially by intermarriage with one of the two co-heiresses of the powerful house of Inverugie, continued to increase.

In the year 1543, Robert Keith, a brother of the fourth Earl Marischal, was appointed Abbot of Deer on the presentation of the Queen Dowager. He died while yet a youth, in the year 1551, and to him succeeded Robert Keith, a son of the Earl, when only fifteen years old.

As Commendator of Deer, he signed a charter, dated at Paris in 1556, confirming one by his father of the lands of Auchrady. These lands were held of the Abbey of Deer, and one of the conditions of the feu-right granted by the abbot was, that the vassals should strive to maintain "orthodoxam seu catholicam fidem."[1]

In 1560, as "now Abbot and Commendator" of Deer, he granted to William, Earl Marischal, his father, a tack of the teind-sheaves of many lands in the parishes of Deer, Peterugy, and Foveran.[2]

[1] Antiquities of the Shires of Aberdeen and Banff, vol. iv. p. 31.

[2] Note from the original in the possession of Patrick Rose, Esq., late sheriff-clerk of Banff.

In 1587, as Abbot and Commendator of the Abbey of Deer, he granted a procuratory for resigning the whole lands, tithes, and other property of the abbey into the king's hands, to be erected into a temporal lordship, to be called the lordship of Altrie, in favour of himself for his lifetime, and after his death to George, Earl Marischal, and his heirs-male and assigns.

In this deed[1] the Abbot states, by way of preamble, "that the monasticall superstitionn for the quhilk the said Abbay of Deer was of auld erectit and foundit is now be the lawis of this realme all uterlie abolischit sua that na memorie thereof sal be heireftir, and considering that the maist pairt of the lands and rentis doittit to the said Abbay proceidit of auld from the dispositioun of the progenitors and predicessors of the richt nobill and potent Lord George, erle Merschell, and that the propertie of the maist pairt thairof is alreddie sett in few ferme to the said erle and his predicessouris."

It appears that the wife of the Earl Marischal entertained scruples about thus interfering with property which had been dedicated to the church, and she dissuaded her husband from the possession of it, but in vain, on which she had a vision of the consequent ruin of the house.[2] The circumstances are thus related by a quaint writer of the seventeenth century :—

[1] Antiquities of the Shires of Aberdeen and Banff, vol. ii. p. 437.

[2] The Commendator seems to have been a lukewarm reformer at first. In 1569 he preferred a request to the General Assembly that he might be relieved from certain payments due by him to the preachers at the Abbey's Churches, to which he got for answer that "the kirk can in no wise demitt the thing that pertains to the poor ministers," especially to such a one as "my lord of Deir who debursed his money to the enemies of God to prosecute his servants and banish them out of the realme."—(The Booke of the Universall Kirk of Scotland, vol. i. pp. 153, 156. Ban. Club ed.)

"This Earle George his first wyfe, dochter to the lord Hom, and grandmother to this present Earle, being a woman both of a high spirit and of a tender conscience, forbids her husband to leave such a consuming moth in his house as was the sacraledgeous medling with the Abisie of Deir. But fourtein scoir chalderes of meill and beir was a sore tentatione; and he could not weel indure the randering back of such a morsell. Upon his absolut refusall of her demand, she had this vission—The night following, in her sleepe, she saw a great number of religious men in their habit, cum forth of that Abbey to the stronge Craige of Dunnoture, which is the principall residence of that familie. She saw them also sett themselves round about the rock, to gett it down and demolishe it, having no instruments, nor toilles, wherewith to perform this work, but only penknyves; wherwith they follishly (as it seemed to her) began to pyk at the Craige. She smyled to sie them intend so frutles ane interpryse; and went to call her husband to scuffe and geyre them out of it. When she had fund him, and brought him to sie these sillie religious monckes at ther foolishe work, behold! the wholl Craige, with all his strong and statly buildings, was by ther pynknyves wndermynded and fallen in the sea, so as ther remained nothing but the wrack of ther riche furniture and stufe flotting on the waves of a raging and tempestuous sea. Som of the wyser sort, divining upon this vission, attrebute to the penknyves the lenth of time befor this should com to pass; and it hath bein observed, by sundrie, that the Earles of that house, befor, wer the richest in the kingdom, having treasure in store besyd them; but ever since the addittion of this so great revenue, they have losed ther stock by heavie burdeines of debt and ingagment."[1]

[1] A short abridgment of Britanes Distemper from the year of God MDCXXXIX

The writer who records this "relacioun of a wonderful vision" did not live to see the events which in the next century ended in the total overthrow of the house, and which he would doubtless have regarded in the light of its literal fulfilment.

An eloquent writer of our own day takes this view, and traces in the destruction of the family, the fulfilment of the saying of St. Columcille, who, when he blessed his infant foundation, left as his word that "Whosoever should come against it should not be many yeared [or] victorious."[1]

to MDCXLIX, p. 113, by Patrick Gordon of Ruthven. Printed for the Spalding Club.

[1] Les Moines d'Occident, par le Comte de Montalembert, Tome Troisième, p. 191. Troisième edition, Paris, 1868.

II.

The Book of Deer.

(1.) The Manuscript.

ITS HISTORY—STYLE OF THE HANDWRITING AND ILLUMINATIONS—WHETHER OF IRISH OR PICTISH EXECUTION—CHARACTERISTICS OF THE MANUSCRIPT.

The remarks on the volume naturally arrange themselves under two heads—first, the history and character of the manuscript; and secondly, the version of the Gospels.

As to the book itself, while its early connection with the Columbian monastery of Deer is unquestionable, we are entirely ignorant of its subsequent history till the end of the seventeenth century. For the following facts illustrative of its later existence I am indebted to Mr. Bradshaw. "In 1697 the Book of Deer formed part of the collection of MSS. of John Moore, then Bishop of Norwich. It came into the possession of the University of Cambridge in 1715, forming part of the library of Moore, Bishop successively of Norwich and Ely, who died in 1714, and whose library was bought (it is believed at the suggestion of Lord Townshend) by King George I. for a sum of six thousand guineas, and presented to the University." It remained there unnoticed till Mr. Bradshaw's research made its real character to be known.

The volume (numbered I. i. b. 32.) is of a small but rather wide 8vo form of eighty-six folios. It contains the Gospel of St. John, and portions of the other three Gospels; the fragment of an office for the Visitation of the sick, the Apostles' Creed; and a charter of King David I. to the clerics of Deer. The notices in Gaelic of grants made to the monastery of Deer are written on blank pages or on the margins.

A reference to the plates of facsimiles will show that the text of the Gospels is written in a character different from and older than that of the Celtic entries.

A comparison of the handwriting used in various early codices of the Gospels has led Professor Westwood to conclude that the date of the Deer Gospels may be ascribed to the ninth century, and I see no reason against accepting this conclusion.

The form of the letters in the Gospels is that which was common to the Irish and Anglo-Saxon schools, being the debased Roman minuscule, and, according to Mr. Westwood, "not very unlike the Bodleian Cædmon."[1]

The style of ornament of the illuminations is similar to that used in many of the early Irish Books of the Gospels, as in the illuminated figures of the four Evangelists in the Book of Dimma (MS. in the Library of Trinity College, Dublin); of St. Mark and St. Luke in the Book of Durrow (MS. in the same collection); and of St. Matthew and St. Luke in the Gospels of Mac Durnan (MS. in the Archiepiscopal Library at Lambeth);[2]—all of which are of a date prior to the ninth century, the Book of Durrow being traditionally ascribed to the penmanship of St. Columba.[3]

[1] Facsimiles of the Miniatures and Ornaments of Anglo-Saxon and Irish Manuscripts, p. 89; Lond. 1868.

[2] Drawings of the last are given in Mr. Westwood's great work just quoted, Plate xxii., and in the "Sculptured Stones of Scotland," vol. ii. Plate iv. of "Illustrations."

[3] Adamnan's Life of St. Columba, by Reeves, *notes*, p. 276.

Of the Book of Deer Mr. Westwood writes, "The initial letter of each Gospel is alone enlarged and ornamented with patches of different colours, being about two inches high, the ends of the principal strokes of the letters terminating in dogs' heads, somewhat in the style of the letters in the Psalter of St. Ouen, and especially like the initials given in my first plate of Irish Biblical MSS., No. 4, from the Harleian Gospels, 1802, and in my second plate, No. 5 of the 'Palæographia Sacra.' These pages, as well as the miniatures in the volume, are surrounded by ornamental borders, chiefly formed of rudely interlaced ribbons, and with some modifications of the Z patterns, both in the lozenge and rectangular forms." * * *

"The figure of St. Matthew[1] is a standing figure in the style of those of the Gospels of Mac Durnan, etc., with the beard of moderate length divided into four points, the feet naked, and the right hand holding a sword of very unusual form, turned downwards, the point of the scabbard resting between the feet. The handle of the sword is guarded not only in the front of the hand (as in Hewitt's 'Ancient Armour,' p. 33, Figs. 9, 10, and 11), but also behind the hand, the guards being curved, but reversed; the scabbard itself appears at first sight, owing to the curved border of the dress, to be shod at the end like Hewitt's Fig. 2, p. 32. The sword is a rare symbol of St. Matthew, but it is given as such in Eusenbeth's lists of the Emblems of the Saints. On either side of the head of the Saint is a small figure, possibly intended for an angel. St. Mark is represented in my second figure.[2] St. Matthew in the Gospels of St. Boniface, represented in my fourth figure of the same plate, 51, is really well drawn as compared with

[1] [Plate vi.] [2] [Plate viii.]

this St. Mark, of which the most noticeable feature is the object held to the breast like a casket, which may represent a book in an ornamental binding, suspended from the neck, with the cumhdach or case in which it is preserved (of which the missal of Corpus Christi College, Oxford, is an example). I need scarcely add that the book is a very constant adjunct to the figure of the Evangelist in those early drawings, as seen in many of my plates."[1]

"My Fig. 3 represents the recto of the last folio, 86,[2] and is probably intended to represent two of the Evangelists with two angels (being analogous to the tessellated pages of the Books of Lindisfarne, etc.); whilst a similar composition, the centre formed of a six-leaved rosette, occupies the verso of the first folio.[3] At the end of St. John (folio 84, verso)[4] is also a group of two of these Evangelists (?), and on the verso of the following folio (85 v.)[5] is a group of four of these figures (without books), two with uplifted, and one with outstretched arms, the fourth without arms. Quaint little flourishes resembling fern-leaves, and small animals

[1] Books, and what appear to be cumhdachs or book-covers, appear on the sculptured stones of Scotland (see "Sculp. Stones of Scotland," vol. ii. Pref. p. 23). I cannot doubt that the figures on the breasts of the Evangelists in the Book of Deer are meant either for cumhdachs, or boxes for relics like the early Celtic example at Monymusk, which is shaped like the present figures, and has an arrangement for suspension (Idem, Plate xi. of "Illustrations"). A different opinion has been expressed by Mr. Paley, who regards the figure as an apparell or rationale suspended from the neck by three strings. He adds, "Assuming that the dress of all these figures is meant to represent the chasuble, considerable interest must attach to a representation, however rude, of the vestments worn by a Gaelic priest in the ninth century. If, as is probable, the chasuble was derived from the toga, which is indicated by the original circular form of both, the appearance of the rounded ends over the knees would be accounted for. The collar or rather the neck-folds seem to be most ample and quite unlike any fashion that we are acquainted with in the middle ages." (Mr. Paley as quoted by Mr. Westwood, p. 90.)

[2] [Plate xx.] [3] [Plate i.]

[4] [Plate xvii.] [5] [Plate xix.]

and birds, occupy many of the open spaces and margins of the pages."[1] (Westwood's "Miniatures and Ornaments," pp. 89, 90.)

A question here naturally suggests itself,—Are we to ascribe the Book of Deer to an Irish or a Pictish origin? and when we recollect the community of religious institutions and art which in their infancy pervaded the churches of both countries, it is one that can only be answered by a consideration of the probabilities and analogies connected with it.

The variety and beauty of the manuscripts of the Gospels, and other works left to us by the early scribes of Ireland, show that the art of writing and illumination was there cultivated and brought to the highest perfection.

There is no reason to doubt that writing was likewise cultivated in the Columbian institutions of Alba, although the productions of the Pictish scribes have not come down to us.

St. Columba was himself a skilful scribe. The copy, which at an early period of his life he made of St. Finian's Gospels, was the remote cause of his mission to Alba from the disputes to which it gave rise. Just before his death, too, as we learn from Adamnan, he was engaged in transcribing the Psalter; and of Connachtach, one of his successors, who died in A.D. 801, it is recorded that he was "scriba selectissimus."[2]

The "Legend of St. Andrew" preserves the name of one Pictish scribe in the following notice:—"Thana filius Dudabrach hoc monumentum scripsit Regi Pherath filio Bergeth in villa Migdele;"[3]

---

1 [Plates xxi. xxii.]

2 Reeves' Adamnan, pp. 233, 388.

3 This is Meigle in Strathmore, which in Pictish times seems to have been a place of high ecclesiastical importance. In no site have so many of the sculptured monuments peculiar to Pictland been discovered. (See "Sculptured Stones of Scotland," vol. i., Notices of the Plates, p. 22; vol. ii., Notices of the Plates, pp. 2, 73.)

and this, with other historical facts, was copied from ancient Pictish books into the Register of St. Andrews about the middle of the twelfth century,—"Hæc ut præfati sumus sicut in veteribus Pictorum libris scripta reperimus, transcripsimus."[1]

In the beginning of the eighth century the letter sent to Nechtan, the Pictish king, by the Abbot of Wearmouth, was first translated into the king's own language, and then, as we learn from Venerable Bede, his order for changing the time of Easter and the shape of the tonsure was transcribed and sent for publication throughout all the provinces of the Picts, while the same author describes the Pictish as one of the five languages of Britain in his day.[2]

St. Ternan, who in our early legends is called Archbishop of the Picts, possessed a copy of the Gospels in four volumes, of which the one containing the Gospel of St. Matthew was preserved at his church of Banchory St. Ternan, on the Dee, till the sixteenth century;[3] and St. Boniface, a missionary to Pictland, was popularly believed to have written 150 books of the Gospels.[4]

The volume of St. Ternan's Gospels was kept in a case of metal, adorned on the surface with silver and gold; and we hear of a copy of the Gospels belonging to Fothad, who was Bishop of the Scots before the middle of the tenth century. The silver cover, which the Bishop made for the volume, remained for admiration on the high altar of St. Andrews in the middle of the fourteenth century.[5]

---

[1] Chronicles of the Picts and Scots, p. 188.

[2] Hist. Eccl. lib. i. cap. i.; lib. v. cap. xxi.

[3] Kalendar in Proceedings of the Society of Antiquaries of Scotland, vol. ii. p. 264.

[4] Breviar. Aberd. Propr. Sanct. Part. Hyem. fol. lxx.

[5] Wyntoun's Cronykil, b. vii. c. x. vol. i. p. 180.

On one of the crosses at St. Vigeans there is an inscription which appears to be the only specimen of writing in the Pictish language that has been preserved. It may be reasonably ascribed to the early part of the eighth century, and the form of the letters agrees with that of the Irish and Saxon writings of the period.[1]

The exquisite ornamental designs of the sculptured crosses of Pictland—which were probably elaborated by the inmates of the Pictish monasteries, and which are identical with those of the early Irish manuscripts and the Book of Deer—fairly entitle us to assume that the men who could carve their intricate patterns on stone with such grace and accuracy would at the same time adorn their writings with similar devices.[2]

On a review of these facts, there seems nothing improbable in concluding that the Book of Deer may have been written by a native scribe of Alba in the ninth century. The existence of a *Fer-leiginn*, or scribe, in the neighbouring monastery of Turriff, would entitle us also to look for one in the monastery of Deer; and we learn from Colgan that the duty of these officials was

[1] See the reading of it given by Professor Sir James Y. Simpson in "Sculptured Stones of Scotland," vol. ii., Notices of the Plates, p. 70. The Pictish character of the inscription is supported by Dr. Petrie and Mr. Whitley Stokes in "Goidilica," by the latter, p. 37. Calcutta, 1866.

[2] "It seems very probable, on the whole, that the sculptor of the crosses, as well as the 'scribe' who prepared the design, was a member of the monastic community, if indeed the offices were not united in one person. Under the rule of St. Benedict every monk was compelled to learn some trade, and many of them became the ablest artists, writers, architects, goldsmiths, blacksmiths, sculptors, and agriculturists in the kingdom. In Ireland the monks were the artificers of the shrines, croziers, book-covers, and bells, which yet excite our wonder by the grace and at the same time the minute intricacy of their style; while they were also the writers of those manuscripts of matchless caligraphy to which I have referred." (Sculptured Stones of Scotland, vol. ii. Pref. p. 16.)

the transcription of manuscripts, the framing of annals, and teaching the schools.

It is reasonable, therefore, to believe that the same aptitude for writing and illuminating which characterised the Irish foundations of St. Columba was manifested in his Pictish monasteries, and that we ought to expect the production of copies of the Gospels in the one as well as in the other.

If it should be suggested that the Irish missionaries, to whom so many of the monasteries in Pictland owed their foundation, probably carried with them copies of the Gospels, and that the Book of Deer may have been one of them, it may be answered that the time for such importations had passed away, and that the intercourse between the churches, originally so close, had been greatly interrupted before the date ascribed to that book.

The comparative abundance of illuminated copies of the Gospels by Irish scribes still remaining, with the almost total want of any Scotch examples, may at first sight suggest the idea that the Book of Deer also should be ascribed to Irish hands. But the circumstances which in Scotland attended the ecclesiastical revolution of the sixteenth century, resulting in an entire breach with the past, led to such a ruthless destruction of the books in any wise associated with the ancient church, that not merely are we without specimens of the books of the early Celtic church of Alba (if we except the Book of Deer); but, even of all that enormous number of service-books used in the offices of the later church of St. Margaret and her sons, we have scarcely a trace beyond a stray volume saved by some happy and rare accident,[1] so that the

[1] As in the case of the missal and other service-books of the church of St. Ternan of Arbuthnott, which were probably rescued from destruction by the lord of the

absence of these later books might with equal justice be adduced as an argument for disbelieving *their* native character, which, however, is beyond doubt.

I think, therefore, we may assume that the Book of Deer was the production of a native scribe, if not of a scribe of the monastery of Deer itself.

The careful facsimiles of the manuscript prepared by Mr. Gibb exhibit the stained and worn appearance of its pages, and prove that the volume has been much in use.

For two centuries it would appear that nothing was added to the original book, for the *credo* and colophon (fol. 85, Pl. xviii.) seem to have been written at the same time as the Gospels.

The fragment of an office for the Visitation of the sick is in a considerably later hand, while the entries in the vernacular Gaelic of Alba, of grants to the monastery, appear to have been inserted at various times in the eleventh and twelfth centuries.[1]

In another chapter ("Celtic Polity") I have suggested the historical circumstances which probably gave rise to *written* notices of grants at this period and not earlier; and it seems likely that

manor, and now belong to his descendant, the Viscount Arbuthnott. We have many references in the accounts of the king's treasurers, and elsewhere, to the breviaries and missals written by the monks of Culross and St. Andrews.

[1] It would seem that the legend of the foundation of Deer, and the grants down to that of Gartnait Mac Cannech (Plates iii. iv. and v.), were written at one time. That of Gartnait is written in different ink, and by a different hand, from those going before, and it was obviously engrossed before the last seven words of the previous note were crowded in. The marginal entries on Plate vi. appear to have been written at one time, except the last two lines, which, judging from the colour of the ink, have been added when the grant of Colbain the mormaer on the following page was recorded (Plate vii.)

similar causes may have led to those records of grants in the Irish language, of the same date, which appear in the Book of Kells.[1]

The writing of the Gospels is all in one uniform hand. The illuminated figures of the Evangelists are designed with different degrees of elaboration—that of St. John being finished with most care. The ornamental borders are in some cases only partially completed (Plates viii. xii. and xiii.)

Occasionally words omitted in the body of the page have been inserted on the margin in the same hand as the rest, the omission being indicated by a mark like that on the margin of Plate xx. (·/.) At times the concluding words of a sentence are written on the line above it, where room had been there left.

The ordinary ink is of a dark brownish colour, and tolerably uniform. In the Celtic grants a marked difference occurs in the colour of the two portions represented on Plates v. and vi.

The writing of the book extends across the page, and the lines are continuous, in which respect its appearance differs from the Gospels of Lindisfarne, where the lines are of unequal length.

The pages generally show marks of horizontal ruled lines, drawn by some sharp instrument, and the writing *hangs from*, instead of *resting on* these, a feature in which this manuscript agrees with the second part of the Book of Armagh. On this point Dr. Reeves remarks: "This was a peculiarity of Oriental writing, and was adopted by the Irish for convenience, inasmuch as the upper

[1] The Book of Kells is one of the earliest of the Irish Gospels, and is ascribed to the hand of St. Columba himself. The charters of endowment of the House of Kells are of the eleventh and twelfth centuries. (The Miscellany of the Irish Arch. Soc., vol. i. p. 127.)

part of many of their letters (as ꞅ, ᵹ, ꞃ, ꞅ, ꞇ,), coincided better with a horizontal line than the lower."[1]

The style of punctuation adopted is exactly reproduced in the printed sheets. Most of the initial letters of paragraphs are capitals, slightly daubed with paint of various colours. In printing, these are represented by ornamental types. Where no paint has been applied to these letters, they are represented by plain types.

The volume contains the first six chapters of St. Matthew's Gospel, and the seventh down to the twenty-second verse, of our common mode of division; the first four of St. Mark's, and the fifth to the middle of the thirty-fifth verse; the first three of St. Luke's, and the first verse of the fourth; with the whole of St. John's; and it obviously never contained more.

The first seventeen verses of St. Matthew's Gospel are treated as a prologue, followed by the inscription "Finit prologus · Item incipit nunc Euangelium secundum Mattheum" (p. 2).[2]

[1] Adamnan's Life of St. Columba, Preface, p. xx. note.

[2] Mr. Westcott thus describes the Gospels of Deer in his valuable article on the Vulgate in Smith's "Dictionary of the Bible," vol. iii. p. 1695:—"Very many old and peculiar readings, nearer Vulgate than *a* [Gospels in Cambr. Univ. Libr. K. k. 1. 24. Sæc. viii. ?], but very carelessly written. No Ammonian Sections or Capitula."

This last statement requires a very slight qualification, inasmuch as a solitary exception occurs in the first chapter of St. John (p. 38), where by the letter u (v), there inserted, is to be understood that here commences the fifth Ammonian Section which belongs to the third canon of Eusebius, thus indicating that the substance occurs in the three Evangelists—St. Matthew, St. Luke, and St. John.

This is the only reference of the kind which occurs in the volume, and it would seem that the letter had been inserted or copied by the scribe without any comprehension of its original meaning. Its occurrence (which was first pointed out to me by Mr. Bradshaw) is worthy of notice in judging of the source from which the Book of Deer may have been derived.

The Book of Deer.

(2.) The Version of the Gospels.

EARLY LATIN VERSIONS—VERSION OF ST. JEROME—"IRISH" GOSPELS—CHARACTERISTICS OF THE DEER CODEX—ITS COLLATION WITH THE VULGATE.

At a very early period in the history of the Christian Church various Latin versions of the Gospels were in use, one of which, as revised by ecclesiastical authority in Italy in the fourth century, was distinguished by the name of *Itala*. Other recensions were made for private use, in which changes were introduced to suit the taste or caprice of the scribe or critic; and from an intermixture of all these, such a corruption of the text took place as to call for an authoritative revision of the current Latin texts by the help of the original Greek.

This was accordingly accomplished by St. Jerome towards the end of the fourth century. His text, however, was not generally received in the Church for some time. In the fifth century it was adopted in Gaul by Eucherius of Lyons, Vincent of Lerins, Sedulius, and Claudianus Mamertus, but the old Latin was still retained in Africa and Britain. At the close of the sixth century, Gregory the Great, while commenting on St. Jerome's version, acknowledged that it was admitted equally with the old by the Apostolic See. But the old version was not authoritatively displaced, though the custom of the Roman Church prevailed also in the other churches of the West. In the seventh century the traces of the old version grew rare, and although the "Italic" was not wholly forgotten, yet the new text came to be generally adopted without any direct ecclesiastical authority.

The Book of Deer is one of the class which has been called "Irish" Gospels, which, while mainly corresponding with the Vulgate, seem to preserve occasional readings from earlier versions.[1]

The most casual examination of this book will show that it is a careless transcript of a corrupt text. The spelling is frequently barbarous and capricious; there are many violations of grammar, with omissions, transpositions, repetitions, and interpolations of various kinds, while the prepositions are almost always joined to the words which they govern.

Generally speaking, the Deer Codex exhibits many of the orthographical peculiarities of the Vulgate as noted by Tischendorf,[2] and especially such as are characteristic of early Irish manuscripts.[3]

The following is a list of some of those of most frequent recurrence:—

ad for ap, as adprehendere for apprehendere.
ae for e, as in Magdalenae for Magdalene.
b for p, as in babtismum for baptismum.
c for qu, as adpropincauit for adpropinquavit.
cc for c, as occulus for oculus.
ch for h, as Abracham for Abraham.
ch for c, as channa for Cana.
cx for x, as uncxit for unxit.
f for ph, as profeta for propheta.

[1] See Mr. Westcott's article on the Vulgate in Smith's "Dictionary of the Bible," vol. iii., pp. 1692, 1696, 1702, 1703.

[2] Novum Testamentum Amiatinum, Prolegomena, pp. xxviii.-xxx. Lipsiæ, 1854.

[3] See a summary of these, with special reference to a MS. Life of St. Columba written in the beginning of the eighth century, now preserved in the public library of Schaffhausen, by Dr. Reeves in his edition of Adamnan's Life of the Saint, Preface, pp. xvi.-xix.

ie for e, as diciens for dicens.
i for y, as sinagoga for synagoga.
i for e, as accipisse for accepisse, Herodis for Herodes, Johannis for Johannes.
ii for i, as nolii for noli.
i for ii, as repudi for repudii.
in for im, as inplere for implere.
zabulus for diabolus.
h added, as horiens for oriens.
h wanting, as aurite for haurite, orreum for horreum.
ll for l, as tullerunt for tulerunt.
o for u, as soffocaverunt for suffocaverunt, monomentum for monumentum.
u for o, as consulare for consolare, parabulas for parabolas.
p omitted, as temtator for temptator.
s for ss, as audisent for audissent.
ss for s, as gauissi for gauisi, Issaiam for Esaiam.
t for d, as illut, aput, for illud, apud.

The division of words and arrangement of paragraphs are very capricious, and could hardly have been made by one familiar with the language.[1] At times words are introduced which entirely destroy the sense, as in the 9th chapter of St. John, where, in the 1st verse, it is written, "et preteriens uidit iohannem cecum," instead of "hominem cecum."[2] In the 35th verse of the same chapter, where the words should have been "credis in filium dei," they are written "dixisset in filium dei."[3] The 10th verse of the 13th chapter of this Gospel in the Vulgate begins, "Dicit ei ihesus qui lotus est," while in Deer the word *lotus* is turned into

[1] The causes which led to that ignorance of Latin in the clergy of the English Church, of which King Alfred complained in the beginning of the tenth century, were generally operative throughout Europe, and the Gaelic clergy of Alba were probably in the same condition as their Saxon brethren in this respect.

[2] The Book of Deer, p. 60.

[3] Idem, p. 62.

"locutus."[1] The 22d verse of the 18th chapter of St. John in the Vulgate concludes with the words, "dicens sic respondis pontifici," while in Deer they appear as "sicrespem dispontifici."[2]

Words are occasionally found in this Codex which do not appear in the Vulgate. Thus in the 4th chapter of St. Matthew, at the 10th verse, where the former have the words "Tunc dicit ei ihesus uade *retro*," the latter omits the word *retro*, and similar omissions occur in the 30th and 40th verses of that chapter.

In the 6th chapter of St. John, after the words "da panem nunc," as in the Vulgate, the scribe of Deer introduces "panem semper hunc." In the 8th chapter at the 10th verse he has "ihesus dixit ei mulier ubi sunt qui te accussabant," while in the Vulgate the last three words do not occur. In the 30th verse of the 19th chapter of the same book, the words "cum autem expirasset uelum templi scisum est medium a sommo usque ad deorsum," which appear in Deer, are omitted in the Vulgate; and in the 6th verse of the 21st chapter, the words "Dixerunt autem per totam noctem laborantes nihil cœpimus in uerbo autem tuo mittimus," which occur in Deer, are not in the Vulgate. A similar case occurs in the 13th verse of the 5th chapter of St. Mark.

The words and passages which appear in the Vulgate, and not in Deer, are very numerous, as will be seen in the collations.

Instances of passages repeated will be found in the 14th verse of the 7th chapter of St. Matthew, and in the 13th verse of the 5th chapter of St. Luke.

A singular one occurs in the 6th chapter of St. John, at the 24th verse, where twenty-three words are repeated with some

[1] Idem, p. 70.

[2] Idem, p. 80.

variations in spelling, of which it seems more difficult to believe that they are merely the result of carelessness in the transcriber, than that they were literally copied by him from another text. The words which are at first written "in naue" are repeated "in nauem;" "a tibriade" becomes "a tiberaide," and "gratias agentes dominum" is turned into "gratias agentes dominus."

But the most grotesque result of the carelessness or ignorance of the transcriber occurs in the genealogy of our Lord in the 3d chapter of St. Luke, where Seth is set down as the first man and grandfather of Adam.[1]

It has been remarked that the whole question of the general character and specific varieties of the Celtic MSS.[2] is very imperfectly known (Smith's Dict. of the Bible, vol. iii. p. 1695); and it is with the view of contributing an addition to the materials for its elucidation that the collation of the Deer Gospels with those of the Vulgate (Codex Amiatinus) has here been made. It does not repeat all the minute literal variations of orthography each time that they occur, but it embraces all words of any importance.

With the same object a table is annexed exhibiting the results of collations of the fourth chapter of St. John, as in the Italic (Codex Brixianus), with the Vulgate (Codex Amiatinus), the Book of Durrow, the Book of Kells, the Book of Dimma, the Book of Moling, and the Book of Armagh, in the library of Trinity College, Dublin; the Lindisfarne Gospels in the British Museum; an

[1] The Book of Deer, p. 36.

[2] See a valuable chapter on this subject in a work which has appeared since the above was written: "Councils and Ecclesiastical Documents relating to Great Britain and Ireland," by Haddan and Stubbs, pp. 170-198, Oxford 1869; and "Descriptive Remarks on Illuminations in certain ancient Irish Manuscripts," by the late lamented Dr. J. H. Todd, in Vetusta Monumenta, vol. vi. p. 1.

early copy of the Gospels (A 2, 17) in the library of the Dean and Chapter at Durham; and the Book of Deer.

The collations of the MSS. in the library of Trinity College, Dublin, were readily completed for me by Mr. William Maunsell Hennessy, of the Public Record Office, Dublin, editor of the Chronicum Scotorum in the Master of the Rolls' Series of Chronicles.

In the collation of the Lindisfarne Gospels I adopted the text of Mr. George Waring in his edition printed for the Surtees Society.

Through the kindness of the Rev. Wm. Greenwell, the librarian of the Dean and Chapter at Durham, I was enabled to collate the text of the original manuscript at Durham,[1] which is thus described by Mr. Westwood:—"This manuscript in its original condition must have been one of the most splendid copies of the Gospels ever written. It may be referred to the early part of the eighth century. It measures about thirteen inches by ten, and is written in a beautiful rounded Hiberno-Saxon minuscule character, intermediate in size between the texts of the Gospels of Kells and Lindisfarne."[2]

[1] This manuscript contains the rare passage, St. John iii. 6: *Quia deus spiritus est et ex deo natus est*, and its mode of punctuation is by three dots in a triangle.

[2] Miniatures and Ornaments of Anglo-Saxon and Irish Manuscripts, p. 48.

Italic Recension; Codex Brixianus. (Sæc. vi.)	The Vulgate; Codex Amiatinus (circ. A.D. 541).	Book of Durrow (Sæc. vi. ?)	Book of Kells.	Book of Dimma (Sæc. vii. ?)
ST. JOHN. [Cap. IV. 1.] Ut ergo cognovit[1] Dominus[2] quia audierunt Pharisaei[3] . quod[4] Jesus plures dis- cipulos facit[5] . et bap- tizat plus[6] quam Johan- nes[7] . (2) quamquam[8] Jesus[9] ipse[10] non bap- tizaret[11] , sed discipuli ejus[12] . (3) relinquid[13] Judaeam[14] et abiit[15] it- erum in Galilaeam[16] . . (4) Oportebat autem[17] eum[18] transire per[19] Samariam . (5) Venit autem[20] in civitatem Samariae[21] . quae[22] dicitur Sychar[23] juxta praedium[24] quod dedit Jacob[25] . Joseph filio suo[26] . (6) Erat autem ibi fons Jacob[27] . Jesus ergo[28] fatigatus . ex[29] itinere . sedebat sic su- per puteum[30] . Erat[31] hora quasi sexta[32] . (7) Venit autem[33] mulier de Samaria . aurire[34] aquam . Et dixit[35] ei Jesus . Da mihi bibere[36] . (8) Dis- cipuli vero[37] ejus . abie- rant[38] in civitatem ut cibos emerent[39] . (9) Di- cit ergo[40] ei mulier illa[41] Samaritana . Quomodo **tu**[42] cum sis Judaeus . **bibere a** me[43] poscis . **quae**[44] **sum** mulier Sa- **maritana . non enim** cou- tuntur Judaei[45] Sama- ritanis[46] . **(10) Respon-**	[2] Iesus. [4] quia. [6] magis. [10] *om.* [13] reliquit. [20] ergo. [30] fontem. [31] hora erat. [33] *om.* [34] haurire. [35] dicit. [37] enim eius. [42] tu, Iudaeus cum sis.	[2] ihesus. [3] farisaei. [4] quia. [6] *om.* [7] Johannis. [10] *om.* [13] Reliquit. [14] iudeam. [16] galileam. [18] *om.* [20] ergo. [22] que. [23] sichar. [28] autem. [30] fontem. [31] hora erat. [33] *om.* [35] dicit. [37] enim eius. [39] quibos emerent. [42] tu iudaeus cum sis.	[2] ihesus. [3] Pharisei. [4] quia. [6] *om.* [7] iohannis. [10] *om.* [13] reliquit. [14] iudeam. [15] abiit. [16] Galileam. [20] ergo. [23] sichar. [30] fontem. [31] hora erat. [33] *om.* [35] dicit. **[37] enim ejus.** **[40] *om.* ei.** **[42]** tu iudaeus cum sis.	[2] ihesus. [3] Pharissei. [4] quia. [6] *om.* [7] iohannis. [8] quanquam. [10] *om.* [13] reliquit. [14] iudeam. [16] galiliam. [20] ergo. [22] que. [23] sichar. [24] predium. [30] fontem. [31] hora erat. [33] *om.* [35] dicit. [37] eius enim. [40] ei ergo. [41] *om.* [42] tu iudaeus cum sis. [43] a me bibere. [44] que. [45] iudei cum.

Book of Moling (Sæc. vii. ?)	Book of Armagh (Sæc. ix.)	The Lindisfarne Gospels (Sæc. vii.)	Gospels at Durham, MS. A 2, 17. (Sæc. viii. ?)	Book of Deer (Sæc. ix. ?)
		1 agnovit.		
2 ihesus.	2 ihesus.	2 Ihesus.	2 ihesus.	2 ihesus.
3 farissei.	3 farisei.	3 Pharisæi.		3 farisei.
4 quia.	4 quia.	4 quia.	4 quia.	4 quia.
			5 facit ∴	
6 *om.*	6 *om.*	6 *om.*	6 *om.*	6 *om.*
7 iohannis.			7 iohannes ∴	
8 quanquam et.				
	9 ipse ihesus.			
10 *om.*		10 *om.*	10 *om.*	10 *om.*
	11 non baptizat			
			12 eius ∴	12 eius ∵ 7
13 reliquit.	13 reliquit.	13 Reliquit.	13 reliquit.	13 Relinquit.
14 *adds* terram	14 iudeam terram.	14 Judæam.	14 iudeam.	14 iudeam.
15 abiit in galiliam iterum.		15 abit.		15 ethabit.
	16 galileam.	16 Galilæam.		16 ingalileam.
				17 enim.
				18 *om.*
19 ad.			19 per samariam ∴	
20 ergo.	20 ergo.	20 ergo.	20 ergo.	20 ergo.
		21 Samariæ.		21 samariæ.
22 que.	22 que.	22 quæ.		22 que.
23 sichar.			23 Sichar ∴	23 sichár.
24 predium.		24 prædium.		24 predium.
			25 *om.*	
			26 suo ∴	
	27 iacobi.			27 iacob ∵ 7 ∵ 7
	28 autem.			
29 ab.				
30 fontem.	30 fontem.	30 fontem.	30 fontem.	30 fontem.
31 horæ erat.	31 hora autem erat.	31 hora erat.	31 hora erat.	31 hora erat.
			32 sexta ∴	
33 *om.*	33 *om.*	33 *om.*	33 *om.*	33 *om.*
		34 haurire.	34 aurire aquam ∴	
35 dicit.	35 dicit.	35 dicit.	35 dicit.	35 dicit.
			36 bibere ∴	
37 autem eius.	37 enim eius.	37 enim ejus.	37 enim eius.	37 enim eius.
	38 abierunt.			
39 emerent sibi.	39 emerent sibi.		39 emerent ∴	
				40 *om.*
	42 tu iudeus cum sis.	**42 tu, Judæus cum sis.**	42 tu iudaeus cum sis.	42 Quomodo iudaeus cum sis.
43 a mé bibere.				
44 que.	44 que.	44 quæ cum.		44 que.
				45 iudei.
			46 Samaritanis ∴	46 samaritanis ∵ 7

Italic Recension ; Codex Brixianus. (Sæc. vi.)	The Vulgate ; Codex Amiatinus (circ. A.D. 541).	Book of Durrow (Sæc. vi. ?)	Book of Kells.	Book of Dimma (Sæc. vii. ?)
dit Jesus . et dixit ei[1] .		**3 domum.**		
Si scires donum[2] Dei .				3 petiisés.
et quis est . qui dicit			* quam (sic).	
tibi Da mihi bibere . tu	**4 neque.**	**4 neque.**	4 neque.	4 neque.
forsitan petisses[3] ab eo .	**5 haurias.**			5 aureas.
et dedisset tibi aquam*				
vivam (11) Dicit ei mulier				
. Domine nec[4] in quo				
aurias[5] habes . et puteus		**7 numquit.**		
altus est . unde ergo habes				
aquam vivam[6] . (12)				
Numquid[7] tu[8] major[9]				
es patre[10] nostro Jacob .	11 *om.*	**11 *om.***	**11 *om.***	**11 istum.**
qui dedit nobis puteum	12 ex eo ipse.			
hunc[11] . et ipse ex eo[12] bi-				
bit . et filii ejus . et peco-	**14 bibit.**	**14 bibet.**	**14 bibit.**	**14 bibit.**
ra ejus . (13) Respondit				
Jesus . et dixit ei[13] **. om-**	**16 hac.**	**16 hac.**	**16 hac.**	**16 hac.**
nis qui biberit[14] **ex aqua**[15]				
ista[16] sitiet[17] **iterum .** qui				
autem **biberit** . ex aqua	**19 dabo.**	**19 dabo.**	**19 dabo.**	19 dabo.
quam **ego**[18] dedero[19] ei[20] .				
non[21] **sitiet** in **aeternum .**				21 *om. from*
(14) sed[22] aqua quam				non *to* ei.
ego dabo ei . fiet in **eo**				
fons aquae[23] salientis **in**		**23 aque.**		23 aque.
vitam aeternam[24] **. (15)**		**24 inuitam**		24 inuitam
Dicit **ad**[25] eum[26] **mulier**		**æternam.**		æternam.
Domine **da** mihi[27] **hanc**		**25 *om.***	25 *om.*	25 *om.*
aquam[28] . ut non **si-**		**26 ei.**	26 ei.	26 ei.
tiam[29] . neque veniam			27 *adds* bibere.	27 *adds* bibere.
huc aurire[30] . (16) Dicit				28 aquam hanc.
ei Jesus Vade voca virum			29 sitiat (sic).	
tuum et veni huc[31] (17)				
Respondit[32] mulier et				30 *adds* aquam.
dixit . Non habeo virum .	**31 *om.***			
Dicit ei Jesus . Bene			**33 *adds* ei.**	
dixisti[33] . quoni-				
am[34] virum non habeo[35] .				
(18) quinque enim[36] viros	**34 quia**	**34 quia.**	34 quia.	34 quia.
habuisti[37] et nunc quem	**35 non habeo**	**35 non habeo**	35 non habes	35 nonhabes
habes[38] non est tuus	**virum.**	**uirum.**	non virum.	uirum.
vir[39] . hoc vere dixisti[40] .				
(19) Dicit ei mulier **. Do-**				
mine **video quia** Pro-				
pheta[41] **es tu**[42] **.** (20)			40 benedixisti.	
Patres **nostri in monte**		41 profeta.		41 profeta.
hoc adoraverunt[43] **. et**				
vos dicitis quia **in Hiero-**				
solymis[44] est[45] **locus** .		44 hyerusoli-	44 hieorusoli-	44 hirusoli-
		mis.	mis.	mis.

Book of Moling (Sæc. vii.?)	Book of Armagh (Sæc. ix.)	The Lindisfarne Gospels. (Sæc. vii.)	Gospels at Durham, MS. A 2, 17. (Sæc. viii. ?)	Book of Deer (Sæc. ix. ?)
	1 *om.*		1 ei ∴	
			3 petisses abeo ∴	
4 neque. 5 aureas.	4 neque.	4 neque. 5 hauris. 6 undam vivam.	4 neque. 5 inquoaurias.	4 neque.
	6 *Repeats entire verse, except* Domine.			
			8 *om.*	
9 major es tú.				
			10 patro^nẽ jacob ∴	
11 *om.*	11 istum.	11 *om.*	11 *om.*	11 *om.*
		13 ei · · · ·	13 ei ∴	
14 bibit.	14 bibit.	14 bibit.	14 bibit.	14 bibit.
		15 *om. from* aqua *to* quam.		
16 hac.	16 hac *and om. to* quam.		16 hac.	16 hác. 17 sitiat. 18 ergo.
19 dabo ego.	**19 dabo.**	19 dabo.	19 dabo. 20 ei ∴	19 dabo.
22 *om. from* aqua *to* ei.				
23 aque. 24 inuitam æternam.	23 aque. 24 inuitam æternam.	23 aquæ. 24 in vitam æternam.	24 in uitam aeternam : :	23 aque. 24 inuitam æternam. 25 *om.* 26 ei. 27 *adds* bibere.
27 da mihi domine, *and adds* bibere.				
29 *adds* iterum.				
		30 haurire. **31 *om.***	30 aurire ∴ 31 huc ∴ 32 *adds* ei.	
				33 benedixisti · · 7
34 quia. 35 nonhabes uirum.	34 quia. 35 non habes uirum. 36 *om.*	34 quia. 35 non habeo virum.	34 quia. 35 non habes uirum. 37 habuisti : : 38 *on margin and in later hand.* 39 uir ∴ 40 dixisti : :	34 quia. 35 non habeo uirum.
41 profeta.	41 profeta.		42 tu ∴ 43 adorauerunt ∴ ·	
44 hierusolimis.	**44 hierusolimis.**		44 hierusolymis.	44 inhierusolimís. 45 *om.*

Italic Recension; Codex Brixianus. (Sæc. vi.)	The Vulgate; Codex Amiatinus (circ. A.D. 541).	Book of Durrow (Sæc. vi. ?)	Book of Kells.	Book of Dimma (Sæc. vii. ?)
ubi adorare oportet [1] .				
(21) Dicit ei Jesus [2]				[3] venit.
Mulier crede mihi . quia	[4] adorabitis.	[4] adorabitis.	[4] adorabitis.	[4] adorabitis.
veniet [3] hora . quando				
neque in monte hoc .	[6] *om.*	[6] *om.*		[6] *om.*
neque in Hierosolymis				
adoravitis [4] Patrem . (22)				
Vos adoratis quod ne-	[10] Iudaeis.	[10] exiudaeis.		[10] exiudeis.
scitis [5] . nos autem [6] ado-				
ramus [7] quod scimus [8] .	[12] venit.	[12] uenit.	[12] venit.	[12] uenit.
quia [9] salus ex Judaeis [10]				
est . (23) Sed [11] veniet [12]				
hora . et nunc est [13]				
quando veri adoratores .				[17] querit eos.
adorabunt Patrem [14] in			* quia.	
spiritu [15] et veritate [16] .				[18] adorant eum
Nam et Pater tales quae-	[20] *adds* eos.	[20] *adds* eos.	[20] *adds* eos.	[20] *adds* eos.
rit [17] qui* adorent eum [18]				[21] eum adorant
. (24) Spiritus [19] est Deus				
. et [20] qui adorant [21]				
eum [22] . in spiritu et				
veritate oportet adorare [23] .	[25] Scio.	[25] scio.	[25] scio.	[25] scio.
(25) Dicit ei mulier [24] .				[26] misias.
Scimus [25] quia Messias [26]	[27] venit.	**[27] venit.**	[27] venit.	[27] *om. verb.*
venturus est [27] . qui dici-				
tur Christus [28] . cum ergo [29]				
venerit [30] . ille nobis ad-				
nuntiabit [31] omnia [32] . (26)				
Dicit ei Jesus Ego sum				
qui loquor tecum [33] . (27)				
Et continuo [34] venerunt [35]				
discipuli ejus . et mira-				
bantur [36] quia cum muliere				
loquebatur [37] . Nemo ta-				
men [38] dixit [39] . Quid				
quaeris [40] · aut quid lo-			[39] *adds* ei.	[39] *adds* ei.
queris [41] cum ea . (28)				[40] queris.
Reliquid [42] ergo ydriam [43]	[42] Reliquit.	[42] Reliquit.	[42] reliquit.	[42] reliquit.
suam mulier [44] . Et abiit [45]	[43] hydriam.	[43] hidriam.	[43] hidriam.	[43] hidriam.
in civitatem [46] . Et dicit				
illis hominibus [47] (29)				
Venite [48] videte hominem				
qui dixit mihi omnia	[48] *adds* et.	[48] *adds* et.	[48] *adds* et.	[48] *adds* et.

Book of Moling (Sæc. vii. ?)	Book of Armagh (Sæc. ix.)	The Lindisfarne Gospels (Sæc. vii.)	Gospels at Durham, MS. A 2, 17. (Sæc. viii. ?)	Book of Deer (Sæc. ix. ?)
			1 oportet ∴	
			2 ihesus ∴	
				3 uiniet.
4 adorabitis.	4 adorabitis.	4 adorabitis.	4 adorabitis.	4 adorabatis.
			5 nescitis : :	5 nescitis · ·
	6 *om.*	6 *om.*	6 *om.*	6 *om.*
7 quodscimus adoramus.				
			8 scimus ∴	
		9 Quod.		
10 exiudaeis.	10 exiudeis.	10 Judæis.	10 exiudaeis.	10 exiudeis.
11 *adds* et.				
12 nenit.		12 venit.	12 ueniet, *corrected to* uenit.	12 uenit.
			13 est ∴	
				14 patrem · ·
				15 INspiritu.
			16 etueritate ∴	
17 *adds* eos.	17 querit.	17 quærit.	17 *adds* eos.	17 querit eos.
18 adorant eum			18 adorent eum ∴	18 eum · ·
19 *om. to* eum.				
	20 *adds* eos.	20 *adds* eos.	20 *adds* eos.	20 *adds* eos.
				21 adorent.
			22 eum ∴	
			23 adorare ∴	
		24 mulier ei.		
25 scio.	25 scio.	25 scio.	25 scio.	25 scio.
	26 myssias.			26 misias.
27 venit.	27 venit.	27 venit.	27 *om. verb.*	27 *om. the verb.*
			28 christus ∴	28 christus · ·
29 *om.*				
	30 verit.		30 uenerit ∴	30 uenit.
	31 annuntiabit		31 adnuntiauit.	31 adnuntiauit
			32 omnia ∴	
		33 tibi.	33 tecum ∴	
	34 contino.			
	35 venieruint.			
			36 admirabantur, *but corrected as in text.*	36 mirabantur · ·
		37 loquebantur.	37 loqueretur ∴	37 loqueretur.
38 autem.	38 autem.			
			39 *adds* ei ∴	39 *adds* ei.
40 queris.	40 queris.	40 quæris.		40 queris.
			41 ea : :	
42 reliquit.	42 reliquit.	42 Reliquit.	42 reliuquit.	42 reliuquit.
43 hidriam.	43 hydriam.	43 hydriam.	43 hidriam.	43 hidriam.
			44 mulier ∴	
45 et abit.				45 ethabiit.
			46 inciuitatem ∴	46 inciuitatem · ·
			47 hominibus ∴	
48 *adds* et.		48 *adds* et.	48 *adds* et.	48 *adds* et.

Italic Recension; Codex Brixianus. (Sæc. vi.)	The Vulgate; Codex Amiatinus (circ. A.D. 541).	Book of Durrow (Sæc. vi. ?)	Book of Kells.	Book of Dimma. (Sæc. vii. ?)
quaecunque[1] feci[2] . num-	[1] quaecum-que.	**[1] quaecum-que.**	[1] quaecum-que.	[1] que cum-que.
quid[3] ipse est Christus[4] .				
(30) Exierunt ergo[5] de		[3] numquit.		
civitate et veniebant[6]				
ad eum[7] . (31) Inter	[5] *om.*	**[5] *om.***	[5] *om.*	[5] *om.*
haec[8] autem[9] rogabant				[6] venebant.
eum . discipuli ejus[10]				
dicentes . Rabbi man-				
duca[11] . (32) Ille autem	[8] Interea.	**[8] interroga-bant.**	**[8] interea.**	[8] interea.
dixit eis . Ego cibum				
habeo[12] manducare quem	[9] *om.*	**[9] *om.***	**[9] *om.***	[9] *om.*
vos nescitis[13] . (33) Di-	[10] *om.*	**[10] *om.***	**[10] *om.***	[10] eius.
cebant ergo discipuli[14]				
ad invicem Numquid[15]	[13] non scitis.			[14] *adds* ejus.
aliquis adtulit[16] ei man-		[15] numquit.		
ducare[17] . (34) Dicit eis	[16] attulit.	[16] attulit.	[16] attulit.	
Jesus . Meus cibus[18]				
est[19] ut faciam voluntatem		**[18] cybus.**	[19] est cibus.	
ejus qui me misit[20] . Et[21]	[20] misit me.	[20] misit me.	[20] misit me.	[20] me missit.
perficiam opus ejus . (35)	[21] ut.	[21] vt.	[21] ut.	[21] vt.
Non ne[22] vos dicitis .	[22] Nonne.		[22] nonne.	
quod adhuc[23] quattuor[24]				
menses[25] supersunt[26] et				
messis[27] venit[28] . Ecce		[25] mensis.		[24] quatuor.
dico vobis . Levate ocu-	[26] sunt.	[26] sunt.		[26] sunt.
los[29] vestros . et videte			**[27] mesis.**	
regiones[30] . quia albae[31]				
sunt jam[32] ad messem .				
(36) Et qui metet[33] , mer-				
cedem[34] accipit[35] . et[36]	[32] iam.	[32] iam.		[32] *om.*
congregat fructum in vi-	[33] metit.	[33] metit.	**[33] metit.**	[33] metit.
tam aeternam . ut et[37]		[34] mercidem.	**[35] accipiet.**	[35] accipiet.
qui seminat simul gau-				
deat[38] et qui metet[39] .				
(37) In hoc enim est[40]	[39] metit.	[39] metit.	[39] metit.	[39] metit.
verbum veritatis[41] . quia				[40] uerbum uerum est.
alius **est qui seminat** .	[41] verum.	**[41] uerum.**	[41] verum.	
et[42] alius est **qui** metet[43]				
. (38) Ego **misi**[44] vos	**[43] metit.**	**[43] metit.**		[43] metit. [44] missi.

Book of Moling (Sæc. vii. ?)	Book of Armagh (Sæc. ix.)	The Lindisfarne Gospels (Sæc. vii.)	Gospels at Durham, MS. A 2, 17. (Sæc. viii. ?)	Book of Deer (Sæc. ix. ?)
[1] que cumque.	[1] que cumque.	[1] quæcumque.	[1] que cumque.	[1] que cumque.
			[2] feci ∴	[2] feci · ·
[3] *adds* non.				
			[4] christus ∴	
[5] *om.*	[5] *om.*	[5] *om.*	[5] *om.*	[5] *om.*
	[6] venierunt, *corrected in margin to* veniebant.		[6] ueniebant.	[6] etuinebant.
			[7] adeum ∴	[7] adeum.
[8] interrogabant.	[8] interea.	[8] Interea.	[8] interea.	[8] interea.
[9] *om.*	[9] *om.*	[9] *om.*	[9] *om.*	[9] *om.*
[10] eius.	[10] eius.	[10] *om.*	[10] *om.*	[10] eius.
			[11] manduca ∴	[11] manduca · ·
				[12] *om.*
		[13] non scitis.	[13] non scitis ∴	
[14] *adds* ejus.	[14] *adds* ejus.			
	[16] ei attulit.	[16] attulit.	[16] attulit.	[16] attulit.
			[17] manducare ∴	
	[19] *om.*		[19] est cibus.	
[20] me misit.	[20] missit me.	[20] misit me.	[20] misit me ∴	[20] missit me.
[21] vt.	[21] vt.	[21] ut.	[21] vt.	[21] vtperficiam.
[22] *from* nonne *to* dico *obliterated.*		[22] Nonne.		
		[23] athuc.		
	[24] quatuor.	[24] quatuor.		[24] quatuor.
	[26] sunt.	[26] sunt.	[26] sunt.	[26] sunt ·
				[27] mensis.
			[28] uenit ∴	[28] uenit · ·
[29] occulos.	[29] occulos.			[29] occulos.
			[30] regiones ∴	
				[31] albi.
[32] iam.	[32] *om.*			[32] *om.*
[33] metit.	[33] metit.	[33] metit.	[33] metit.	[33] mitit.
			[34] mercidem.	[34] mercidem.
			[35] accipiet .	[35] accipiet · ·
	[36] *adds* qui.			
		[37] *om.*		
[38] congaudeat				
[39] metit.	[39] metit.	[39] metit.	[39] metit ∴	[39] metit.
[40] *om.*				
[41] uerum.	[41] uerum.	[41] verum.	[41] uerum ∴	[41] uerum · ·
				[42] *om.*
[43] metit.	[43] metit.	[43] metit.	[43] mettet ∴	[43] mettit · ·
[44] Ergo ego vós misi.	[44] vos missi.			

Italic Recension; Codex Brixianus. (Sæc. vi.)	The Vulgate; Codex Amiatinus (circ. A.D. 541).	Book of Durrow (Sæc. vi. ?)	Book of Kells.	Book of Dimma (Sæc. vii. ?)
metere[1] in[2] quo[3] vos				
non laborastis . alii labor-	[2] *om.*	[2] *om.*	[2] *om.*	[2] *om.*
averunt . et vos in la-	[3] quod.	[3] quod.	[3] quod.	[3] quod.
bores[4] eorum introistis	[4] laborem.		[4] laborem.	
(39) Ex[5] civitate autem[6]				
illa[7] multi crediderunt in				
eum Samaritanorum .				
propter verbum mulieris .				
testimonium perhibentis .				
quia dixit mihi . omnia	[8] illum.	[8] illum.	[8] **illum.**	[8] **illum.**
quaecunque feci . (40)				
cum venissent ergo ad	[10] *om.*	[10] *om.*	[10] *om.*	[10] *om.*
eum[8] Samaritani . roga-				
verunt eum . ut ibi[9] ma-	[13] *adds* quia.	[13] *adds* quia.	[13] ***adds* quia.**	[13] *adds* quia non.
neret aput[10] eos[10] . Et				
mansit ibi duos dies . (41)				
Et[11] multo[12] **plures** cre-				[15] ***om. the rest of the verse, and has* ab eo et credimus.**
diderunt **in**[10] eum[10] .				
propter sermonem ejus .				
(42) Et mulieri dicebant[13]				
Jam **non propter** tuam lo-	[16] vere hic est.			
quellam[14] **credimus .** ipsi				
enim audivimus[15] et sci-		[18] *puts verse 44 before v. 43.*		
mus . quia hic est vere[16]				
Salvator mundi[17] **Chris-**				
tus[10]. (43)[18] **Post** duos	[19] **exiit.**	[19] exiit.	[19] exiit.	[19] exiit.
autem dies profectus est[19]	[20] ***adds* et abiit**	[20] *adds* et abiit.	[20] *adds* **et abiit.**	[20] et abiit.
inde[20] in Galilaeam[21] .		[21] galileam.	[21] galileam.	[21] **galiliam.**
(44) Ipse enim Jesus testi-				
monium perhibuit . quia[22]				[23] *om.*
Propheta in sua patria		[24] exciperunt.		[24] exciperunt.
honorem[23] non habet				[25] galilei.
(45) Cum ergo venisset in	[26] cum omnia vidissent.	[26] cum omnia vidissent.	[26] **cum omnia vidissent.**	[26] cum omnia uidissent.
Galilaeam . exceperunt[24]				
eum Galilaei[25] . videntes[26]			[27] **que fecerait.**	[27] que.
omnia quae[27] fecerat in[28]	[28] *om.*	[28] *om.*		[28] *om.*
Hierosolymis[29] . in die		[29] hyerusolimis.		[29] hirusolimis.
festo . et ipsi enim **vene-**			[30] **venerunt.**	
rant[30] **in**[31] diem festum .	[31] **ad.**		[31] **ad.**	
(46) Venit[32] **ergo iterum**				
Jesus[33] **in Chana**[34] **Gali-**	[33] ***om.***	[33] *om.*	[33] *om.*	[33] *om.*
leae . ubi fecerat[35] **aquam**	[34] **Cana.**	[34] channa.	[34] Channan.	[34] Cannan.
vinum . Erat[36] **autem**[10]	[35] **fecit.**	[33] fecit.	[35] fecit.	[35] fecit.
ibi[10] quidam **Regulus**[37]	[36] **Et erat.**	[36] Et erat.	[36] et erat.	[36] Et erat.
cujus filius infirmabatur .				
in Cafarnaum[38] . (47) Hic	[38] **Capharnaum.**	[38] ***om.* in.**	[38] Capharnaum.	

Book of Moling (Sæc. vii. ?)	Book of Armagh (Sæc. ix.)	The Lindisfarne Gospels (Sæc. vii.)	Gospels at Durham, MS. A 2, 17. (Sæc. viii. ?)	Book of Deer (Sæc. ix. ?)
				[1] me tere.
[2] *om.*	[2] *om.*	[2] *om.*	[2] *om.*	[2] *om.*
[3] quod.	[3] quod.	[3] quod.	[3] quod.	[3] quod.
		[4] laborem.	[4] laborem.	[4] laborem.
[5] et ex.				
[6] *om.*				
		[7] illam; *so in MS., but corrected by a later hand.*		
[8] illum.	[8] illum.	[8] illum.	[8] illum.	[8] illum.
				[9] utubi.
[10] *om.*	[10] *om.*	[10] *om.*	[10] *om.*	[10] *om.*
				[11] *om.*
	[12] multi.			
[13] *adds* quia.	[13] *adds* quia.	[13] *adds* quia.	[13] *adds* quia.	[13] *adds* Quia.
[14] loquelam.	[14] loquelam.	[14] loquelam.		
[16] *om.*	[16] *om.*	[16] vere hic est.		
[17] mondi.			[17] mundi ∴	[17] mundi · · ·
[19] exit.	[19] exiit.	[19] exiit.	[19] exiit.	[19] exiit.
[20] et abit.	[20] et fugit.	[20] et abiit.	[20] et abiit.	[20] *adds* ethabiit.
[21] galileam.	[21] galileam.	[21] Galilæam.	[21] galileam ∴	[21] galilæam.
		[22] *om.*		[22] qua.
				[23] *om.*
[24] exciperunt.	[24] exciperunt.		[24] excoeperunt.	
[25] galilei.	[25] Galilei.	[25] Galilæi.	[25] galiliaei.	[25] galilaei.
[26] cum omnia audissent.	[26] cum omnia audissent.	[26] cum omnia vidissent.	[26] cum omnia uidissent.	[26] cum omnia uidissent.
[27] que.	[27] que.			[27] que.
	[28] *om.*	[28] *om.*		[28] *om.*
[29] hierusolimis.	[29] hyerusolimis.	[29] Hierosolimis.	[29] **hierusolimis.**	[29] hierusolimis.
	[30] venierunt.			
			[31] **ad.**	
		[32] venerat.		
[33] ***om.***	[33] *om.*	[33] *om.*	[33] *om.*	[33] *om.*
	[34] Kanna.	[34] Cana.	[34] channan.	[34] channa.
[35] fecit.	[35] fecit.		[35] fecit.	[35] fecit.
[36] Et erat.	[36] Et erat.	[36] Et erat.	[36] Et erat.	[36] Et erat.
[37] regulus quidam.		[37] quidem regulus.	[37] regulus quidam.	
		[38] Capharnaum.	[38] Capharnaum ∴	

Italic Recension; Codex Brixianus. (Sæc. vi.)	The Vulgate; Codex Amiatinus (circ. A.D. 541).	Book of Durrow (Sæc. ix. ?)	Book of Kells.	Book of Dimma (Sæc. vii. ?)
cum audisset quia Jesus a Judea[1] in Galilaeam ve- nisset . abiit[2] ad eum .	[1] Iesus adveniret a Iudaea.	[1] ihesus adueniret a iudaea.	[1] Ihesus advenieret a iudea.	[1] ihesus aduenieret a iudea.
et rogabat eum[*]. ut de- scenderet[3] . et sanaret		[3] discenderet.	[*] ad eum. [3] discenderet.	[3] discenderet.
filium ejus . incipiebat[4] enim mori . (48) Dixit	[5] Iesus ad eum.	**[5] ihesus ad eum.**	[5] Iesus ad eum.	[5] ihesus ad eum.
ergo ad eum Jesus[5] nisi[6] signa et[7] prodigia videritis non creditis[8] . (49) Dicit ad eum Regulus[9]		**[10] discende.**	[10] discende.	[10] discende.
Domine descende[10] prius quam moriatur filius meus	[12] *om.* [13] sermoni.	[12] *om.* [13] sermoni.	[12] *om.* [13] sermoni.	[12] *om.* [13] sermoni.
(50) Dicit ei Jesus Vade filius tuus vivit[11] . Et[12]				
credidit homo . verbo[13] quem[14] dixit[15] ei Jesus . et abiit[16] (51) Descendente autem eo[17] occurrerunt ei	[16] ibat. [17] Iam autem eo descendente. [18] servi occurrerunt ei.	[16] ibat. [17] iam autem eo discendente. [18] serui occurrerunt ei.	[16] ibat. [17] iam autem eo discendente. [18] servi occurrerunt ei.	[16] ibat. [17] iam autem eo discendente. [18] serui occurrerunt ei.
servi[18] et[19] nuntiave-		**[20] adds ei.**		
runt[20] dicentes[21], quod[22] filius ejus vivit[23] . (52)				[21] *om.*
Interrogabat ergo eos[24] in quam oram melius habu- erit[25] . Et dixerunt ei	[22] quia. [23] viveret. [24] horam **ab** eis in qua.	[22] quia. [23] uiueret. [24] horam ab eis in qua.	[22] quia. [23] viveret. [24] horam ab eis in qua.	[23] uiueret. [24] horam ab eis in qua.
Quia heri hora septima .			[25] habuerat.	
reliquid[26] eum febris .	[26] reliquit.	[26] reliquit.	[26] reliquit.	[26] reliquit.
(53) Cognovit ergo pater	[27] quod.		† erat in.	
ejus[12]. quia[27] in[12] illa[28]				[29] dixissit.
hora† qua dixit[29] illi[30] Je- **sus** . Quod[31] filius tuus	[30] ei. [31] *om.*	[30] ei. **[31] *om.***	**[30] ei.** **[31] *om.*** **‡ *om.***	[30] ei.
vivit[32]. et‡ credidit[33] ipse **et domus** ejus tota[34] .				[33] crededit.
(54) Hoc iterum . secun-		[35] saecundum.		
dum[35] signum fecit Jesus · **veniens[36] a** Judaea[37] in **Galilaeam.[38]**	[36] cum venisset.	[36] cum uenisset. [37] a iudaea. [38] galileam.	[36] cum venisset. [37] iudea. [38] galiliam.	[36] cum uenisset.

Book of Moling (Sæc. vii. ?)	Book of Armagh (Sæc. ix.)	The Lindisfarne Gospels (Sæc. vii.)	Gospels at Durham, MS. A 2, 17. (Sæc. viii. ?)	Book of Deer (Sæc. ix. ?)
1 ihesus ueniret a iudea.	1 ihesus aduenirei a iudeis.	1 Ihesus venisset a Judæa.	1 ihesus adueniret a iudaea.	1 ihesus adueniret a iudea.
2 et abit.				
3 discenderet.	3 discenderet.		3 discenderet.	3 discenderet.
				4 INcipiebat.
5 ihesus ad eum.	5 ihesus ad eum.	5 Ihesus ad eum.	5 ihesus adeum.	5 ihesus adeum.
	8 nissi.			
			7 ad prod.	7 adprodigia.
	9 credetis.			
			9 regulus ∴	9 regulus ∴
10 discende.	10 discende.	10 discende.	10 discende.	10 discende.
			11 uiuit ∴	11 uidit.
12 *om.*	12 *om.*	**12** ***om.***	12 *om.*	12 *om.*
13 sermoni Ihesu.	13 sermoni.	**13 sermoni.**	13 sermoni.	13 sermoni.
14 quenim.				
15 dixerat.				
16 ibat.	16 ibat.	16 ibat.	16 ibat ∴	16 ibat.
17 iam eo discendente.	17 iam autem eo discendente.	17 Jam autem eo descendente.	17 iam autem eo discendente.	17 iam autem eo discendente.
18 serui occurrerunt ei.	18 serui occurrerunt ei.	18 servi occurrerunt ei.	18 serui occurreruut ei ∴	18 serui occurrerunt ei.
				19 *om.*
20 adnuntiauerunt.				20 adnuntiauerunt, *and adds* ei.
22 quia.	22 quia.	**22 quia.**	22 quia.	22 quia.
23 uiueret.	23 uiueret.	**23 viveret.**	23 uiueret ∴	23 uiueret.
24 horam ab eis in qua.	24 horam ab eis in qua.	**24 horam ab eis in qua.**	24 horam ab eis in qua.	24 horam ab eis inqua.
25 habuerat.				
26 reliquit.	26 reliquit.	26 reliquit.	26 reliquit.	26 reliquit.
		27 quod.		
28 *om.*				
30 ei.	30 ei.	**30 ei.**	**30 ei.**	30 ei.
31 *om.*	31 *om.*	**31** ***om.***	**31** ***om.***	31 *om.*
			32 uiuit.	32 uidit.
			34 tota ∴	
			35 signum secundum.	
36 cúm uenisset.	36 cum uenisset.	36 cum venisset.	36 cum uenisset.	36 cum uenisset.
37 a iudaea.		37 a Judæa.	37 a iudaea.	37 aiudea.
38 galileam.		38 Galilæam.	38 galilaeam.	38 ingaliliam

III.

Celtic Entries in the Book of Deer.

NOTES OF GIFTS AND IMMUNITIES TO ST. COLUMBA, AND DROSTAN, BY THE MORMAERS AND TOISECHS OF BUCHAN—BY THE KING OF ALBA—AND BY THE MORMAERS OF MORAY.

THESE entries, in the vernacular Gaelic of Alba, in the eleventh and twelfth centuries, are represented in facsimile on Plates III. IV. V. VI. and VII.

[THE FOUNDATION OF DEER.]

The legend which records the foundation of the monastery is begun on a spare half of folio 3, and is continued on the following folio. It is in the following terms:—

Columcille acusdrostán mac cósgreg adálta tangator áhí marroalseg día doib goníc abbordobóir acusbéde cruthnec robomormáer búchan aragínn acusessé rothídnáíg dóib ingathráig sáin insaere gobraíth ómormaer acusóthóséc tangator asááthle sen incathraig ele acusdoráten ricolumcille sí iarfallán dórath dé acusdorodloeg arinmormáer . i . bédé gondas tabrád dó acusnithárat acusrogáb mac dó galár iarńeré nagleréc acusrobomarᵭb act mádbec iarsen dochúid inmormaer dattác naglerec góndéndæs ernacde les inmac gondisád slánte dó acusdórat inedbaírt dóib úaćloic intiprat goníce chlóic pette meic garnáit doronsat inernacde acustaníc slante dó; Iarsén dorat collumcille dódrostán inchadráig sén acusrosbenact acusforacaib imbrether gebe tisad ris nabad blienec buadacc tangatar déara drostán arscartháin fri collumcille rolaboir columcille bedeár ánim óhúnń ímácć;

Columcille, and Drostán son of Cosgrach, his pupil, came from Hí, as God had shown to them, unto Abbordoboir, and Bede the Pict was mormaer of Buchan before them, and it was he that gave them that town in freedom for ever from mormaer and toisech. They came after that to the other town, and it was pleasing to Columcille because it was full of God's grace, and he asked of the mormaer, to wit Bede, that he should give it to him; and he did not give it, and a son of his took an illness after [or in consequence of] refusing the clerics, and he was nearly dead [lit. *he was dead but if it were a little*]. *After this the mormaer went to entreat the clerics that they should make prayer for the son, that health should come to him; and he gave in offering to them from Cloch in tiprat to Cloch pette meic Garnait. They made the prayer, and health came to him. After that Columcille gave to Drostán that town, and blessed it, and left as (his) word, "Whosoever should come against it, let him not be many-yeared [or] victorious." Drostán's tears came on parting from Columcille. Said Columcille, "Let* DÉAR *be its name henceforward."*

Two of St. Columba's great monastic foundations in Ireland were at Durrow, in King's County, and at Derry, places which in the Latin of Adamnan appear as *Roboreti Campus* (Dair-mag), and *Roboretum Calgachi* (Daire Calgaich). In both cases the sites derived their names from the surrounding oak-woods, and the latter *Daire* seems to have been the royal fort of Aedh, son of Ainmire, King of Erin, within which St. Columba founded his church after the royal grant of it.[1]

It seems in every way probable that the Deer of Buchan took its name, in like manner, from the surrounding oak-woods. The parish is believed to have been at one time covered with wood, and the names of such places as Aikichill and Aikiebrae still preserve the recollection of the oaks which once grew there. The site of

[1] Reeves' Adamnan, p. 160. Venerable Bede speaks of the "*copia roborum*" at St. Columba's monastery of Dearmach or Durrow, which, he says, in the language of the Scots means "*campus roborum*" (lib. iii. c. 4). Of Derry, Dr. Petrie tells us that the chief fact connected with its state in Pagan times which has been recorded is, that it was a pleasant eminence covered with oaks. (Ordnance Survey of Londonderry—Parish of Templemore—p. 18.) The same eminent antiquary, in treating of the *dartheachs*, *duirtheachs*, or *dearteachs* of the Irish Annals, adopts the etymology which

Deer would have much to attract the susceptible nature of St. Columba. With rich pasture on the banks of the river, and the surrounding hills crowned with oaks, he would often be reminded of his own dearly-loved monastery of Durrow and its woods, in which, as he sings to Cormac, he used to listen to the sighing of the winds and the blackbird's joyous note.[1]

[Of the Offerings made to God and to Drostan.]

The following entries, down to that of Gartnait, son of Canneeh, are written in a consecutive order on folio 3 *b* and folio 4, and are represented on Plates IV. and V. They are here broken up for the sake of convenient reference :—

Cómgeall mac éda dórat úaorti [go] nice fúrené docolumcille acusdodrostán.

Comgeall son of Aed gave from Orte to Furene to Columcille and to Drostán.

The names here mentioned were the extreme points of the boundary. No name resembling the first is now to be found, but it is probable that the last, "Furene," may have been the Hill of Pitfour, which rises on the north side of the flat ground on the river-bank, where the monastery of Drostan was placed.

Moridac mac morcunn dorat pett meic garnáit acus áchád toche temní acusbahé robomormáir acus robothosec.

Moridach son of Morcunn[2] *gave Pett meic Garnait and Achad toche temni; and it was he that was mormaer and was chief.*[3]

derives the word from *dair-thech*, a house of oak.—(Origin and Uses of the Round Towers of Ireland, p. 342.)

[1] Reeves' Adamnan, App. p. 275.

[2] Donnchadh mac Morgaind is one of three mormaers of Alba, whose deaths are recorded in the Annals of Tighernac, A.D. 976. (Chronicles of the Picts and Scots, p. 77.)

[3] Mr. Skene is inclined to adopt a different reading of the last passage, for the reasons stated in the following memorandum, with which he has favoured me:—"The instance I think wrongly rendered is—

"'Comgeall son of Aed gave from Orte to Furene to Columeille and to Drostan.'

"'Moridach son of Morcunn gave Pett-meic-Garnait and Achad-toche-temni; and it was he that was mormaer and toisech.'

Matáin mac caerill dorat cuit mormoir inálteri acus culii mac batín dorat cúit tóiség.

Matáin son of Caerill gave the mormaer's share in Altere, and Culii son of Baten gave the toisech's share.

The lands here referred to are doubtless those of Altrie, about two miles westward from the church of Deer.

Domnall mac gíric acus malbrigte mac chathail dorat pett inmulenn do drostán.
Domnall son of Giric and Malbrigte son of Chathail[1] *gave Pett-in-Mulenn*[2] *to Drostán.*

An old mill stood on the bank of the Ugie, a short way to the north of the church, with a "sheelin'-hill" beside it, and it may have represented the mill of which the "Pet" or portion is here granted to the clerics.

It is possible that the joint gift may convey the respective shares of the mormaer and toisech, but this can only be an inference.

Cathal mac morcunt dorat áchád naglerec dodrostán.
Cathal son of Morcunt gave the clerics' field to Drostán.

This would seem to be the gift of Cathal's share as toisech in lands

---

"Now this gives Comgell no designation, and gives to Moridach both titles of mormaer and toisech. This is at variance with the whole scope of the passages, which invariably distinguish between mormaers and toisechs, and the positions of each. The two are mentioned first without designation to either, and then comes the statement 'and it was he.' Now, if it had been meant that Moridac was both mormaer and toisech, the text would have been '7 bahe robomormair 7 toisech.' The text, however, is 'robo mormair 7 *robo* thosec:' 'robo' is the past tense of the word to be, 'he was,' and its being repeated shows that the real meaning is, 'and it was he (Comgell) that was mormaer, and he (Moridac) that was toisech.'

"Whether Moridac were mormaer or toisech, it will be seen that his brother Cathal was toisech, when, as *Cathal mac Morcunt*, he mortified the toisech's share.'

[1] Malbrigte mac Chathail may have been the son of Cathal the toisech.

[2] Muilenn, a mill.—(O'Brien's Dict.)

already belonging to the clerics, but not "freed" at the time of the grant in their favour.

Domnall mac rúadri acus malcolum mac culéon doratsat bidbín dó día acus dó drostán.

Domnall son of Ruadre and Malcoluim son of Culéon gave Bidbin to God and to Drostán.

Bidbin seems to be the Biffie of the present day. It lies about a mile west of the church, and the gift must be held to convey only the interests of the donors, as the king's share is granted in the subsequent entry. Although they are not designated, we are led to infer that the granters were respectively the mormaer and the toisech.

Malcoloum mac cinathá dorat cúit ríig íbbidbín acus inpett meic gobróig acus dá dabég uactaír rósábard.

Maelcoluim son of Kenneth gave (the) king's share in Bidbin and in Pett meic Gobroig and two davochs of Upper Rosabard.

This grant of the royal share by the King of Alba out of his lands of Bidbin, and the subject of co-existing rights of different officials in the same lands, are commented on in a subsequent chapter headed "Celtic Grants." The interest of the mormaer in these lands of Pett-meic-Cobroig was subsequently granted to the clerics.

Malcolum mac moilbrigtæ dorat indelerc. Málsnecte mac lulóig dorat pett maldúib dó drostán.

Malcolum son of Maelbrigte gave the Delerc. Malsnecte son of Lulóeg gave Pett Malduib to Drostán.

The first of these grants is by Malcolm, mormaer of Moray, son of Maelbride, who was also mormaer of that province,[1] and the

[1] The first mormaer of Moray on record is Ruaidhri or Rory, who was succeeded by his son Malbride. He was followed by his brother Finlay, who fought with Earl Sigurd between A.D. 1005-1009. Finlay was slain by his nephews Malcolm and Gilcomgain, sons of Malbride, on which Malcolm, mentioned in the text, became

second is by Malsnechte, son of Lulach, who, as representing the house of Moray, is styled "King of Moray" by the Irish Annalists, in recording his death A.D. 1085.[1] If the lands conveyed by them were in the neighbourhood of Deer, as is likely, it is not easy to understand how the mormaers of Moray could have any title, as such, to lands in a province obviously subject to their rivals the Kings of Alba.

No such local names as *the Delerc* or *Pett Malduib* are now to be found in the district; but if the lands consisted of small portions which afterwards were merged in larger possessions with definite names, this could hardly be expected. It does not seem likely that the lands were isolated fields lying in Moray and at a distance from the monastery; nor do I think the difficulty is removed by Mr. Robertson's remark,[2] that "the grants of Malcolm mac Malbride, and of Lulach's son Malsnechtan, would appear to mark the tenacity with which the family of Moray clung to their claim of exercising proprietary rights in that province, in which both the kings who sprang from their race met their death," as the province of Moray was always confined within the limits of the Spey as its southern boundary.[3]

Domnall mac méic dubbacín robáith nahúle edbarta rodrostan [do drostán] arthabárt áhule dó.

Domnall son of Mac Dubbacin mortified [robaith[4]] all the offerings to Drostán, giving the whole of it to him.

mormaer, and died A.D. 1029. Gilcomgain, his brother, then became mormaer, and was slain in his rath A.D. 1032, leaving a son, Lulach, who was killed A.D. 1058.

[1] Chronicles of the Picts and Scots, p. 370.

[2] Scotland under her Early Kings, vol. ii. p. 500.

[3] Chronicles of the Picts and Scots, pp. lxxxiv. lxxxvii.

[4] "Wherever the word *robaith* is used, of which the literal meaning is 'drowned,' and which is rendered 'mortified' or 'sacrificed,' it will be found that the grant is made for 'receiving the whole;' meaning, perhaps, that in return for the

Robáith cathál árachoir chetna acuitid thoisíg acus dorat próinn chét cecnolloce acus cecease dó día acus dó drostán.

Cathal immolated in (the) same way his chief's share, and gave a dinner of a hundred every Christmas and every Easter to God and to Drostan.[1]

Cainnech mac meic dobarchon acus cathál doratsat ar alterín alla úethé na camone gonice inbéith edarda álterin.

Cainnech son of Mac Dobarchon [waterdog or otter] gave Alterin-alla-uethe na camone as far as the birch between the two Alterins.

The subject of this grant seems to have formed part of Altrie, lands which in recent times have come to be known by the name of Bruxie.[2]

Dorat domnall acus cathál étdanin dó dia acus dó drostán.

Domnall and Cathal gave Etdanin to God and to Drostán.

This place is not recognisable in any modern name.

Robaíth cainnec acus domnall acus cathál nahulc edbarta ridía acus rí drostan óthósach goderad *issære omór[maer] acus othesech culaithi brátha.*

Cainnech and Domnall and Cathal mortified all these offerings to God and to

---

land, or for some similar advantages, the 'mortifier' guaranteed all the dues and offerings belonging to the abbey, just as the Bishops of St. Andrews guaranteed food and clothing to the community of Kirkness in return for the lands of the little priory."—(Scotland under her Early Kings, vol. ii. p. 500.)

[1] This was probably an obligation to entertain a hundred of those of the province of Buchan, who were assembled at Deer to celebrate these great festivals.

In the registry of Clonmacnoise, among the dues payable to the house was one "to intertaine and cherish all those of the clanna Neills as should have come for pilgrimadg to Cluain uppon every Good Fryday."—(Mac Firbis's translation, with notes by Dr. Donovan, in Trans. Kilkenny Arch. Soc. 1856-57, p. 449.)

[2] In the rental of the abbey-lands in 1554, those of Altrie are entered as also Mill of Bruxie; and when the lands of the abbey were erected into a temporal lordship, in the year 1587, in favour of Robert, Commendator of Deer, it was under the title of the Lordship of Altrie.

Drostán, from beginning to end, in freedom from mormaer and from toisech to (the) day of judgment.

The clause translated by the words in Roman type is written with ink of a different colour from that used in the previous part of the entry,—at a later time,—and after the succeeding entry had been engrossed. This may be seen by referring to Plate V., where it will be observed that the writing of the words in question is closer than the rest of the entry, and that its conclusion is carried above the line, the space below having previously been filled up. Cathal, who, as we have seen, had already mortified his share as toisech in certain subjects previously dedicated to Drostan, is now associated with Domnall and Cathal in "freeing" other subjects from the claims of mormaer and toisech. Domnall and Cainnech seem to have been mormaers, or at least in right of the mormaer's dues, so as to be entitled to surrender them.

Gartnait mac cannech acus éte ingengillemíchel dóratsat pet mec cóbrig ricosecrad éclasi críst acus petir abstoil acus docolumcille acus dodrostan sér ónáhulib dolodib cónánascad dócormac éscob dunicallenn ínócmad blíádin rígi da[bid] Testibus istis néctan escob abb[erdeon] acus léot áb brecini acus máledonn mac meic bead acus álgune mac árcill acus rúadri mórmaer márr acus matadin bríthem acus gillecríst mac córmaic acus malpetir mac domnaill acus domongart ferleginn turbruad . acus gillecolaim mac muredig . acus dubni mac málcolaim.

Gartnait son of Cainnech, and Ete daughter of Gille Michel, gave Pett mac Cobrig for (the) consecration of a church of Christ and Peter (the) apostle both to Columcille and to Drostán free from all the exactions, with the gift of them to Cormac Bishop of Dunkeld in the eighth year of David's reign. Testibus istis *Nectán Bishop of Aberdeen, and Leot Abbot of Brechin, and Maledonn son of Mac Be[th]ad, and Algune, son of Arcell, and Ruadri, mormaer of Marr, and Matadin the brehon,*[1] *and Gillechrist son of Cormac, and Maelpetir son of Domnall, and*

[1] A later brehon of the province, Farhard, "judex de Buchan," witnesses a charter of William, Earl of Buchan, to Cospatrick Mac Madethyn (Registr. Episcop. Aberd. vol. i. p. 14); and Ferchard is one of three "judices" who were present at a perambulation of the lands of Tarves in A.D. 1236. —(Registr. de Aberbrothoc, p. 161.)

Domongart ferleighin of Turriff, and Gillecolaim son of Muredach, and Dubni son of Maelcolaim.

This entry is probably the abstract of a *written* grant, dated A.D. 1131-32, but the transaction retains the appearance of the earlier unwritten gift, and seems to have been completed at a great gathering of the country, probably held on the Moot Hill at Ellon, where, as we shall see, a similar gift was afterwards made at a like meeting.

On the release of the lands from all exactions, and the gift of them to Cormac, Bishop of Dunkeld, some remarks will be found in connection with the general subject of burdens in a subsequent chapter ("Celtic Polity.") Among the witnesses we find Nectan, the first bishop of the see of Aberdeen, on its foundation or translation from Mortlach about the year 1125; and Leot or Leod, Abbot of Brechin, was one of the lay abbots of that place, by whom, and by Dovenald his grandson, also abbot, portions of the church property were alienated.[1]

Dorat gartnait acus ingengillemicel ball domin ipet ipáir docrist acus docolimcilli acus dodrostan, Teste gille calline sacart acus feradac mac málbhricin acus málgirc mac tralin.

Gartnait and [Ete] the daughter of Gillemichel gave Ball-Domín in Pet Ipair to Christ and to Columcille and to Drostan. Witness, Gillecaline, priest, and Feradach, son of Malbhricin, and Maelgirc, son of Tralin.

No spot in the district now corresponds with the name of the place here granted.

Acus bennact inchomded arcecnormar acus arcectosech chomallfas acus dansfl daneis.

[1] Registr. de Dunfermelyn, p. 8; Registr. Episcopat. Brechinen. vol. i. p. 3; Registr. Vet. de Aberbrothoc, p. 49.

And the Lord's blessing on every mormaer and on every toisech who shall fulfil (this), and to their seed after them.

This invocation, which is on the upper margin of the illumination of St. Matthew (Plate VI.), appears to have been written at a different time and by a different hand from the entries on the previous folios.

The side marginal entries on Plates VI. and VII. (fols. 4 *b* and 5), beginning with the grants of Donchad, son of Mac Bead, and ending with that of Colbain, the mormaer, seem to have been written at one time. The last two lines at the bottom of Plate VI., granting freedom from the toisech, have been inserted after the other writing.

On the upper margin of Plate VII. have been written the words, "in nomine sc͠te Trinitatis," which have been partially pared off in binding the volume.

Donchad mac mec bead mec hídid dorat acchad madchor docrist acus dodrostan acus do choluimchille in sóre gobrád malechi acus cómgell acus gille crist mac fingúni innaíenasi intestus . acus malcoluim mac molini.

Donchad, son of Mac Bethad, son of Hided, gave Achad Madchor to Christ and to Drostán and to Columcille in freedom for ever · Malechi and Comgell and Gillechrist, son of Fingune in witness thereof, in testimony, and Maelcoluim son of Molíne.

The lands in this grant are obviously those of Auchmachar lying about three miles north-west from the church of Deer.

Cormac mac cennedig dorat gonígc scáli merlec.

Cormac son of Cennedig gave as far as Scale Merlech.

The place here indicated is that now known as Skillymarno, a farm about a mile beyond Auchmachar to the north.

Comgell mac cáennaig taesec clande canan dorát docrist acus dodrostán acus dócholuim cille gonige ingort lie mór igginn infíus isnesu daldín alenn ódabací gólurchári et arsliab acus achad issaere othesseach cubráth acus abennacht arcachhén chomallfas araes cubrath acus amallact arcachén ticfa ris.

Comgell, son of Caennech, toisech of Clan Canan, gave to Christ and to Drostan, and to Columcille as far as the Gort lie mór (Great-rock field) at (the) hither (?) end which is nearest to Aldin Alenn from Dobaci to Lurchari both mountain and field in freedom from toisech for ever; and his blessing on every one who shall fulfil (this) after him, and his curse on every one who shall go against it.

The lands here conveyed adjoined those of Aden (of old *Alneden*), which lie along the river Ugie eastward from the church; but from the additional description, "both mountain and field," I infer that they must have comprehended part of the high ground at Pitfour. The granter was toisech of the Clan Canan.

Robhaid colbain mormáer búchan acus eua ingen garnait **abenphústa acus** donnachac mac sithig tœsech clenni morgainn nahuli edbarta rí día acus ridrostán acus ria columcilli acus rí petar apstal onahulib dolaidib archuit cetri dabach do ni thíssad arardmandaidib alban cucotchenn acus arardchellaib. testibus his brocin et cormac abb turbrúaid et morgunn mac donnchaid acus gilli petair mac donnchaid acus malæchín acus da mac matni acus mathe buchan huli naíaidnaisse in helain.

Colbáin, mormaer of Buchan, and Eva, daughter of Gartnat, his wedded wife, and Donnachac, son of Sithech, toisech of Clann Morgainn, immolated all the offerings to God and to Drostán and to Columcille and to Peter the apostle from all the burthens for a share of four davochs of what would come on the chief residences [monasteries] of Scotland generally and on chief churches. Testibus his Broccin, and Cormac, Abbot of Turbruaid, and Morgunn, son of Donnchad, and Gille Petair, son of Donnchad, and Malaechin and Matne's two sons, and the nobles of Buchan, all in witness hereof in Elan.

This solemn mortmaining of all the offerings was executed by Colban, who was mormaer through his marriage with Eva, the daughter of Gartnat, the previous mormaer. Eva, "his wedded wife," joined in it, and the toisech of Clann Morgainn. Some remarks on the exception from the release from burdens, and the expressions "chief monasteries" and "chief churches," will be found in the chapter No. IV., "Celtic Polity."

The act took place at Ellon, which was of old the capital of the province and earldom of Buchan, at a meeting of the officials, and "good men" or proprietors of the district. This was doubtless held on the Moothill, a green mount at Ellon on the banks of the Ythan, where the Earls of Buchan administered justice and took investiture of their great fief.

One obvious inference may be drawn from the grants now recited—namely, that the annexation of the province to the Crown did not infer the uprooting of the primitive state of society, or the destruction of the early proprietary of the soil, for it is clear that the population and institutions of Buchan were wholly Celtic in the time of David I., and that the influences which led to a change in both must be traced to a later time, and to a concurrence of causes gradually working out their issues throughout the kingdom.

On two blank pages of the Book of Deer (folios 28 *b* and 29; Plates X. XI.) is written in a somewhat later hand than the colophon, the concluding portion of an office for the Visitation of the sick.[1]

It agrees in character with two similar offices for the visitation of the sick which are found in the Book of Dimma and the Book of Moling, two early copies of the Gospels in the Library of Trinity College, Dublin.

In a luminous notice and a careful collation of the three offices by the Bishop of Brechin,[2] it has been shown that they all belong to the Ephesine family of offices, thus establishing the very important and interesting fact of the Gallican origin of the liturgy of the

[1] The office is printed at p. 89, *et seq.*

[2] Liber Ecclesie Beati Terrenani de Arbuthnott. Preface, pp. x-xxiv. Burntisland, 1864.

early Celtic churches of St. Patrick in Ireland and St. Columba in Scotland.

The thoroughly Celtic character of the clerics of Deer plainly appears from a rubric which in their "book" is given in Gaelic, "Hisund dubeir sacorfaice dau," or "Here give the sacrifice to him." In the Book of Dimma the corresponding direction is expressed in Latin, "Das ei eucharistiam."[1]

The last document engrossed in the book (folio 40, Plate XIV.) is in a different hand from that used in the Celtic grants, while it yet partakes to a considerable extent of the same character. It is a charter in Latin by David I.,[2] wherein the king declares the clerics to be free from all lay interference and undue exaction, *as it is written in their Book*—expressions evidently referring to the grants just recited—*and as they pleaded at Banff and swore at Aberdeen.*

I have elsewhere remarked on the secularising process which marked the history of the eleventh century, and the lay usurpations which overtook the monastic institutions of Ireland and Scotland (Chapter V., "The Early Scottish Church"). It is plain, from the tenor of King David's charter, that the clerics of Deer had suffered from attempts of this nature, and that in order to preserve their immunities they had been compelled to obtain the written charter of the King of Alba, as they formerly resorted to the "freedoms" of the mormaers and toisechs of the district, guaranteed at the provincial assemblies.

The witnesses to this grant, dated at Aberdeen, include Cormac, the first diocesan Bishop of Dunkeld; Andrew, the first Bishop

[1] Liber Ecclesie Beati Terrenani de Arbuthnott. Preface, p. xiii. [2] Printed at p. 95.

of Caithness; Samson, the first Bishop of Brechin;[1] Duncan, Earl of Fife; Malmore of Athol; Gillebrite, Earl of Angus; with Brocin and Cormac of Turriff, the last two being associated together, as in the previous grant of Colbain the mormaer (p. xxvii.)

At the end of the volume (fol. 85; Plate XVIII.) is inserted, in writing of the same period as the Gospels, the Apostles' Creed.[2]

After this comes the following colophon, written apparently at the same time as the Gospels:—

Forchubus caichduini imbia arrath in lebrán collí aratardda bendacht foranmain intruagaín rodscribai.

It is thus translated by Mr. Stokes, who says of it, "In point of language this is identical with the oldest Irish glosses in Zeuss' *Grammatica Celtica*."—(Saturday Review, Dec. 8, 1860.)

"*Be it on (the) conscience of every one in whom shall be for grace the booklet with splendour, that he give a blessing on the soul of the wretchock (misellus) who wrote it.*"

For the sake of convenient reference, the matter of the grants is exhibited under the various heads in the following table:—

---

[1] This charter proves the foundation of the See of Brechin by King David. "There is," says Dr. Grub, in his valuable Ecclesiastical History of Scotland, writing before the Book of Deer had become known, "no contemporary evidence of this, nor am I aware that any of his charters are attested by a Bishop of Brechin. But in the reign of Malcolm IV., and during the episcopate of Arnold, Bishop of St. Andrews, we find mention of Samson, Bishop of Brechin, whence it may reasonably be inferred that the traditional date of the erection is correct."—Vol. i. p. 268.

[2] Printed, p. 89.

Abstract of the Grants in the Book of Deer.

Names of Granters.	To whom granted.	Subject and object of Grants.	Witnesses of Grants.
Bede the Mormaer of Buchan	To Columcille and Drostán, the clerics	(1) The "town" of Abbordoboir. (2) From Cloch in Tiprat to Cloch pett mic Garnait,—"that town."	
Comgeall, son of Aed	To Columcille and Drostán	From Orte to Furene.	
Moridach, son of Morcunn	. . .	Pett meic Garnait and Achad toche temni.	
Matáin, son of Caerell	. . .	The mormaer's share in Alteri.	
Culi, son of Baten	. . .	The toisech's share in the same.	
Domnal, son of Giric; and Maelbrigte, son of Cathal	To Drostán . .	Pett in Mulenn.	
Cathal, son of Morcunt	To Drostán . .	Achad naglérech.	
Domnal, son of Ruadre; and Maelcoluim, son of Culeon	To God and to Drostán	Bidbin.	
Maelcoluim, son of Cinaed	. . .	The King's share in Bidbin and in Pett mac Gobroig and two davochs of Upper Rosabard.	
Maelcoluim, son of Maelbrigte	. . .	The Delere.	
Maelsnechte, son of Lúlóeg	To Drostán .	Pett Maelduib.	
Domnal, son of Mac Dubbacin	To Drostán .	Immolates all the offering to Drostan, giving the whole of it to him.	

Names of Granters.	To whom granted.	Subject and object of Grant.	Witnesses of Grants.
Cathal . .	To God and to Drostán	Immolates in the same way his toisech's share, and gives a dinner of a hundred every Christmas and every Easter to God and to Drostán.	
Cainnech, son of Mac Dobarcon	. . .	Alterin alla bhethe na camone. "As far as the birch-tree between the two Alterins."	
Domnal and Cathal	To God and to Drostán	Etdanin.	
Cainnech and Domnall and Cathal	To God and to Drostán	Immolate all these offerings from beginning to end, in freedom from mormaer and from toisech, to the day of judgment.	
Gartnait, son of Cainnech, and Ete, daughter of Gille Michel	Both to Columcille and to Drostán	Pet mac Cobrig; granted for the consecration of a church of Christ and Peter the Apostle, free from all the exactions, with the gift of them to Cormac, Bishop of Dunkeld, in the eighth year of David's reign.	Nectán, Bishop of Aberdeen. Leot, Abbot of Brechin. Maledonn, son of Mac Bethad. Algune, son of Arcell. Ruadri, mormaer of Mar. Matadin the Brehon. Gille Christ, son of Cormac. Mael Peter, son of Domnall. Domongart, ferleginn of Turriff. Gillicolaim, son of Muredach, and Dubni, son of Maelcolaim.
Gartnait and the daughter of Gille Michel	To Christ and to Columcille and to Drostán	Báll Dómin in Pet Ipair	Gillecaline, priest, and Feradach, son of Maelbricin; and Maelgire, son of Tralin.
Donnchad, son of Mac Bethad, son of Hided	To Christ and to Drostán and to Columcille	Achad Madchor in freedom for ever	Malechi and Comgell, and Gille-Christ, son of Fingune; and Maelcoluim, son of Molíne.
Cormac, son of Cennedig	. . .	As far as Scale Merlech.	
Comgell, son of Caennech, toisech of Clan Canan	To Christ and to Drostán and to Columcille	As far as the Gort-lie-mór at the hither end, which is nearest to Aldin Alenn from Dobaci to Lurchari, both mountain and field, in freedom from chief for ever.	

Names of Granters.	To whom granted.	Subject and object of Grant.	Witnesses of Grants.
Colban, mormaer of Buchan, and Eva, daughter of Gartnait, and Donnachac, son of Sithec, toisech of Clann Morgainn	To God and to Drostán, and to Columcille and to Peter the Apostle	Immolation of all the offerings [free] from all the burthens for a share of four davochs of what would come on the chief monasteries or residences of Alba generally, and on chief churches.	Broccin, and Cormac, abbot of Turbruaid, and Morgunn son of Donchad, and Gille-Petair son of Donchad, and Maelechin, and two sons of Matni, and the nobles of Buchan. At Elan or Ellon.
David, King of the Scots	The Clerics of Dér	Declaration that the clerics are free from all service of laymen and undue exaction, as it is written in their "Book," on which they pleaded at Banff and swore at Aberdeen.	Cormac, Bishop of Dunkeld. Andrew, Bishop of Cathnes. Samson, Bishop of Brechin. Duncan, Earl of Fife. Malmore of Athole. Gillebrite, Earl of Angus. Gillecomded, son of Aed. Brocin, and Cormac of Turbrud or Tureff. Adam, son of ferdomnac. Gillendrias, son of Mátni. At Aberdeen.

IV.

Celtic Polity.

VERBAL GRANTS OF LAND WITH SYMBOLICAL INVESTITURE—NOTITIÆ—MEMORANDA OF GRANTS IN THE BOOK OF DEER: IN THE REGISTER OF ST. ANDREWS—INTRODUCTION OF CHARTERS IN SCOTLAND—TRIBAL POLITY OF SCOTLAND—PICTISH PROVINCES AND RULERS—GRADUAL CONSOLIDATION OF THE PROVINCES INTO A KINGDOM—ROYAL MAERS, ARDMAERS, OR MORMAERS—TOISECHS—CONDITION OF LAND—RENTS—JOINT RIGHTS IN LAND—GRANTS OF LAND WITH "FREEDOM"—SERVICES AND BURDENS ON LAND—"SLAVERY" OF CHURCHES AND MONASTERIES.

THE earlier condition of society, when land was rather the property of the tribe or community than of individuals, did not admit of grants either symbolical or written. But when this state of things had passed away, and individual rights in land came to be recognised, these were not constituted by writings, but by a verbal gift, with the use of some appropriate symbol of investiture, as shadowed out in a statement of the so-called Chronicle of the Abbey of Croyland, by Ingulf—"Conferebantur etiam primo multa prædia nudo verbo absque scripto vel charta, tantum cum domini gladio, vel galea, vel cornu, vel cratera; et plurima tenementa cum calcari, cum strigili, cum arcu, et nonnulla cum sagitta;"[1] and

[1] Hist. Croyland, p. 70. However little weight we may now attach to the authenticity of Ingulf's charters and chronicle, in the light of Mr. Riley's masterly exposure (Arch. Journal, vol. xix. pp. 32, 114), the extract in the text correctly expresses the early conditions of investiture, and has been adopted by Ducange, Gloss. voce *Investitura*.

many such articles, delivered at the time when grants were made, are yet to be found in repositories of early muniments.

A knife was a common symbol, and occasionally the act of delivery was accompanied by the opening and shutting of the blade, after which it was laid on the altar.[1]

In the life of St. Grellan, a contemporary of St. Patrick, we find a gift of land to the saint by the King of Connaught noticed, and the delivery of a branch in token of possession.[2]

When Hungus, the Pictish king, bestowed on the church of St. Andrew a territory freed from secular services, the grant was accompanied by the "altar sod," "In memoriale datæ libertatis Rex Hungus cespitem arreptum coram nobilibus Pictis hominibus suis usque ad altare Sancti Andreæ detulit et super illud cespitem eundem obtulit."[3]

The conformity of ceremonial which accompanied the Pictish grant, with that of other countries at the time, does not end here; for the procession by which the ground of Chilrymont, at St. Andrews, was solemnly set apart for purposes of religion is exactly analogous to that used in a like case by the congenerous people of Wales. Seven times, as we learn from the Register of St. Andrews (quoting from the ancient Chronicles of the Picts), did the solemn procession wind round the land thus bestowed—St. Regulus the missionary bearing on his head the relics of St. Andrew, followed by the king

[1] Of this character apparently was the sword by which the lands of Lany, in Menteith, were held. It is thus referred to in a charter of Alexander II., to Alan de Lany and his wife, declaring that the lands were to be held "adeo libere et quiete sicut ipsa Margareta tenuit seu possedit ante hanc resignationem, virtute gladii parvi quem Culenus rex olim symbolice dedit Gillespic Moir predecessori sue pro dicto singulari servitio.—(Archæologia, vol. xi. p. 45.)

[2] The Tribes and Customs of Hy-Many, by O'Donovan, p. 9.—(Irish Arch. Soc.)

[3] Chronicles of the Picts and Scots, p. 187.

on foot, with the nobles of his country; and thus "locum ipsum Deo commendarunt et pace regia munierunt."[1]

When King Iddon, son of Ynyr Gwent, granted to the church of Llandaff his town and territory of Llanñ Garth, "Rex circumiens totum territorium, et portans evangelium in dorso, cum clericis ferentibus cruces in manibus, et aspersa aqua benedicta simul cum pulvere pavimenti ecclesiæ et sepulchri, in omnibus finibus perambulavit per totum."[2]

Other examples occur in the Register of Llandaff, in one of which the king, carrying the Gospels on his back, went round the territory in presence of the bishop and his clergy, thereby "confirmans eleemosinam factam pro anima patris sui Mourici in perpetuo."[3]

The first approach to written evidence of grants is to be found in short *memoranda* or *notitiæ*, in which the gift is described, and the names of the witnesses before whom it took place are specified.[4]

These notitiæ are of frequent occurrence in the chartularies of religious houses on the continent, and are described by Mabillon in his dissertation "de origine atque usu veterum notitiarum" as "notitiæ privatæ."[5]

The earliest specimens of such memoranda among ourselves,

[1] Chronicles of the Picts and Scots, p. 186.

[2] Liber Landavensis, p. 114, printed for the Welsh MSS. Society, 1840.

[3] Idem, pp. 152, 157, 358.

[4] Unless we should regard as a still earlier step the descriptive titles attached to the symbols of investiture. To these Mabillon refers, quoting Sirmundus—"Quin etiam extant hodieque in Sancti Albini cœnobio, et in aliis plerisque veteris moris monumenta; baculi, inquam, et chirothecæ, et alia investiturarum traditionumque quas signarant titulis inscripta."—(De Re Diplomatica, lib. iii. cap. 4, edition 1681. Ducange, voce *Investitura*.)

[5] Acta SS. ord. Benedict. Sæc. iv. pars prima, p. 714; and De Re Diplomatica, lib. iii. cap. 4. See also Ducange, Glossar. voce *Notitia*.

hitherto known, occur in the Chartulary of St. Andrews.[1] They appear to have been engrossed in that register in the twelfth century, but profess to have been extracted at that time from an ancient volume, "antiquo Scotorum idiomate conscripto." These record the foundation, in the island of Lochleven, by Brude, the Pictish king, of a monastery for St. Serf and the Culdee hermits abiding there, and describe gifts of various lands and franchises subsequently conferred on the house by Macbeth and other Kings of Scotland.

They are destitute of the formality of charters, and are rather notes, in which are recorded, by the receivers of the grants, the names of the donors, and of the witnesses who were present at the time when delivery was given.

Verbal grants were of frequent occurrence among the Celtic people of Brittany; and in the Chartulary of the monastery of St. Salvator of Redon they are recorded under the name of "Notitia,"[2] in the same style as the memoranda of the Register of St. Andrews.

Of this nature are many of the grants in the Book of Llandaff, already quoted, describing the subject of the gift, with its boundaries, and the names of those who witnessed the grant.

The Irish entries in the Book of Kells, which record various grants of lands and privileges to the ecclesiastics of Kells, dating

[1] Registr. Priorat. S. Andree, p. 113.

[2] Cartulaire de L'Abbaye de Redon en Bretagne, pp. 290, 303, 331, 369. In these early times we have instances of such memoranda being entered in the register of a religious house, not to establish the rights of the monastery, but to preserve the evidence of a private title. Thus the record of a shire-moot, in the year 1036, where a disputed point about certain lands was settled, sets forth that after the Court, the gainer of the plea, with the consent of all the folk, rode to St. Ethelbert's monastery, and caused the judgment to be set in Christ's Book (the Gospels).—(Thorpe's Diplomatar. Angliæ, Ævi Saxonici, p. 338. London, 1865.)

from the end of the eleventh to the middle of the twelfth century, are of this nature.[1]

In all these cases the grant was made with suitable solemnity before witnesses, and the written entries are memoranda of the facts, but are not such deeds or instruments as in a later time would have been the means and evidence of the transfer.

The earliest entries in the Book of Deer are memoranda of offerings thus made to God and to Drostan (pp. 92, 93), without reference to any formal instrument connected with them; while the grants by Gartnait mac Cannech, and Ete, the daughter of Gillemichel (p. 92), and those Gaelic entries which follow, appear to be abstracts of such written documents—the deed of immunity in favour of the clerics by King David I. being the only record with the formality of a regular charter.

In the time of this monarch the charter in confirmation of

[1] "Conchobar O'Maelsechlainn gave Cill-delga, with its territory and lands, to God and to Columbkille for ever, no king or chieftain having rent, tribute, hosting, coigny, or any other claim on it. [A.D. 1021-1050.]"

"The freedom of Ard Breacain, granted by the King of Ireland—*i.e.* Muirchertach O'Lochlainn—and by Diarmaid O'Maelsechlainn, King of Meath, and by the King of Loeghaire, Aedh, the son of Cu Uladh O'Caenulbhain."

"The Loegrians [*i.e.* the race of Loeghaire, monarch of Ireland] had a certain tribute on the church—viz. one night's coinmhe every quarter of a year. O'Lochlainn, King of Ireland, and Diarmaid O'Maelsechlain, King of Meath, induced the King of Loeghaire to sell this night's coinmhe for ever, for three ounces of gold. The church, therefore, with its territory and lands, is free for two reasons—viz. on account of the general freedom of all churches, and on account of this purchase."

"These are the guarantees of this freedom and liberty—viz. Gilla-mac-Liag, the comharba of Patrick [etc.], for the perfect freedom of the church for ever, without liberty of roads or woods, but to be common to the family of Ardbreacan as to every Meathian in like manner [*circa* A.D. 1150]."—(Miscellany of the Irish Archæological Society, vol. i. pp. 139-143.)

grants came into general use in the country north of the Forth, and had been partially introduced in the time of his brother, Alexander the Fierce.[1]

When that monarch restored to the church of St. Andrews the territory which at an earlier time had been dedicated to it by King Hungus, but had afterwards become secularised in the persons of the royal coarbs, or hereditary abbots of the monastery, the transaction was completed by a symbolical ceremony, without any written confirmation.

In the *History of St. Regulus, and the Foundation of the Church of St. Andrews*, written within twenty years after King Alexander's death, his grant of the Boar's Chase to the church, with many privileges, is narrated, and the striking ceremony by which it was completed and witnessed is thus described:—"Ob cujus etiam donationis monumentum, regium equum Arabicum,[2] cum proprio freno et sella et scuto et lancea argentea, opertum pallio grandi, et pretioso, præcepit rex usque ad altare adduci; et de predictis donis, libertatibus et consuetudinibus omnibus regalibus,

[1] It may be thought that such a notice as the following would support the idea that *charters* were not unknown in the time of Malcolm Canmore, the father of King Alexander. David II., by his charter dated at Scone, in a Parliament held there 10th June 1344, confirmed to the Prior of Restennet what had been granted by the charters of his predecessors, Malcolm, Alexander, and David, kings of Scotland; but it is most probable that the charters referred to were those of Malcolm's sons; and that in the case of Malcolm himself the gifts were made with "usuale and auld custommys," without writing, other than a notice in the book of the monastery. —(Acts of the Parliaments of Scotland, vol. i. p. 156.)

[2] In the Chartulary of Redon, in Armorica, already quoted, the gift of a horse is recorded, A.D. 1066, when, on a knight becoming a monk in that house, "armatus accessit ad altare sanctum, ibique arma malicie reliquit, deponens veterem hominem, novumque induens. Tunc tradidit equum valentem x libras cum proprio alodo de Treihidic."—(Cartular. de Redon, p. 312.)

ecclesiam investiri; arma quoque Turchensia diversi generis dedit, quæ cum ipsius scuto et sella in memoriam regiæ munificentiæ usque hodie in ecclesia Sancti Andreæ conservantur. Quæ undecumque advenientibus populis ostenduntur, ne oblivione ullatenus deleantur, quod tam crebro ad memoriam revocatur."[1]

The Prior of St. Serf's Inch composed his "Cronykil" about three centuries later, and has introduced into it much matter from the Registers of St. Andrews—those precious monuments of our early history—which in his day were complete, but of which we now only possess the fragments. The ceremonial at the restoration of the Boar's Chase is thus described by him:—

"In wytnes and in taknyng
That in this purpos stud the Kyng
And on full condytyown
Al Saynct Andrewys to be Relygyown
Be-for the Lordis all the Kyng
Gert than to the Awtare bryng
Hys cumly sted of Araby
Sadelyd and brydelyd costlykly
Coveryd wyth a fayre mantlete
Of pretyows and fyne welvet
Wyth hys Armwris of Turky
That Pryncys than oysyd generely
And chesyd mast for thare delyte
Wyth scheld and spere of Sylver qwhyt
Wyth mony a pretyows fayre Jowele
That now I leve for caus to tele.
Wyth the Regale, and al the lave
That to the Kyrk that tyme he gave
Wyth wsuale and awld custowmys

[1] Historia beati Reguli et fundationis ecclesie Sancti Andree.—(Chronicles of the Picts and Scots, p. 190.)

Rychtis Essays and Fredwmys
In Bill titlyd and thare rede
Wyth Hors arayed he gert be lede."

Wyntownis Cronykil, B. vii. c. 5.

The account of the chronicler is substantially that of the Register; but he conjoins, "wyth wsuale and awld custwmys" attending the grant, a statement that "the rychtis Essays and Fredwmys" "were in Bill tytled and thare rede." Whether this is descriptive of a "notice" or "memorandum" such as those previously described, or is an addition suggested by the customs of a somewhat later time, may be doubted; but, in any event, it does not appear that the grant was the subject of a formal charter, but that its memory lived in the tale of the impressive ceremony which accompanied it, and by the exhibition of its symbols, like the pillar-stones—those unwritten records of early times—which, although of themselves mute, served to preserve the memory of events, by suggesting the question, *What mean these stones?*

Charters were in common use among the Saxons in England long before this time, and the grants by Duncan and Edgar, kings of Scotland, to the monks of St. Cuthbert, in the end of the eleventh century, were expressed in charters which are yet preserved in the Chapter-House at Durham;[1] but the subjects of their gifts lay in the country on the south of the Forth, which at this time was entirely Anglian—the Saxony of the Celtic chroniclers of Alba—and the documents are obviously the work of Saxon scribes, and are attested by witnesses of that race.

In the same way, when King Alexander I., about the year

[1] See Anderson's Diplomata Scotiæ, Plates IV. and VI. National MSS. of Scotland, Part I., Plates II. and III.

1114, refounded a house of religion at Scone, for a body of canons-regular from St. Oswald's, near Pontefract, the charter, which in this case records his gifts, in its recital and other clauses bears evidence of its having been the production of an ecclesiastical scribe, familiar with Saxon documents of the same nature.[1]

David, the king's brother and successor, founded, or more probably refounded, the monastery of Dunfermelyn; and in his charter, which conveys many possessions to the clerics, he confirms the gifts or grants (*dona*) of Malcolm Canmore, his father, and Margaret, his saintly mother, as well as of his brethren, Duncan, Edgar, Ethelred, and Alexander. The reference to these grants is unaccompanied by the clause which is soon found in such recitals, "sicut carta istius testatur;" and we may conclude that they had been made after the "wsuale and awld custumys," without charters, which otherwise would have been engrossed in the register, or referred to in the later writ.[2]

Most of the Gaelic entries in the Book of Deer record gifts of this nature, and they are of the highest interest and value as the only specimens left to us of the records of our forefathers, at a time when the people and polity were Celtic, and just before the introduction of elements which changed the aspect and character of both.

From them we are enabled to form conclusions on points which have hitherto been more the subject of speculation than of historical certainty.

In considering the questions thus suggested, it must be borne in mind, that the entries appear to have been written in the end of the eleventh and early part of the following century, while the

[1] Liber Ecclesie de Scon, p. 1.

[2] Registr. de Dunfermelyn, p. 3.

subject of the first relates to a period more than five centuries before.

It is possible, therefore, that the scribe, in recording the traditional account of the foundation of the monastery, may have to some extent used terms expressing conditions of later growth.

Thus, in the legend of Columkille and Drostan, we are told that Bede the Pict was "mormaer of Buchan" at the time when the clerics entered on their mission in that country, at some period between A.D. 563 and A.D. 597.

In the time of the Roman occupation, North Britain was possessed by many independent tribes, whose names and position we learn from the geographer Ptolemy. In the progress of time these tribes came to be grouped into seven confederacies or provinces, ruled over by seven kings or chiefs, having under them seven "reguli" or inferior chiefs, with a king supreme over the whole.[1]

Of these kingdoms, the country between the Dee and the Spey formed one. In a description of Scotland, written in the twelfth century, it appears in two forms. In one case it is said, "Quartum regnum [fuit] ex De usque ad magnum et mirabile flumen quod vocatur Spe, majorem et meliorem tocius Scocie;" and in the other, it is spoken of as one of seven districts into which Scotland was divided, and as composed of Marr with Buchan.

Probably the last refers to the latest arrangement, when the country had been divided into two provinces.

[1] The memory of a sevenfold division was revived on various occasions long afterwards. See "De Situ Albanie," and "Legend of St. Andrew," in Chronicles of the Picts and Scots, pp. 135, 139; Palgrave's Documents and Records of Scotland, p. ix.; and Registrum de Dunfermelyn, p. 235.

The position of the ardrigh among the Northern Picts had come to be established at the time of St. Columba's mission, and then he doubtless ruled over the provincial chiefs or kings in much the same way as the monarch of Tara ruled over the provincial kings of Ireland, receiving from them a stipulated tribute, and entertainment in his occasional circuit or visitation.

After the union of the two branches of the Celtic people under one sovereign, towards the middle of the ninth century, "the next step in the progress of amalgamation was to confirm the preponderance of one state, and thus render the elective monarchy hereditary in one family. In the attempts to accomplish this object, which were made by the elder Angus and his successors, the ancient sevenfold division of the nation appears to have been destroyed, and the real conquest of the Pictish people to have been effected."[1]

When Columba and Drostan appeared in Buchan, it is probable that the country was governed by an under-king of the Pictish race; and it is not unnatural that one, writing at a later period, when the name of *Pict* had died out, should refer to the fact of his lineage as a distinguishing mark.[2]

At the time when the memoranda in the Book of Deer were written, a great consolidation of the power of the supreme king, especially under the reigns of Malcolm II. and his father Kenneth, had taken place by conquests over the provincial rulers.

This resulted not merely in the royal aggrandisement in a

[1] Scotland under her Early Kings, by E. W. Robertson, vol. i. p. 38. Edinburgh, 1862.

[2] "From the opening of the tenth century, the ancient name of *Pict*, gradually dying out, was superseded by the more familiar appellation of *Scot*."—(Scotland under her Early Kings, vol. i. p. 23.)

political view, but in a great addition to the property of the king. At an earlier period, the land thus acquired would have been portioned out among the conquerors as free allod—untaxed freehold held by right of blood; but when the importance of the supreme head came to be more prominent, and his power recognised, considerable portions of land in newly-annexed districts were reserved for the use of the crown.[1] In this case the older proprietary seem to have remained undisturbed as a tributary class.

"Like Wales and Ireland, the whole kingdom was probably divided in theory into *Triocha-ceds*, *Cantreds*, or Thanages—the tribe-lands held by chieftains as untaxed duchas, the crown-lands by maors or thanes, answerable for the rents and dues; and if Malcolm, by cancelling '*Duchas right*,' as far as it lay in his power, assimilated the tenure of the whole kingdom to that of the royal maor, or, in other words, taxed the hitherto untaxed duchasach, he only brought about the same change which Harfagr had already effected in Norway, and which the ministers of the Frank kings were continually aiming at, five or six centuries before his era."[2]

The royal lands appear to have been under the charge of a maer or steward, and when a new province was annexed to the crown, it was subjected to the government of an official called a mor-

[1] It is thus that we can account for the numerous estates throughout Pictland held in demesne by the Kings of Alba, which appear in the records of later times, out of which they founded monasteries and endowed churches; see as an instance the remarkable grant by Malcolm III. of the lands of Keig and Monymusk to the Church of St. Andrews.—(Collections for a History of the Shires of Aberdeen and Banff, vol. i. p. 171; Spalding Club.)

[2] Scotland under her Early Kings, vol. i. p. 107.

maer,[1] or great steward, coming in place of the "king," who had formerly been to some extent an independent ruler; and it is only after the period of the national consolidation that the term of mormaer

[1] In the Irish Annals we find occasional references to officials who are styled ard-maers, or high stewards; but whose office, like that of the toisech, gave them authority over *the clann*, not as with the mormaer of Alba, who combined with personal rule the charge of a territory or district. Thus, A.D. 922, the Annals of Ulster record the death of Murray, son of Donnell, Abbot of Monasterboice, head of the counsel of all the men of Bregia [the country between the Boyne and the Liffey, north of Dublin], lay and ecclesiastical, and stewards of Patrick's family, from Slieve Fuaid [south of Armagh]. In the Annals of Ulster the Murray here mentioned is called "Tanist Abbot of Armagh and ard-maer [or high steward] of the O'Neills of the South [or men of Meath], and coarb of Boice." "Muredhach mac Domhnaill tanuse Ab Airdmacha 7 ardmaer oa Neill in deisceirt 7 comharba Buiti mc Bronaigh, cenn adcomaire fer m Breg nuile Ocaib, Cleirchibh."—(O'Conor, Rer. Hib. SS. vol. iv. p. 256; King's Memoir of the Primacy of Armagh, p. 74.) *As steward of the family of Patrick*, "he appears to have been the authorised receiver of the tribute and offerings available for the support of the Armagh clergy from the inhabitants of the district committed to his charge."—(King, p. 75.) The Four Masters, A.D. 927, record the death of Kencorach, son of Maelweer, Abbot and Bishop of Derry-Calgy (*i.e.* Derry), and Steward of Adamnan's Law. "The abbot and bishop here named would seem to have discharged a similar office in connection with St. Adamnan's (or Eunan's) tribute—*i.e.* the offerings presented in memory of St. Adamnan to the Abbot of Raphoe for the support of his church and clergy."—(Idem.) In the account of the inauguration of Cathal Crobhdhearg O'Connor, King of Connaught, A.D. 1224, there is a list of the various officers under the king, of whom the first was the ard-maer, or high steward.—(Dr. O'Donovan's translation from the Celtic, in Transactions of the Kilkenny Archæological Society, vol. ii. p. 344.)

These ard-maers appear to have been the receivers of dues, both lay and ecclesiastical, and the term *exactores*, in the Annals of Ulster, used to describe certain officers of the Pictish King Nechtan, who fell at the battle of Monitcarno, A.D. 729, is probably meant for some of his great stewards or maers.—(Chronicles of the Picts and Scots, p. 356.) The word occurs in the Saxon Charters, as in that of Bishop Túnbriht, dated A.D. 877, where he frees the land conveyed by it from all burdens, "sive a pastu regis, principis, *exactoris*," etc. (Kemble, Codex Diplomat. No. 1063.)

The term *satrapas*, applied in the Pictish Chronicle to Dubdou, the ruler of Atholl in A.D. 965, seems to mean *minister* or

occurs in the Annals as applied to provincial rulers; while in Galloway and Lothian, which were not annexed to Alba till after the period of mormaers, no such officers appear. The notice of the death of Dubucan, mormaer of Angus, in 939, is the first in a Scottish record where the term is applied to an individual.[1] In the Annals of Ulster the mormaers of Alba are spoken of as a class, A.D. 917.[2]

As to the office of the mormaer, "there seems little doubt that, like the maor, he was a royal official resembling the graphio amongst the early Franks, and the Scandinavian jarl, acting as a royal deputy, and retaining in early times the third part of the royal revenue and prerogatives. The substitution of this species of tenure for pure duchas must have been gradually brought about, as in Norway, by the growth and increase of the royal authority—oirrighs and lesser chieftains often exchanging their earlier condition of partial or complete independence for that direct dependence upon the central authority which converted them into mormaers and maors; a change which was much facilitated by the great increase of wealth which must have resulted from extending taxation to the classes hitherto untaxed, and in which both mormaer and maor, like the royal officials of the north, must have participated."[3] In Armorica, the Mactyerns were hereditary lords of districts, and received from their vassals rents which corresponded in all appearance to the imposts levied by the chiefs of districts in Gaul.

officer, and to be an equivalent of mormaer, the term applied by the same Chronicle to Dubucan, the ruler of Angus, who died A.D. 939.—(Ducange, Gloss. in voc. *Satrapa*, *Ministri*. Chron. of the Picts and Scots, pp. 9, 10.)

[1] Chronicles of Picts and Scots, p. 9.

[2] "But neither their king nor any of the mormaers fell by him."—(Chron. of Picts and Scots, pp. 363-4.)

[3] Scotland under her Early Kings, vol. ii. p. 469.

Under the Carlovingians the Mactyerns lost much of their importance. Some placed themselves under the authority of the Frank count set over the government of the Peninsula; while others, such as Portitoe and Wrbili, held directly of the emperor, with the title of *vassi dominici*.[1]

We may, I think, infer that the rights of the mormaer were less absolute than those of the ruler of an earlier period, consisting in a hereditary claim to certain lands in the province, and an official title (which in process of time seems also to have become hereditary) to a share of the royal dues, for which, as steward, he accounted to the King of Alba.[2]

It would seem probable, on the whole, that Bede, the Pictish ruler of Buchan in the sixth century, was an oirrigh or under-king when he conferred on the clerics the towns of Aberdour and Deer, with full freedom, as if they were his own sole property.

At a later period we find grants by several mormaers of townlands, which also appear to have been their absolute property; but in other cases "the share" or interest of the mormaer in the lands is only granted; probably consisting of that part of the royal returns which fell to him.

Malcolm [Mac-Kenneth], King of Alba, gave the royal share

[1] Cartulaire de Redon. Prolegom. p. cclxix.

[2] The office of the mormaer was expressive of a more direct dependence on the ardrigh than had been the case with the provincial ruler; but, as the royal representative in the district over which he ruled, he naturally combined with his stewardship some of the functions of the earlier rulers, such as the leadership of the provincial subsidies in the king's host. It would be the policy of the supreme king to continue the administration of the provinces in the families of the former rulers where that was possible; and the natural tendency of Celtic institutions towards hereditary official tenures (as instanced in the case of many of the thanes) would in time practically confine the office to the descendants of the first mormaers, although, doubtless, with the sanction of the royal authority.

or portion in Bidben and other lands;[1] while Bidben was also granted to the clerics by Domnal Mac Ruadri and Malcolm Mac Culeon, thus showing the co-existing rights of different persons in the same lands.

Again, we find that the mormaer and toisech had joint rights in the same townlands.[2] Thus Matain mac Caerill gave the share of

[1] This shows that the King of Alba had certain defined rights in lands lying in a province only recently added to his kingdom, rights which accrued to him in virtue of his conquest, and as "ardrigh," while it is obvious that his conquest or annexation left the Celtic proprietary in the enjoyment of their lands. There are indications in our earliest records of a fluctuating period, showing traces of the gradually widening claims of the supreme King of Alba, and yet shadowing out an earlier condition, when the rights of property were to some extent vested in the community.

When Macbeth confirmed to the monks of Lochleven the lands of Kirkness, *with freedom from the king, or the king's son, or the sheriff*, his title to grant resulted from his position as King of Alba, his own inheritance lying in Moray—thus witnessing to the rights of the crown in the lands.

When King David confirmed to the monks of Dunfermline, "auctoritate regia et potestate," the grants of his father, mother, and brethren, it was with the ratification not only of his bishops, earls, and barons, but with the consent of the clergy and people; "clero etiam adquiescenteet populo."—(Registrumde Dunfermelyn, p. 3.)

His son, Alexander I., who granted a charter of foundation to the abbey of Scone, did so with consent of his seven Gaelic mormaers or earls.—(Liber de Scon, p. 1.)

When Ethelred, another of the sons of Malcolm, Abbot of Dunkeld and Earl of Fife, conferred on the monks of St. Serf the lands of Admore, his grant was confirmed at Abernethy by his brothers David and Alexander, at a great convention of the country both of clergy and laity, with freedom from both, and with the usual malediction against those who should infringe the gift. The transaction was concluded with a popular ratification: "Omni populo respondente, Fiat. Amen."—(Registr. Priorat. S. Andree, p. 116.)

[2] An instance of the concurrence of parties having separate interests in land to its surrender to the monastery of Redon, occurs in the Chartulary of that house, A.D. 1105, where we find the granter "habito consilio cum dominis suis, id est, Herveo Juscel, et Guaterio, atque Erardo filiis ejus—et Hamelino de Armalle super eos domino,—et Guaterio Hai domino super omnes, communi assensu," gave to the abbey the land in question.—(Cartul. Redon, p. 322.)

the mormaer in Alteri, and Culí mac Baten gave the share of the toisech.[1]

In one case the same person is styled both mormaer and toisech, and his grant must have included the shares of both in the lands which it conveyed.[2]

[1] "The word *Toshach* simply means 'captain' or 'leader,'—*dux;* the Irish *Taisigeacht* meaning 'captaincy,' 'leadership,' or 'precedency.' When the office of *dux*, originally elective, became hereditary, according to the invariable principle of 'divided authority' so characteristic of all the Celtic communities, it remained permanently in the family of the eldest cadet of the clan, the Tighern farthest removed from the chieftainship. The 'Captains of Galloway,' and the 'Thanes of Ross,' were probably known in their native tongue as *Toshachs*—captains by right of office—for though the oldest cadet, and the thane in his military capacity, were known as *Toshachs*, it by no means follows that a Toshach was necessarily either one or the other."—(Scotland under her Early Kings, vol. i. p. 104, *note.*) "The theory of a toshach over every Triocha-ced, or group of thirty *Baile-biataghs*, was familiar to the Irish Gael" (Idem); and the Toshachs of Buchan were probably chiefs of clans or families, and as such possessed of rights in certain lands which could be made the subject of grants. The name, however, long survived the existence of the important officials to whom it was originally applied. The *Toshach* of our later records had sunk into the position of something between a ground-officer or bailiff, and a sheriff-officer.

In a charter by Alexander Stewart, Earl of Marr, in favour of Sir Alexander Irvine of Drum, of the lands of Davachindore and Fidelmonth, dated in 1410, the office of tosach, and its dues, appear alongside of those of the hereditary smith of the barony. The lands in the charter are declared to be free of all services, "et sine aliqua custuma danda, fabrisdera vel tosachdera."—(Illustr. of Antiquities of the Shires of Aberdeen and Banff, vol. iv. p. 453. See Skene, De verb. signif. voce *Tocheoderache;* Dr. Jamieson's Scott. Dict. voce *Mair.*)

[2] See p. xlix. The rights of the mormaer as a royal official representing the crown in the district over which he presided, and accounting to the ard-righ for his rents and dues, were eclipsed by the introduction of the vicecomes or sheriff, soon after the time when the entries in the Book of Deer were written. When this took place, the prerogatives of the royal maer devolved on this officer, who was directly dependent on the sovereign, and accounted for the rents of the demesne lands of the crown, standing in the same relation to the royal Thanes, and the tenantry in demesne lands, as the baron by military service did to the

The lands in the grants were probably of varying extent, some of them being described as fields, as achad naglérech (the field of the clerics). The descriptions imply recognised boundaries, defined at times by prominent rocks, and stones or trees, which could only have been temporary landmarks.[1]

knights and tenantry of the barony.—(Scotland under her Early Kings, vol. ii. pp. 252-3.) At this period the title of mormaer fluctuates, until it finally becomes earl; thus Gartnait, Mormaer of Buchan, whose grant to the clerics about the year 1132 is recorded in the Book of Deer, appears in the foundation-charter of the monastery of Scone, about A.D. 1120, as *Earl* Gartnait; and Ruadri, who, as a witness to the grant of Gartnait, is styled Mormaer of Mar, appears in the charter of Scone as Earl Rotheri.—(Liber Eccles. de Scon, p. 3.) Long after the mormaers or earls had generally ceased to have any claims over the king's tenants, an exception survived in the case of the Earl of Fife, who was still entitled to exact from all the freeholders within his earldom his rights as *King's Mair* of the province of Fife; "Forsuth na erl, na seriand of the erlis, in the land of ony man haldand of the Kyng aw for to cum, for to rais that defalt, bot the erl of Fyffe, and he sal not cum as erl, bot as the mair of the Kyng, of his rychtis to be rasyt wythin the erldome of Fyffe."—(See Acts of the Parliaments of Scotland, vol. i. p. 68. The Book of Deer, p. 93.)

[1] The land given by Bede the mormaer, is said to lie between Cloch in Tiprait and Cloch pette mic Garnait, which may probably mean between "the stone of the well" and the "stone of the portion of Garnait's Son." In the same way we learn from the Pictish Chronicle that Nectan, king of all the provinces of the Picts, dedicated to St. Brigid the territory of Abernethy, with its boundaries, which ran from "the stone in Apurfeirt to the stone near Cairfuill, that is Lethfoss."—(Chronicles of the Picts and Scots, p. 6.)

The boundaries of the lands conveyed in the first grants are in many cases vague and indeterminate, and of a temporary character; but as the country was brought under cultivation and settled, the boundaries became specific, and are distinguished by marks of a permanent description. Thus the boundaries of the three davochs of Fedreth [now Feddernt] in the neighbourhood of Deer, which are given with great minuteness in a charter by Fergus, Earl of Buchan, to John, the son of Uthred, before the year 1214, consist in many instances of the natural features of the country, such as burns and hills; but in others of such remarkable objects as the *Crux Medici* or Cross of the Doctor, the sheep-fold of Ruthri mac Oan of Allathan, the fold of horses, etc.

The davochs comprised Eastir Auheoch

In some cases the extent is more determinate, reference being made to a davoch, which implies a measure of arable land.

In others the description "both mountain and field"[1] would lead us to understand a townland of varying size, which would be determined by the circumstances of the locality. The general idea, however, of the townland is thus shadowed out by Dr. Reeves:—"If we suppose a widely-diffused population to have existed in the island [Ireland] at an early date, which the thick interspersion of the earthen duns, rathes, and lisses authorises us to do, we can easily understand how, among a people semi-pastoral semi-agricultural, each occupation of land would acquire a severalty, and become defined by ascertained limits. Our idea of a primitive settler would be of one who obtained a tract of land, so circumstanced as to be clear in part, and have a fair supply of running water, near which a habitation might be erected, together with a

Auhetherb, Auhethas and Conwiltes, "cum omnibus limitibus suis et rectis diuisis, videlicet a riuulo currente ex parte orientali de Estir Auhioch in oriente vsque ad fossam concauam ex occidentali costa montis de Derevan in occidente, et inter viam altam supra Clochnily sicut extenditur in austro vsque ad Crucem Medici in aquilone et iterum . . . ndo in oriente a vado riuuli de Huskethuire inter Auhelit et Auhitherb vsque riuulum de Giht in occidente, et in predicto oriente a . . . li inter duas Aubcrauthis vsque in dictum riuulum de Giht subter ouili Ruthri Mac Oan de Allethan in occidente, et progrediendo . . . do inter dicta ouilia equitum versus austrum vsque ad predictam viam altam supra Clochnuly et etiam a fossa magna propinquius adiacente ville de Carnebennach ex parte aquilonali occidentaliter extendente in riuulum de Giht vsque ad concursum . . . de Lethalge . . . n aquilone et sicut fossa concaua que dicitur Holleresky Lech jacet inter Buchangy et montem de De . . . n sub occidentali parte de Derevan et sic a fossa vadi concaui de Auhakorty ex parte occidentali vsque in costam aquilonalem de Crageultyr et de Crageultyr vsque ad predictam Crucem Medici et . . . de ipsa Cruce vsque in costam aquilonalem de Derevan.—(Collections on the Antiquities of the Shires of Aberdeen and Banff, vol. i. p. 407.)

[1] The Book of Deer, p. 94.

proportion of mountain, wood, or bog, as the case might be. Should circumstances lead the neighbouring occupants to a community of abode, their several farms, while they retained their distinctive appellations, would naturally acquire a generic name borrowed from their joint habitation."

"An Irish memorandum in the Book of Armagh, written before the year 800, furnishes us with a sketch which may fairly be understood as representing the characteristics of a primitive townland: Cummen and Brethan purchased Ochter-n-achid [upper field], with its appurtenances, both wood, and plain, and meadow, together with its habitation and its garden."[1]

The lands described by the prefix *Pet* seem to have been divisions or portions, known from their connection with an individual, or their special use. In the first sense we have Pett-mic-Garnait, or Pett of the Son of Garnait, Pet in Mulenn, the Pet of the Mill, for which probably the equivalent is now the Mill Town.[2]

[1] Of the Townland Distribution of Ireland, by the Rev. Wm. Reeves, D.D.; Proceedings, Royal Irish Acad. vol. vii. p. 473.

[2] It has been at times suggested that *Pet*, which is a very prominent feature in the topography of Pictland, should be translated "the hollow;" but it occurs in such varying circumstances of site as to preclude this idea.

In the parish of Migvie, in Aberdeenshire, we have the church-lands called Pettentagart, or the Pette of the Priest; in Fife, Pittenweem, or the Pitt of the Cave. In Athol there is Pet mac dufgille, or the Pet of the son of dufgille. In some cases we find Pit and Bal used indiscriminately, as in Pitskellie in the parish of Barry, Forfarshire, which in the records is also spelt Balskellie; and in Pitgerso, which also appears as Balgerso, in the parish of Foveran, in Aberdeenshire.

Mr. Jervise informs me that the same occurs in the case of Balgersho in the parish of Kettins, in Forfarshire, which is also known as Pitgersho. He adds that *Pit* and *Bal* are used indiscriminately, as the names of the following lands in Forfarshire:—

In the parish of—

Panbride	Balmachie—Pitmachie.
Tealing	Balargus—Pitargus.
Forfar	Pitruchie—Baltruchie.
Newtyle	Balkeerie—Pitkeerie.
Aberlemno	Balglassie—Pitglassie;

and that most of these places are on rising grounds.

The fluctuating character of property among the early tribes under the law of gavel, which led to continued redistribution, was adverse to any enduring boundaries; and in Ireland the evils of this system survived to be deplored by Sir John Davis in the beginning of the seventeenth century:—

"Again, in England, and all well-ordered commonwealths, men have certain estates in their lands and possessions, and their inheritances descend from father to son, which doth give them encouragement to build, and to plant and to improve their lands, and to make them better for their posterities. But by the Irish custom of tanistry, the chieftains of every country, and the chief of every sept, had no longer estate than for life in their chiefries, the inheritance whereof did vest in no man. And these chiefries, though they had some portions of land allotted unto them, did consist chiefly in cuttings and cosheries, and other Irish exactions, whereby they did spoil and impoverish the people at their pleasure. And when their chieftains were dead, their sons or next heirs did not succeed to them, but their tanistes, who were elective, and purchased their elections by strong hand; and by the Irish custom of gavelkind, the inferior tenanties were partible among all the males of the sept, both bastard and legitimate; and after partition made, if any one of the sept had died, his portion was not divided among his sons, but the chief of the sept made a new partition of all the lands belonging to that sept, and gave every one his part according to his antiquity."[1]

As the formal charter may be said practically to have been introduced into Alba in the time of David I., so that change was accompanied by more fixed rights of property in the land, and by

[1] Historical Tracts, p. 12.

more careful adjustment of boundaries, than had prevailed before his time, of which we find tokens in the numerous perambulations and settlements of marches recorded in the chartularies of our religious houses.[1]

The terms of the grants are suggestive of other points of interest in connection with the institutions of the time and the condition of the people.

It will have been observed that many of them convey the lands

1 The lands to which a general name is given, as including both mountain and field, are evidently of an indeterminate extent. Such descriptions seem to imply rights of commonty, of which many illustrations occur in the charters even of later times. David I. granted to the monks of May one-half of the lands of Ballegallin, with common pasture in the shire or parish of Kellin and the shire of Crail.—(Records of the Priory of the Isle of May, p. 2.)

When William the Lion gave to the monks of Arbroath the church of Monikie, with its lands and tithes, he added "with common pasturage of the whole parish of Muniekky."—(Registr. vet. Aberbroth. p. 18.)

The same monarch confirmed to the Hospital of St. Andrews a grant by David I. of the lands of Kenaleken, which included "communitatem eciam in pascuis de Fif pecoribus hospitalis."—(Registr. Priorat. S. Andr. p. 212.)

He granted to the Priory of St. Andrews the church of Eglisgirg, with the land of the Abbey of Eglisgirg, "et cum communi pastura eisdem canonicis et hominibus eorum in predictis terris manentibus cum theyno meo et c̄ hominibus meis per totam parochiam de Eglisgirg.—(Idem, p. 192.)

The perambulations by which the boundaries of lands were settled by the goodmen of the country were often presided over by the king in person.

Alexander II. confirmed to the monks of Kinloss the lands of Kinloss and Inverlochty, granted to them by King David, "et preterea terram quam ipse rex David perambulavit."—(Registr. Morav. p. 457.)

David I. granted to the monks of Coldingham a charter confirming the boundaries between the lands of Coldingham and Bonekel "quas ego cum probis hominibus meis perambulare feci."—(Raines' North Durham, App. p. 4.)

In a settlement of disputed marches between the monks of Kelso and Melrose, a ditch along the top of a hill, made by order of David I., is referred to.—(Liber de Calchou, vol. i. p. 22; Munimenta de Melros, p. 136.)

with clauses of "freedom," or exemption from burdens of various kinds.

Pet-mac-Cobrig was granted "free from all the exactions or burdens," and Achad-Madchor was conveyed "in freedom for ever;" while a general confirmation of the offerings declares them to be "in freedom from mormaer, and from toisech, to the day of judgment" (pp. 93, 94).

The freedom from mormaer and toisech is obviously an exemption from the rents, tributes, or customs[1] exigible by these officials

[1] Rents were probably mostly paid in kind; and "can," which forms so prominent a feature in our early charters, seems generally to mean the portion of the produce paid as rent to the owner of the land, and in this sense the name is not yet altogether unknown in leasehold arrangements in Scotland—the fowls which form part of the rent being termed *kain fowls*.

A considerable part, however, of the rent consisted in the personal services of the tenant, as in the tillage of the landlord's ground, the sowing and reaping of his crop, digging and carrying his fuel, carrying materials for his buildings, and the like. This resulted from the want of trade, and consequently of capital.

But there is reason to believe that in Celtic times, besides the rents payable by occupiers of the soil, there was a poll-tax or tribute, which might be demanded from the people generally, and at special times from the occupants of certain lands, to which the word *can* was also applied. Of this last we find a trace in a charter granted in the year 1467, by Alexander Wardropar of Gothnys to Henry Forbes of Kynnellour, conveying to him certain lands in the Thanage of Kintore, in Aberdeenshire, with his cane of barley and cheese, "et totam pecuniam michi vel heredibus meis racione fer chane [mancane] contingentem de terris de Kynkell, et de Dyse infra thanagium predictum."—(Collections on the Shires of Aberdeen and Banff, vol. i. p. 575.) A similar tax was known among the Celtic people of Brittany. Alan, the earl of that country, had "quandam consuetudinem quam super homines S. Salvatoris qui morantur in plebe que vocatur Penkerac et in guerram habebat quam vulgo tallia nuncupatur, nos incisionem nominamus;" which, by a charter granted in the year 1122, he released, commanding "ne quis villicus nec prepositus nec etiam aliquis suorum clientum ullo modo sit ausus super hac re aliquid querere nec incisionem quando erit facta colligere, sed in arbitrio et potestate abbatis sit, ut quotiescunque comes suos homines inciderit, hoc est censum a suis exigerit, abbas suos secundum velle suum

from those over whom they ruled. By such payments the polity of the tribe was maintained, and after the provincial arrangement had passed into that of the consolidated kingdom, certain public necessities of the state were met by a tax which formed a burden on landholders.

These burdens were inherent in the possession of land, unless a special "freedom" was conferred by competent authority. Even in grants of land to the church *in free alms,* the burden of contributing towards the maintenance of the national fabric was implied, unless accompanied by an express exemption.

According to a statement in the Register of St. Andrews, the land which King Hungus gave to St. Regulus was to be held "in eliemosynam perpetuo; et tanta libertate, ut illius inhabitatores liberi et quieti semper existerent *de exercitu, et de operibus castel-*

incidat, et potestative ut concessum est colligat et habeat."—(Chartular. Redon, p. 324.)

Of the tribute exigible on certain occasions from the people of a district we seem to have an example in the *can* leviable by the King of the Scots, not from his demesnes, of which he had none in Galloway, but from the people of that country, his right to which was determined by the judges of Galloway, in presence of Roland, its Celtic chief.—(Acts of the Parliaments of Scotland, vol. i. p. 56.) In this sense the word was known to Skene, being used, he says, to describe a tribute "payed be the servand or subject to the maister, as I haue read in ane auld authentic register of the Bishoprick of Dunkeld, quhair it is called *chan* or *chanum*."—(De verb. signif. voce *canum.*)

Conveth, which so constantly occurs in our early charters in association with *can,* seems to be synonymous with the right of refection, or the Irish *coigny.*

We find that the Bishops of St. Andrews, in the twelfth century, were wont to receive refection for themselves and their followers from the men of the Kirktown of Arbuthnott, in the Mearns, which formed part of the Episcopal inheritance.

In the document which records the exercise of the right, two expressions are used in reference to it. It is said that the Bishops Arnald and Richard, "*hospitatos* fuisse pluries apud Aberbuthenot in terra illa, tanquam in propria;" that Bishop Hugh "ibidem tanquam in propriis *hospitatus* est, et de hominibus illis terre sicut de hominibus suis necessaria recipisse et munera."

lorum et pontium, et de inquietatione omnium secularium exactionum.[1]

Some of these "freedoms" may be expressed in the language of a later age than that of Hungus; but they consisted in exemptions from payments or burdens which no doubt were exigible in his time, and had come to be expressed in the terms just quoted.

When Macbeth, as King of the Scots, and Gruoch, his Queen, conferred on the Culdee hermits in Lochleven the lands of Kyrkenes, it was "cum omni libertate," "absque omni munere et onere et exactione Regis, et filii Regis, vicecomitis et alicuius,—et sine refectione pontis, et sine exercitu, et venacione;"[2] and other grants, with the like exemption, were made by Malcolm, Edgar, Duncan, Alexander, and later kings.[3]

Even when the charters by which churches were conveyed to religious houses contained remissions of some of the burdens which had most the appearance of personal payments to the granters, they occasionally reserved in force those which contributed to the national support.

Thus David I. confirmed to the monks of Coldingham the churches of Ederham and Nesebit, which had been granted by Gospatric, brother of Dolfin—"liberas ab omni servitio et omni con-

Again, the right is expressed thus—viz. That the Bishops Richard and Hugh were wont "in terra illa tanquam in propria *conevetum suum*, ab hominibus illius terre recipere tanquam ab hominibus propriis;" and that the same Bishops "ibidem *conevetum suum* tanquam in terra propria et ab hominibus propriis recepisse;" while Bishop Roger "per paupertatem eorum in quodam itinere suo *conevetum suum* omisit accipere."—(Miscellany of the Spalding Club, vol. v. pp. 212, 213.)

[1] Legend of St. Andrew, in Chronicles of the Picts and Scots, p. 187.

[2] Registr. Priorat. S. Andree, p. 114.

[3] Idem, p. 115. David I. granted to the monks of Dunfermelyn "ut homines sui sint liberi ab omni operacione castellorum et poncium et omnium aliorum operum.—(Registr. de Dunferm. p. 14.)

suetudine, exceptis triginta solidis quos prefati monachi dabunt filio ejus Gospatricio et heredibus suis post eum pro conredio[1] regis, . . . et excepto exercitu Regis, unde monachi erunt attendentes ipsi Regi, et ipse Gospatricius de exercitu erit quietus in perpetuum.[2]

Under this exception, the monks were bound to attend the king's host. They were bound in the same way to afford aid from the twelfth town of Coldinghamshyre—viz. that within which the church of Coldingham was founded; and this burden continued in force till it was remitted to them by King Alexander II. by a charter[3] dated in the thirteenth year of his reign, A.D. 1226.[4]

William the Lion, by his charter founding the Abbey of Arbroath, in the year A.D. 1178, conveyed to the monks many churches free "ab exercitu et expedicione et operacione et auxilio et ab omnibus consuetudinibus et omni servicio et exacione." He then confirmed the grants made by various individuals to the abbey "in liberam elemosinam," adding to his confirmation the words "salvo servicio meo," and concluding "omnia autem dona predicta ita liberaliter et quiete prefate ecclesie concedo sicut ego terras meas proprias possideo, *defensione regni mei excepta* et regali justicia."[5]

The nature of the burdens then falling on land may be gathered from a charter by Gillecrist, Earl of Angus, confirming to the monks of Arbroath the lands of Portincraig, which had been pre-

[1] Conredium interdum pro *Procuratione* seu conviviis quæ Dominis præstabantur a vassallis ex jure definito quoties per illorum terras pergebant.—(Duncange, Glossar. *sub voce.*)

[2] Raine's North Durham, App. p. 5.

[3] Raine's North Durham, App. p. 14.

[4] The Irish clergy were released from personal attendance on the hostings, A.D. 799.—(Annals of the Four Masters by O'Donovan, vol. i. p. 409.)

[5] Registr. de Aberbroth. pp. 5-7.

viously granted to them by his father for the erection of an hospital, "in liberam elemosinam libere et quiete, ab exercitu, et expedicione, et exaccione multure, et ab omnibus auxiliis et geldis, et omnibus serviciis, et secularibus exaccionibus."

All these burdens the Earl took upon himself, and the freedom thus bestowed was confirmed by the king's charter, without which it would have been inept.[1]

William the Lion confirmed to the Hospital of St. Andrews a ploughgate of land granted by Simon Fitz Michael, free from secular services or customs, all of which were undertaken by the granter and his heirs, with this exception, "quod idem hospitale adquietabit illam carrucatam terre de Gildo regio quod communiter capictur de terris et de elemosinis per regnum Scocie."[2]

In various cases of national emergency, aids were demanded even from the holders of enfranchised lands, but they were followed by formal acknowledgments from the Crown that such aids were exceptional, and should not infer any loss of privilege.[3]

One of these by Robert the Steward, on the part of David II. to the Abbot of Arbroath, is remarkable. After reciting the exemption of the abbot, his men, and lands, from common aids and contributions, by reason of their enfranchisement and privileges, as well by reason of their regality as of pure alms, and that they had

[1] Registr. de Aberbroth. p. 35.

[2] Registr. Priorat. S. Andree, p. 212.

[3] At the request of William the Lion, the men of the Abbot of Dunfermline assisted in fortifying the king's castles in Ross, and his writ was issued that this instance of their good will should not be used to their prejudice in future.—(Registr. de Dunferm. p. 32.) The men of the Abbot of Arbroath, at the request of King Alexander II., contributed aid "ad coria adquietanda que in Anglia vendidimus quando usque ad Douerum profecti fuimus,"—and a like writ was issued by the king.—(Registr. Vet. de Aberbroth. p. 224.)

of their own will contributed a subsidy of the twentieth mark of their lands at the siege of Perth, because through the wasting of the country, those who were liable in the common aid could not then fully perform what the exigency of the time required, yet this act of grace should not be used to their prejudice thereafter ("quod qui erant sub jure communi non valebant plene perficere quod regni necessitas tunc temporis requirebat").[1]

The early condition of landed property in England was similar in respect of the burdens laid on it. Of the change of the folcland into bocland, or from a condition of commonalty to that of individual property, Kemble writes, "In whatever form the usufruct may have been granted, it was accompanied by various settled burthens. In the first place were the inevitable charges from which no land was ever released, namely military service, alluded to by Beda, and no doubt in early times performed in person, the repair of roads, bridges, and fortifications."[2]

We find that many charters were granted by the authority of the king and his witan, freeing lands and churches belonging to monasteries from the burthens thus incident to them.[3]

One of these, granted by Ceolwulf, King of Mercia (A.D. 822), to Uulfred the Archbishop, contains a list of the dues and services from which the lands were exempted; some of which seem to be analogous to those grants in the Book of Deer, which free the lands from mormaer and toisech, and to that in favour of St. Serf's monks

[1] Registr. Priorat. S. Andree, p. 224.

[2] The Saxons in England, vol. i. p. 293.

[3] See Epistola ad Ecgbertum Antistitem, where Bede describes the monasteries of laymen as obtaining freedoms which made them independent "a divino simul et humano servitio," and withdrew from the defence of the country against pagan invasions those who ought to have protected it.—(Bede, Hist. Eccl., ed. Hussey, pp. 338-9.)

at Lochleven, in the Register of St. Andrews, already quoted. The lands in King Ceolwulf's charter are freed "ab omni servitute secularium rerum, a pastu regis, episcopi, principum, seu prefectum, exactorum, ducorum canorum vel æquorum seu accipitrum, ab refectione et habitu illorum omnium, qui dicuntur fæstingmen, ab omnibus laboribus, operibus, et oneribus sive difficultatibus, quot plus minusve numerabo vel dico, ab omni gravitatibus magioribus minoriis notis ignotis, undeque liberata permaneat in æfum, nisi in quattuor causis que nunc nominabo; expeditione contra paganos ostes, et pontis constructione seu arcis munitione vel destructione in eodem gente et singulare pretium foras reddat, secundum ritum gentis illius."[1]

Among the Celtic people of Brittany similar burdens on land were common, and the charters which give freedom from them have clauses like those just referred to. One conveying complete freedom, dated A.D. 842, is thus expressed:—"Sine fine, sine commutacione, sine jubileo anno, sine exactore, satrapaque, sine censu, et sine tributo sine opere alicui homini sub cælo nisi Sulcomino presbytero (the purchaser) et cui voluerit post se commendare, præter censum regis."[2]

In this case, as in some of the Scotch instances just quoted, the land was freed from all tributes to chiefs and officers, except the tax for national purposes, "preter censum regis."

In the year A.D. 866, Solomon, Count of Brittany, granted to the monastery of Redon certain lands, "sine censu, et sine renda, et sine tributo, et pastu caballis, et sine ulla re ulli homini sub cælo, nisi supradicto Salvatori et supradictis monachis."[3]

---

[1] Thorpe's Diplomatar. Anglic. Ævi Saxonici, p. 65: Lond. 1865.

[2] Chartular. de Redon, p. 103.

[3] Idem, p. 42.

The *consuetudines* and *servicia* in the clauses of enfranchisement of the Scotch charters probably included some burdens like those specified in the grants of the Mercian Ceolwulf just quoted.

Among these, besides personal services, was the burden of receiving the king or chief on his annual progress, and affording refection to him and his followers for a limited time.[1]

This right of refection forms a prominent feature in the early Irish system, and is described by Sir John Davis among the exactions extorted by the chieftains and tanists, in virtue of their barbarous seignory, by the term of *coshering*—viz. "visitations or progresses made by the lord and his followers among his tenants, wherein he did eat them out of house and home."[2]

In Brittany it appears in the charters as marjerium, prandium, pastus, procuratio.[3]

---

[1] Long after the migratory king, quartering himself during his yearly progresses upon the provincial aristocracy, and upon the steward of the royal lands, had passed into a stationary monarch, we find traces of the early custom. In the Parliament held at Cambuskenneth in 1326, King Robert Bruce undertook, in consideration of the liberal aid given to him, not to insist on the ancient exactions of provisions and conveyance in his journeys through the country, without making immediate payment. Another provision in the parliament of David II. at Perth, A.D. 1369, for equalising the burden of the royal household, points also to the results of the earlier royal circuits.—(Acts of the Parliaments of Scotland, vol. i. pp. 115, 150.)

[2] Historical Tracts, p. 134.

[3] Chartular. Redon, Prolegom. p. cccvi. There are notices in some of the charters of Inchaffray, which seem to indicate the existence of exactions of this nature, payable to the church of Dunkeld from the monastery of Madderty, one of our early Celtic foundations, which became secularised in the persons of the Earls of Strathearn. The monastic territory under the name of "Maddyryn que antiquitus Abbacia vocabatur," was towards the end of the twelfth century conferred on the monks of Inchaffray by Earl Gilbert, the founder of their house.—(Registr. de Inchaffery, p. 13.) Thereafter Hugh, Bishop of Dunkeld, remitted to Inchaffery the can and coneveth which the clerics of Dunkeld had been in use to receive at Maddirdyn "qui Scotice dicitur Abthan."—(Idem, p. 73.)

There, as in Ireland and among the Saxons of England, the burden of refection fell not only on the lay proprietors and occupiers of the soil, but on churches and monasteries, in which case the right is expressed in the charters by different terms, as cibus, circada, parata.[1]

Among the Saxons in England the burden of furnishing refection to the king on his progresses, and to his officials and followers, was well understood, and in many cases became a fixed charge upon the lands whether the king actually visited them or not.

"Many of the charters granted to monasteries record the exemption from these claims, purchased at a heavy price by prelates, from his avarice or piety; and as the king himself gradually ceased to undertake these distant expeditions, and entrusted to his messengers to see and hear for him; so they in time established a claim to harbourage and reception in the same places. This was extended to all public officers going on the king's affairs, and not only to them, but to servants of the royal household."[2] "The huntsman, stable-keepers, and falconers of the court, could demand bed and board in the monasteries, where they were often unwelcome enough; and this royal right, no doubt frequently used by the ealderman or sheriff as an engine of oppression, was also bought off at very high prices."[3]

[1] Chartular. Redon, Prolegom. p. cccvi.

[2] In Scotland we find traces of the ancient system in such claims as the following, made by James of Kyninmond on the monks of St. Andrews, A.D. 1438:—"Item yheure bailzery landsteuartry marschalry, I clame thir poynetis in fee and heritage, wyth houshald for me and twa gentilmen, twa yhemen, wyth the boyis folowand, my wyfe, and twa gentill women wyth hir, wyth sic houshald as efferis, a falcoune and a goishauk, a brais of greyhundis, and a coppil of Rachis, the best chaumer, the best stabill next my lordis, with fourty pund of fee folowand thir offices."—(Registr. Priorat. S. Andree, p. 430.)

[3] Kemble's Saxons in England, vol. ii. pp. 60, 61. We have an instance of the

At the beginning of the system, not only were the lands, dedicated to the church by temporal chieftains, held to be free from such an exaction, but many of those in their own occupation were subjected to payment of tributes and rents *to* the church;[1] but long before the twelfth century a change in this, as in other particulars, had taken place, as we may gather from denunciations against the usurped rights by the synods of the church.

The fourth act of the Synod of Cashel, A.D. 1172, enacts that all church lands, and possessions belonging to them, be wholly free from exaction on the part of all secular persons, and especially that neither petty kings nor chieftains, nor any other powerful men in Ireland, nor their sons, with their families, are to exact, as has been customary, victuals and hospitality, in lands belonging to the church, or presume any longer to extort them by force. And that those detestable contributions, which are wont to be exacted from lands belonging to the church four times in the year by the neighbouring chieftains, are to be exacted no more.[2]

The "freedom" conferred in some of the Irish grants in the Book of Kells,[3] includes a release from this burden of lay refection. Thus the King of Tara granted Cill-delga, with its territory and

purchase of exemption from payment of the earl's dues in the Chartulary of Redon, A.D. 1114-39, which shows that a certain knight Geoffrey bestowed on the abbey thirty measures of salt, and two men with their land, which were free from all custom to the earl or any one else, "quia ipse dum sospes et in prosperitate erat, a comite Alano emerat, et octo libras pro immunicione eorum ut notum est omnibus habitantibus in terra ipsa, dederat (p. 325).

[1] An example of such tributes payable by the Hy-Many to St. Grellan will be found in O'Donovan's Tribes and Customs of Hy Many, p. 13.

[2] Giraldus Cambrensis, Hibern. Expug. c. 34. Lanigan's Ecc. Hist. of Ireland, iv. pp. 206-210.

[3] Miscellany of the Irish Arch. Soc. vol. i. pp. 139, 143.

lands, to God and to Columbkille for ever, no king or chieftain having "rent, hosting, coigny on it as . . . before, for no chief durst touch it while [staying] in the territory."

The "freedom" of Ard Breacain was confirmed by the Kings of Ireland, the King of Meath, and the King of Loeghaire. The race of Loeghaire had a certain tribute on the church, viz. one night's coinmhe every quarter of a year, and this right the King Loeghaire surrendered for three ounces of gold. The church, therefore, was declared by all means to be separated from the Loegrians, and with its territory and lands to be free for two reasons—viz. on account of the general freedom of all churches, and on account of this purchase.[1]

Some of the grants in the Book of Deer confer "freedom" from the claims of the mormaer and the toisech. In one of them, however, the freedom is said to be from "all burdens except the proportion affecting four davochs of land, of such burdens as would fall on all chief monasteries [literally residences] of Alba generally, and upon all chief churches" (p. 95).

Another, after mortifying the chief's share, gave a dinner of a hundred every Christmas and every Easter to God and to Drostan (p. 93).

Among these burdens was doubtless that of refection, and while the monks were relieved of it and the other tributes and customs, they were declared to be still liable for a tax imposed on chief monasteries and churches in general, their proportion of which was regulated by the extent of their land.

Such grants of exemption from customary tributes and services were said to confer "freedom" on the monasteries and churches to

[1] Miscellany of the Irish Arch. Soc. vol. i. pp. 139, 143.

which they were granted; and after the gift of the Boar's Chase to St. Andrews by Hungus, with these immunities, it is said that "in memoriale *datæ libertatis*," the king placed on the altar a sod of the land.[1]

On the other hand, churches and monasteries, while they were paying such exactions and tribute, were said to be "sub servitute" and "enslaved."[2]

Thus, A.D. 1161, it is recorded that the churches of Columcille, in Meath and Leinster, were freed by the successor of Columcille Flaithbheartach Ua Brolchain, and "their tributes and jurisdiction were given him; for they had been previously enslaved."[3]

This "slavery" or subjection often inferred rights and privileges of considerable value to the superior. Thus, in A.D. 985, Maelseachlainn, the King of Ireland, having carried off for a time the shrine of St. Patrick, had to submit to the award of the successor of St. Patrick, the Abbot of Armagh, for his sacrilege—viz. "the visitation of Meath, both church and state, and a banquet for every fort from Maelseachlainn himself, besides seven cumhals [*i.e.* twenty-one cows, or their value], and every demand in full;[4] and on his first visitation of Munster, A.D. 1008, the successor of Patrick obtained a full visitation, both in screaballs and offerings.[5]

In the same way, tribes liable in payment of tributes and rents to other tribes were said to be "enslaved."[6]

In A.D. 854 the Saxon king Ethelwulf granted a charter reliev-

[1] Chronicles of Picts and Scots, p. 187.

[2] O'Donovan's Annals of the Four Masters, vol. ii. p. 1143.

[3] Idem, p. 1143.

[4] Idem, p. 719.

[5] Idem, p. 894. The offerings referred to in this passage meant valuable property—such as goblets, cattle, rings, etc.—(Note by O'Donovan, referring (as to the screaball) to Petrie's Round Towers, pp. 214, 215.)

[6] Tribes and Customs of Hy Many, p. 83.

ing the tenth part of the lands throughout his kingdom from all secular services and burdens, which narrates that he had resolved to grant the said tenth "in perpetuam libertatem," and free "ab omni regali seruitio et omnium saecularium absoluta seruitute."[1]

In A.D. 1048, Radulfus, a priest, granted to the monastery of Redon the church of St. Mary of Montalter. The gift was confirmed by Conan, Duke of Brittany, with freedom from rent and tribute, and a declaration that the men of the monastery were "ab *omni servitute liberi*."[2]

By an undated charter of William the Conqueror, granted at Winchester, to the monastery of Battle, printed from the original by Selden, in his edition of Eadmer's Historiæ Novorum (p. 165), he declares that it should be "libera et quieta in perpetuum ab *omni seruitute*, et omnibus quæcunque humana mens excogitare potest;" and again, that the church, with its territory, "libera sit ab omni dominatione et oppressione Episcoporum sicut illa quæ mihi coronam tribuit," "Nec liceat Episcopo Cicestrensi quamuis in illius Diœcesi sit, in Ecclesia illa, vel in maneriis ad eam pertinentibus ex consuetudine *hospitari* contra voluntatem Abbatis."

When, therefore, we come to consider the following entry in the Chronicle of the Picts and Scots, bearing on the state of the Pictish Church, it will be seen that the writer makes use of expressions which were common in the contemporary records of other countries. In the lists of the Pictish kings, from the Register of St. Andrews, it is said of Girg or Grig, "Et hic primus dedit *libertatem* ecclesiæ Scoticanæ, quæ *sub servitute* erat usque ad illud tempus ex consuetudine et more Pictorum.[3]

[1] Kemble, Codex Diplomat. Anglo-Saxon, vol. ii. p. 52.

[2] Chartular. Redon, p. 144.

[3] Chronicles of the Picts and Scots, p.

From the uniform application of the words in the chronicles and charters just quoted, where the meaning is obvious, there seems every probability that the terms "servitude" and "liberty," just quoted, are meant for some tribute or service customarily exacted from the church by the Pictish chiefs, of which it was released in the time of Grig.[1]

We discover, from the grants in the Book of Deer, that there yet remained burdens exigible from the chief monasteries and chief churches of Alba, which the mormaer excepts from the general enfranchisement of his grant.[2]

One of the memoranda in the Book of Deer, dated in the eighth year of the reign of David I., preserves the record of a grant by Gartnait the mormaer, and Ete his wife, to Columcille and to Drostan, of Pet-meic-Cobrig, for the consecration of the church of Christ and the apostle Peter;[3] with a declaration that the

174. See also p. 305, where the expression is "et dedit libertatem ecclesie Scoticane."

[1] In the Chartulary of Redon, quoted in the text, where the men of the abbey are said to be free "ab omni servitute," there is a contemporary gloss of "servicio" above the last word; and in the same sense of "services," the word is explained by Ducange as "census, præstatio, quæ serviri seu præstari et exsolvi debet" (voc. *Servitudo*, *Servitus*).

[2] About the same time we find that a payment of some kind continued to be paid by the monasteries of Brittany to the chief of the province. In the year 1040, Alan, Duke of Brittany, standing before the altar of St. Salvator at Redon, granted to that monastery the revenues payable to him by all the abbeys of the country, "gualoir tocius abbatie per totum Britannie regnum diffuse, illam scilicet partem que principibus usque ad illud tempus solvi consueverat;" at the same time enjoining on his officers, "ne quis eorum ingredi ulterius presumeret abbatiam Sancti Salvatoris pro hoc debito exigendo."—(Chartular. de Redon, p. 250.)

[3] The Pictish nation adopted the Roman usages, and, as we are told by Venerable Bede, rejoiced in being placed under the direction of St. Peter in the reign of King Nechtan, A.D. 710. Some of the Columbite churches at first refused to accept the usages, but soon conformed.—(H. E., lib. v. c. 21. Annals of Ulster, in Chronicles of the Picts and Scots, p. 354.)

lands were "free from all the exactions with the gift of them to Cormac, bishop of Dunkeld."

The *king's* share of Pet-meic-Gobroig had been already granted to the clerics by King Malcolm mac Kenneth;[1] so it would seem that the "share" of the mormaer was now granted as a gift at the dedication of a newly-erected church at Deer.

It is not clear what is here conferred on the Bishop of Dunkeld, but probably we are to understand the subjection of the lands to his jurisdiction, and to his rights of visitation.[2]

The establishment of a bishop at Dunkeld, over a defined diocese, was then of recent date—having occurred less than twenty years previously.

Before this time Dunkeld was the site of a royal monastery,

[1] The king's grant consisted of his *share in* the lands—not of the lands themselves, as seems to be assumed by Mr. Robertson (Scotland under her Early Kings, vol. ii. p. 499).

[2] Writing of early Episcopal visitations, Dr. Reeves remarks—"The first rudiment of the Irish system of visitation is to be discovered in the practice of the abbots of chief monasteries, who occasionally made a circuit of a particular district where the memory of their patron saint was held in esteem, carrying with them his reliques or insignia, and levying contributions from churches and people."—(Primate Colton's Visitation of Derry, p. iii.) It followed that churches and lands in different parts of the country might thus be subjected to a bishop in consequence of the connection being frequently the result of merely personal considerations. Thus, A.D. 1140, the Coarb of Patrick (Bishop of Armagh) went on a visitation-tour in Connaught for the first time, and obtained a liberal tribute; and it was agreed by Turlough O'Connor and the nobles of Connaught to place their churches in subjection to his control."—(O'Donovan's Annals of the Four Masters, vol. ii. p. 1063.) In the early Irish Church the right of refection in visitations formed the principal means of support to the bishop, "and indeed by these refections did the Byshops chiefly mayntayne themselves and their followers, spending the most part of the yeare in this wandring kind of lyfe among their tenents and receaving from them meate and drink for 100 and some tymes 200 people that followed the Bp."—(MS. of Bishop Montgomery, quoted in the Ordnance Survey Memoir of Templemore, p. 50.)

founded about the middle of the ninth century. It was dedicated to St. Columba, and was rendered illustrious by its possession of some of the relics of that great saint. For a time the abbot of Dunkeld seems to have exercised that primacy over the church of Alba which originally belonged to the abbots of Hy. The Annals of Ulster, in A.D. 864, record the death of Tuathal, son of Artgus, chief Bishop of Pictland and Abbot of Duncaillenn. About a century later, the primacy was transferred to the Abbot of St. Andrews; and amid the distractions incident to the desolations of the Norsemen, and other causes which were at work throughout Europe, the abbacy fell into the hands of laymen, who assumed the name of abbots, and transmitted the inheritance to their children.

The idea of defined territorial dioceses was foreign to the ecclesiastical system of the Celtic people of Ireland and Scotland; and when Dunkeld was erected into the see of a bishop, his diocese was not a continuous territory, with boundaries suggested by the natural features of the country, but rather consisted of districts without any such relation, and of churches on opposite sides of the kingdom, destitute of any connection with Dunkeld, except that arising from circumstances of personal and religious affinity.

In this way the newly-created bishopric of Dunkeld comprehended within its spiritual jurisdiction Argyle, with Iona, in continuation of the primacy with which the abbey of Dunkeld had been invested.

It would seem, then, that the gift to Cormac, Bishop of Dunkeld, expressed in the grant of the mormaer of Buchan, was a token of veneration for the memory of the great Columba, and a memorial of the original connection of Deer with him as its founder.

The lands granted by Gartnait lay within the still more recently created diocese of the bishop whom King David had established at Aberdeen;[1] but it is plain that the subjection to the Bishop of Dunkeld did not infer any breach of diocesan privileges, and we may readily believe that these were as yet too undetermined, and the old feelings of *personal* connection too common, to render such an arrangement in any way unsuitable.

There is a remarkable exception from a general confirmation of the offerings to the clerics of Deer (p. 95), in which Colban and his wife mortmained the whole from every burden for ever, except *as much as would fall on four davochs of the gross burdens exigible from the chief monasteries and chief churches of Alba.*[2]

[1] Nectan, the first Bishop of Aberdeen after the transfer of the See from Mortlach, is a witness to the grant of the mormaer.

[2] What constituted a chief monastery or chief church was probably the importance arising from antiquity of foundation and extent of endowments. Some monasteries had under them dependent houses and churches, as Mortlach, which had a subordinate monastery at Cloveth, and five churches. The monastery of Dull, in Athole, seems to have been subject to that of Dunkeld, and a payment continued to be made out of the *abthania* of Dull to the Bishop of Dunkeld, apparently as in place of the earlier abbots, in the year 1361.—(Chamberlain Rolls, vol. i. p. 381.) The Culdee monastery at Madderty seems also to have been subject to Dunkeld, whose "clerics" had right to certain payments from the abthania of Madderty.—(Registr. de Inchaffray, pp. 15, 71, 72.) The church of Kinkell had under it seven churches.

In the matter of jurisdiction as apart from extent of endowment, the monastery of Hy was chief of all the monasteries of the Columban order both among the Scots and Picts of Alba, as well as in Ireland. Venerable Bede, writing of the foundation of Durrow and Iona, says, "Ex utroque monasterio plurima exinde monasteria per discipulos ejus et in Brittania et in Hibernia propagata sunt; in quibus omnibus idem monasterium insulanum in quo ipse requiescit corpore principatum tenet."—(H. E. iii. c. 4; see also c. 21.) The primacy was afterwards vested in the monastery of Dunkeld, and lastly in that of St. Andrews.

Precedency among churches was sometimes acquired from circumstances connected with their foundation. Thus of

Thus, notwithstanding the freedom from mormaer and toisech conferred in the grants, the lands of the clerics would still be liable for their proportion of a tax for the public or national support—"those inevitable charges" from which, according to Kemble, "no land was ever relieved" (see p. xcii.); and the clause of the grant which restricts their liability to the amount leviable from four davochs, would lead us to conclude that some scheme for the allocation of such public burdens, dependent on the *extent* of the land, was in operation at this early period.[1]

Clogher we learn from Dr. Reeves that the nucleus of this ecclesiastical settlement was an earthen fort in the episcopal demesne, which was the seat of the Kings of Airghialla, and when St. Maccarthen founded the see of Clogher at this place it was in compliance with the instructions of St. Patrick: "Vade in pace fili et monasterium ibi construe in platea antea regalem sedem Urgallensium." Hence it was that this church, being grafted on the lordship, acquired precedency in the dominions of Airghialla, so that in after ages *Episcopus Ergalliæ* became a common designation of the Bishops of Clogher."—(Reeves' Adamnan, p. 112, *note.*)

[1] The term "old extent," as applied to land, was known in the time of King Alexander III. For traces of some early general valuation or extent of all the lands in the kingdom subject to aids, see an Historical Inquiry regarding the Imposition of Taxes upon Land in Scotland, by Thomas Thomson, Esq., pp. 14, 15. Edinburgh, 1816. Mr. Thomson there remarks that "very early indications of such extents may be traced in the local denominations of *carrucata terræ, bovata terræ* (ploughgates and oxgangs), to be found in writings of the eleventh century; and the more precise and intelligible description of merk-land and pound-land (*mercata terræ, librata terræ*), and others of the same sort, give clear demonstration of the existence of a general extent of lands."—(Idem, p. 14.) Traces of something similar occur in the description of the lands granted to St. Kieran by the chief of Hy Many, which concludes with "a quarter in Kiltuma, and the portion proportionable to five ungaes or ounces of silver in Carnagh, that is, a quarter and a half in Cluain Acha Leaga,—viz. in Acha Obhair, and the Creagga, and in Killiarainn and town-lands of Ruan."—(Tribes and Customs of Hy Many, p. 15, *note.*)

V.

The Early Scottish Church.

THE PICTISH CHURCH: ITS PECULIARITIES—ABIDING REVERENCE FOR CHURCH FOUNDERS—LAY USURPATIONS—WARRIOR ABBOTS—CHANGES INAUGURATED BY ST. MARGARET—CHARACTER OF THE CULDEES, AT ST. ANDREWS, MONYMUSK, BRECHIN, DUNBLANE, ABERNETHY, ST. SERF'S INCH—CHANGE OF ABBATIAL INTO EPISCOPAL JURISDICTION.

THE Church of St. Columba, which he founded in Alba, inherited with its Irish origin, the monastic system and ecclesiastical usages which prevailed in that country. In the beginning of the eighth century, under the influence of Nectan, King of the Picts, some of these usages were exchanged for those of the Church of Rome; and after this conformity, in the language of Venerable Bede, the nation rejoiced as being placed under the new discipleship of St. Peter, and safe under his protection.[1]

If the system of the Pictish Church was at this time brought into harmony with that of other branches of the Western Church, it is certain that, in the course of the three centuries and a half which followed, she had again become estranged from that influence, and, in the end of the eleventh century, presented to the

[1] "Et quasi novo se discipulatui beatissimi apostolorum principis Petri subditam ejusque tutandam patrocinio gens correcta gaudebat."—(Hist. Eccles. v. 21.)

view of the Saxon princess Margaret, the queen of Malcolm Canmore, a picture of corruption and stagnation.

About the middle of the following century, St. Bernard bewailed the corrupt state of the Irish Church, which in many respects corresponded with that of her sister in Scotland.

In both countries the ecclesiastical arrangements were grafted on the patriarchal system of society, in which nearness of blood to the founder of the clan, secured privileges and rights which were denied to those whose connection with him was more remote.[1]

---

[1] We can detect similar results flowing from relationship of a different description to great church saints, like St. Cuthbert.

Thus the monks who were the bearers of his body, when it finally reposed at Durham, came to enjoy portions of his patrimony, and transmitted them to their descendants. Of four of these bearers, we gather from Reginald the nicknames or surnames. One of them, who was guilty of hiding a cheese from his brethren, was believed to have been for a time changed into a fox, whence his descendants were named "*Tod* quod vulpeculam sonat." At that time, says the same lively writer, "cætus Clericorum qui usus in canendo monachorum eotenus tantummodo retinuerat, in eadem ecclesia, sub Episcopo, dominii privilegium obtinebat." He goes on to add that the bearers of the saint's body were of the same kind and training. They possessed prebends of the church "de more Canonicorum, qui nunc dicuntur Secularium, . . . et exercitia monastica in officiis ecclesiasticis persolvebant." From thence it happened, says Reginald, of him who was called *Tod*, "jam tunc temporis, tali religionis scemate, Ecclesiam de Bethligtune cum pertinentiis suis jure canonicali in sua progenie possidebat."—(Reginaldi Monach. Dunelm. Libellus, cap. xvi. p. 29—Surt. Soc.) The descendants of another of the bearers of St. Cuthbert's body acquired hereditary rights over the church of Hexham.—(See Mr. Longstaffe's valuable paper, entitled The Hereditary Sacerdotage of Hexham, Arch. Ælian. (new series), vol. iv. pp. 11-28.)

The "family" of St. Cuthbert soon degenerated in discipline, not merely through the decay of their first fervour, but from the distractions of the time, and the want of ecclesiastical oversight. Symeon thus describes them:—"Seculariter itaque omnino viventes, carni et sanguini inserviebant, filios et filias generantes: quorum posteri per successionem in ecclesia Dunelmensi fuerunt, nimis remisse viventes, nec ullam nisi carnalem vitam quam ducebant scientes, nec scire volentes. Clerici vocabantur, sed

In the same way, the memory of those saints who founded monasteries was so esteemed in later times, that the abbots who succeeded them derived much of their importance from being regarded as "heirs" or successors[1] of the founder, not merely in office, but as of the same blood.[2]

There was in both a gradually-increasing tendency to render every office, from the most important to the most trivial, hereditary in certain tribe-families.[3]

nec habitu nec conversatione clericatum prætendebant.—(De Dunelmensi Ecclesia, Prefatio Symeonis, ap. Twysden, Decem Scriptores.)

Another mode by which a church became hereditary, was when the founder entailed it on a priest and his issue, of which Kemble gives an example, where a lady grants a church hereditarily to "Wæulfmr preost and his bearnteam," as long as he shall have any in orders.—(Codex Diplomat. vol. iv. p. 282.) In Scotland, so late as the latter part of the twelfth century, Pope Urban III., while he pronounced against the hereditary succession of a son to his father's benefice, yet permitted its recognition in certain cases.—(Registr. Episcopat. Glasguen. vol. i. p. 59.)

[1] The word comarba or successor, applied by the Irish Annalists to the succeeding abbots, was restricted in its application. It did not mean that the one abbot was successor of his predecessor, but of the founder of the monastery: "Hinc apud nostrates vocari cœpit illius *successor comhorbanus;* non tamen cujuscumque cui sic succedebat, sed solius primi fundatoris illius loci vocabatur *comhorbanus.*—(Colgan. Trias. Th. p. 630, col. 1, in Reeves' Eccles. Ant. of Down, Connor, and Dromore, p. 145, note.)

[2] The spirit of jealousy, which prevailed between rival clans, and led to incessant conflicts and bloodshed, was equally powerful among the monastic bodies, whose battles with each other fill a prominent page in the Celtic Annals. A very ample list of ecclesiastical battles, drawn from these sources, is given by Dr. Reeves in Primate Colton's Visitation, Appendix B, pp. 93-97. Of the warrior abbots of Scotland, the same Annals preserve notices. Duncan, Abbot of Dunkeld, was slain in battle, A.D. 965. Crinan, Abbot of Dunkeld, was married to Bethoc, the only daughter of Malcolm II., and he fell in supporting the claims of his grandson, Malcolm, against Macbeth, A.D. 1045.—(Annals of Ulster, in Chronicles of the Picts and Scots, pp. 364, 369.)

[3] So late as the beginning of the seventeenth century, Camden writes of the Irish nobility: "They have their historians, who record their exploits; physicians;

Thus the abbatial succession came to be confined to members of the clan of the founder; and although originally the abbots were elected from the "founder's kin," and were distinct from those of the clan who possessed the abbatial lands, yet in process of time the ecclesiastical line was merged in the secular, and both were united in one lay official, like the successors of St. Patrick at Armagh, who were the objects of St. Bernard's denunciations.[1]

In the Scotch monasteries of the twelfth century we find that the evils complained of by St. Bernard, in the case of Armagh, had been reproduced. This may probably be said of most of them,—and certainly of the more important institutions of which we have the history. The abbots had come to be ecclesiastics in nothing but the name;[2] they themselves were not ordained; and their

poets (called bards), and harpers, each of whom have lands assigned them, and each of these possessions in every territory form distinct families; as the Breahans of one lineage and name, the historians of another, and so of the rest, who each bring up their children or relations in their respective arts, and are always succeeded by them."—(Britannia, by Gough, vol. iv. p. 467.)

[1] "Verum mos pessimus inoleverat quorumdam diabolica ambitione potentum sedem sanctam obtentum iri hereditaria successione. Nec enim patiebantur episcopari nisi qui essent de tribu et familia sua. Nec parum processerat execranda successio decursis jam in hac malitia quasi generationibus quindecim. Et eousque firmaverat sibi jus pravum imo omni morte puniendam injuriam, generatio mala et adultera, ut etsi interdum defecissent clerici de sanguine illo, sed episcopi nunquam. Denique jam octo extiterant ante Celsum viri uxorati, et absque ordinibus, litterati tamen."—(Vita S. Malachiæ, S. Bernardi Opera, ed. Migne, tom. i. col. 1086.) See an instructive paper, by Dr. Reeves, on the Early System of Abbatial Succession in the Irish Monasteries, in Proc. R. I. Acad. vol. vi. p. 447; and his Adamnan's Life of St. Columba, p. 342.

[2] The usurpation of spiritual benefices by laymen was so inveterate in Scotland, that even in the commencement of the thirteenth century it was necessary for the Scotch Church to enact that rectors of churches should be ordained "Item irrefragabili constitutione sancimus, ut rectores ecclesiarum ad primos ordines veniant ordinandi ita quod quam cito fieri

spiritual duties, which they neglected, were performed by stipendiary priors; while those which specially belonged to the episcopal office were fulfilled by bishops living within the monasteries, and subject to the jurisdiction of the abbots. Monastic rules were set at nought by those who were called monks, and their share

poterit commode ordinentur."—(Registr. Aberdon. vol. ii. p. 34.)

In England the same abuse prevailed, of which we have an instance at Whalley, in Lancashire, where the rectors or "deans" were for generations also lords of the town and married men, who held the benefice not by presentation from any other patron, but as their own patrimonial estate, being compounded of patron, incumbent, ordinary, and lord of the manor, and not in priest's orders.—(Whitaker's History of Whalley, pp. 32, 41, 42. Lond. 1806.)

In the year 1226 the rector of the church of Wickington was accused of having succeeded to his father in the benefice, and under a writ issued by the Archbishop of York, it was proved "quod pater ejus firmarius tantum ecclesiæ memoratæ extitit et non rector," on which ground the archbishop decreed "memoratum Willelmum ab hujusmodi successione immunem."—(Rot. Major, Walteri Gray, Archiep. Ebor. (1216-1255, No. 9, noted for me by my friend Canon James Raine of York.) The same state of lay usurpation sometimes arose from different causes.*

In the case of Bobbio, one of the houses founded by the great Irish missionary St. Columbanus, the steps can easily be traced in the records of the monastery,* by which the lay character was attained. One of these narrates a grant, dated A.D. 602, by Agilulf, King of the Lombards, of the basilica of St. Peter of Bobbio, with a territory, to St. Columbanus, who by a subsequent deed resigns it to the Roman See. This is signed by St. Columbanus and eleven brethren, of whom three appear to have been of his own Celtic blood:—Conanus sacerdos et monacus; Gurgarus genere brittonum, Domcialis humilis diaconus Scotto [sic] et monacus (p. 2).

About forty years afterwards, Pope Theodore conferred various privileges on the monastery of Bobbio, which is said then to contain 150 monks under the rule of St. Benedict, or of its founder St. Columbanus.†

Somewhat later the successors of the humble Irishman coveted the addition of temporal lordship to their spiritual privileges, and various deeds of the Kings of Italy and Emperors of Germany occur, constituting the abbots *counts* of Bobbio.‡

* For some of these, see Mabillon, Act. Sanct. Ord. Bened. tom. iii. pref. p. lvi. Venet. 1734.

* Printed in the great work of the Sardinian government, Historiæ Patriæ Monumenta, vol. i. Turin, 1836.

† Idem, p. 6.

‡ Idem, pp. 66, 252.

of the monastic revenues was transmitted to their families and relatives.

Under this system the episcopal arm was powerless to control or correct the usurpations of the lay element; and so long as the system of clanship remained unbroken, there was no opening for that episcopal interference which, in the diocesan and parochial institutions, had become influential in other parts of Europe.

Like results had indeed prevailed in the ecclesiastical arrangements of most European countries for a time; but in these the progress of events had introduced many changes, and ameliorating influences.

In Ireland and Scotland the corruptions seemed so naturally adapted to those national tendencies which prompted them to look back with chief regard to the *founders* of their polity, whether spiritual or civil,[1] that no foreign element of improvement could

[1] A reverence for St. Columba was the great obstacle to the adoption of the Roman usages, when the systems of the Roman and Pictish Churches were discussed at the Synod of Whitby in the year A.D. 664. Colman, the champion of the latter, asked if it was credible that St. Columba and his successors kept their Easter contrary to the Divine writings (Bede, H. E. iii. 25); and in describing the conformity of the monks at Hy to the Roman use, through the preaching of the holy father and priest, Egberct, Venerable Bede calls it a surrender of the inveterate tradition of their forefathers.—(H. E. iii. 25, v. 22.) This reverence assumed many forms. In Ireland objects associated with the Saint were for many centuries carried into battle by the men of his clan, in the belief that thereby victory would be secured.—(Reeves' Adamnan, pp. 249, 319, 332.) In the tenth century we read that the men of Alba would have as their standard at the head of every battle the crozier of Columcille (Chron. of Picts and Scots, p. 406, note); and in the twelfth century we find a fair barony belonging to the keeper of the brecbennoche, a banner of St. Columba (Reeves' Adamnan, p. 330); while in the same age the highest sanction to an obligation with some was an oath *per sanctum Columbam.*—(Registr. de Passelet, pp. 125, 126.)

Among the arguments used by St.

obtain access; and in these countries the evils which had been more or less prevalent in all, remained unabated[1] after they had been supplanted elsewhere.

In Scotland this system of inherited peculiarity, both civil and ecclesiastical, was first confronted with one founded on entirely different principles, when the Celtic clergy of Scotland met in council, to listen, during three days, to the addresses of Margaret, the Saxon princess, translated out of her own tongue by her Gaelic husband, King Malcolm.

The portrait of the Saxon princess, as it is drawn in the pages of Turgot, her friend and spiritual adviser, commends her to our admiration, as one of the purest, the most humble and beneficent of women; while, as a queen, she appears to have combined with her personal graces, admirable majesty of conduct, and true love of her adopted country.

The rugged but generous nature of her husband, through her tender influences, became at once softened and elevated. Through these he was predisposed to welcome those numerous emigrants driven from England by the violence of the Conqueror, or attracted to a new country by the hopes of better fortunes, whose settlement was so influential in remoulding the structure of society in Scotland.

While Margaret's own life was marked by the austerity of an

Columbanus to sustain his practice of celebrating Easter after the Scotic custom, long after he had forsaken his monastery of Bangor for missionary toil among the Franks and in Italy, are prominent references "traditioni patriæ meæ," "regulis nostrorum seniorum," and the like.—(S. Columban. Abb. Epist. ap. Migne, Scriptor. Eccles. sec. vii. coll. 266, 269.)

[1] For a notice of the "servitude" under which the Scottish Church was placed by the custom of the Picts, and its release by King Grig in the end of the ninth century, see p. c. *supra*.

ascetic, she deemed it right to add to the dignity and splendour of her husband's court, encouraging merchants to bring from abroad costly garments, and gold and silver dishes.[1]

The gentleness and purity with which she sought for improvement, were new influences in the government of the country, and to some extent disarmed the first feeling of aversion to all change which characterised her Celtic subjects; while the steady adherence by her children to the policy which she had inaugurated, led to a more rapid yet less violent overthrow of the clan system, both in church and state, than could have otherwise been anticipated.

Besides the usages and corruptions[2] in the church, which, through her influence, were altered and corrected, she led to the introduction of institutions which, as their influence became powerful, broke up the narrow and divided polity of the Celtic

[1] The gifts of Malcolm Canmore to Edgar, the brother of his wife, show that the statements of Turgot on this point, which I have quoted in the text, are well founded. They comprehended "skins decked with purple, pelisses of marten skin, and weasel skin, and ermine skin, palls, and golden and silver vessels."—(The Anglo-Saxon Chronicle, ad an. 1074, by Thorpe, vol. ii. p. 180.)

[2] Among these errors of the Scotch clergy, one consisted in their time of beginning the Lenten fast, which resulted in this, that they only fasted thirty-six, instead of forty days. Others were, their declining to receive the sacrament of Christ's body at Easter, and certain barbarous rites connected with the celebration of the mysteries, "contra totius ecclesiæ morem." The queen persuaded them to abandon those, and to give up unlawful marriages, such as that between a brother and his brother's wife, "multa quoque alia contra morem ecclesiæ inoleverant, quæ in eodem concilio damnans, de regni finibus extirpavit." While the church, as a body, was thus corrupted, we hear of the strict lives of many hermits living in caves or cells throughout Scotland. These the queen venerated, as seeing Christ in them, visiting them in their abodes, and soliciting the blessing of their prayers.—(Vita. S. Marg. Scotor. Regin. by Turgot, ap. Symeonis Dunelm. Opera, vol. i. p. 247—Surt. Soc.)

people,[1] to make way for one founded on the ideas of corporate unity and diffused sympathy.

Soon, dioceses and parishes, such as had been established in England at an earlier period, begin to appear in our records. We discover new civil divisions, through the change of the old "countries" or "provinces" into shires; the transition of the mormaers into earls; the beginning of towns; the growth of feudal law, in the rules of succession and the tenure of land. A race of Saxon settlers was introduced into the country, the result of the whole being a quickening of the national life, and the awakening of a feeling of unity, such as could find no place among the divided clans of a Celtic people.

The corrupted state of Scottish monasticism is well illustrated in the history of the house of St. Regulus at St. Andrews. It is impossible, however, to advert to this history without reference to the Culdees, who are so intimately connected with the fortunes of the establishment; and as the system of those clerics was still a prominent feature of the religious polity of Scotland when we become acquainted with the house of Deer in the eleventh century, I have thought it permissible to collect in this chapter the more important facts relating both to the monastery of St. Andrews, and to the Culdees generally.

The rubric of "the legend of St. Andrew," written shortly after the middle of the twelfth century, tells us of the many monasteries of early foundation in the country of the Picts, and by what means

[1] In Ireland foreign ecclesiastical influences led, about the same time, to the formation of territorial dioceses and parishes, which were unknown in that country prior to the Synod of Rathbreasil, held in 1110.

many of them had come to be possessed by secular men of hereditary right.[1]

At St. Andrews, the monastery of St. Regulus, on which the piety of Hungus, the Pictish king, had conferred extensive lands and privileges, had become almost wholly secularised. Of its inmates, thirteen were commonly called Culdees. These transmitted their office "per successionem carnalem," by which we are probably to understand that the office was confined to members of a sept, in conformity with the arrangements in many of the Irish monasteries.[2]

After they were made Culdees, it was not lawful for them to keep their wives in their houses, nor any other woman through whom evil suspicions might arise.[3]

Although it was their duty to serve at the altar of the apostle, yet it was deserted by them, nor was mass celebrated there, except on the rare occasions when the king or the bishop was present, for the Culdees celebrated their office after their own fashion in a certain corner of their church, which was exceedingly small.

---

[1] "Qualiter acciderit quod memoria Sancti Andree apostoli amplius in regione Pictorum, que nunc Scotia dicitur, quam in ceteris regionibus sit; et quomodo contigerit tante abbatie ibi facte antiquitus fuerint quas multi adhuc seculares viri jure hereditario possident."—(Chronicles of the Picts and Scots, p. 138.)

[2] King's Early History of the Primacy of Armagh, p. 23. The monks of Lindisfarne, who towards the end of the ninth century had borne away from Holy Island the body of their great saint, thereby established for their descendants a hereditary right to their clerical position and estates.—(Reginaldi Liber de B. Cuthbert. cap. xvi. p. 29.)

[3] Apparently when in residence, and while performing their duties. The popular belief about the Culdees of Dunkeld is preserved by Mylne in his History of the Bishops of Dunkeld, of whom he writes, "habentes tamen secundum orientalis ecclesiae ritum conjuges a quibus dum vicissim ministrabunt abstinebant; sicut postea in ecclesia Beati Reguli, nunc Sancti Andreae, consuetum tunc fuit."—(Vitæ Episcop. Dunkelden. p. 4; Bann. Club.)

Besides the Culdees, the ecclesiastical community of St. Andrews consisted of seven "personæ" or parsons, who, after allotting to the bishop one-seventh, and to the hospital another, divided among themselves the other five portions of the oblations of the altar, although they performed none of its duties, or of the church, beyond receiving such strangers as could not be received into the hospital.

These *parsons* (who may have been the lay inheritors of the seven churches founded by St. Rule at Kilrimont), besides receiving the oblations, were possessed of separate rents and property, which, on their death, their wives, whom they publicly maintained, and their sons or daughters, their relatives or sons-in-law, divided among themselves.[1]

The lands thus abstracted from their religious destination included the territory granted with such solemnity by Hungus, and called the Boar's Chase.

This condition of things has been thus described by Dr. Reeves:— "From this laboured and ill-digested statement we learn that at some period anterior to 1107, the ecclesiastical community of Cill-

[1] This was contrary to monastic discipline. The great Columbanus, in the fourth chapter of his *Regula Cœnobialis*, "De paupertate ac de cupiditate calcanda," lays down "Ideo ergo nuditas et facultatum contemptus prima perfectio est monachorum." The Rule of St. Columkille also enjoined, "Be always naked, in imitation of Christ and the Evangelists." "Whatsoever little or much thou possessest of anything,—whether clothing, or food, or drink,—let it be at the command of the Senior and at his disposal, for it is not befitting a religious to have any distinction of property with his own free brother."—(S. Columbani Abbatis Regula Cœnobialis apud Migne, Sæculi VII. Scriptor. Ecclesiast. Opera, col. 211, Paris, 1863. Reeves, Archbishop Colton's Visitation, A.D. 1397, pp. 109-10, where the Rule of St. Columbkille is printed for the first time. St. Chrodegang's Rules for Canon-Clerics, dated about the middle of the eighth century, allowed them the liferent use of their private estate, and a right to dispose of half of it by will.—(Statuta Eccles. Scotic. p. ccx. *note*.)

Righmonaigh had become parted into two sections, and that each carried with it a portion of the spiritualities and temporalities, which we may reasonably conceive had been originally combined. One party was the Keledei, consisting of a prior and twelve brethren, who numerically represented the old foundation, and as clerical vicars performed divine service, having official residences, and enjoying certain estates as well as the minor dues of the sacerdotal office. With them also, as the clerical portion of the society, rested the election of the bishop when a vacancy occurred in the see. The other party included the bishop, the eleemosynary establishment, and the representatives of the abbot, and other greater officers now secularised, yet enjoying by prescription another portion of the estates and the greater ecclesiastical dues."[1]

It is paralleled by the case of Winchester, where the canon-clerics in the same way deserted the altar, and consumed the monastic revenues in riotous living and all kinds of excess. At Durham also the canon-clerics left the church desolate, and led scandalous lives.

The remedy in these and like cases in England, was the expulsion of the canon-clerics or secular canons, and the introduction of regular canons.

A choice was, however, given to them in both the cases just referred to, between ejectment from their churches and submission to monastic rule. At Winchester three, and at Durham one, of their number conformed.[2]

[1] The Culdees of the British Islands, p. 39.

[2] At Winchester, A.D. 964, King Edgar, by the mouth of one of his attendants, and of the bishop, "mandavit clericis ocissime dare locum monachis, aut monachicum suscipere habitum. At illi execrantes monachicam vitam, illico exierunt de ecclesia; sed tamen postmodum tres ex illis conversi

When Alexander I. ascended the Scottish throne in the year 1107, the corruption at St. Andrews was unabated, presenting to him much which was in entire conflict with the new ecclesiastical customs and ideas of the period.

Accordingly the king began by conferring on the church of St. Andrews many gifts and privileges, restoring for the establishment of "religyoun," the lands which had formerly been granted for that purpose, but had been in the possession of the crown as royal coarbs, or hereditary abbots of the monastery of St. Regulus.

The intention of the king for the institution of a monastic "family" at St. Andrews was not fully effected till about twenty years after his death, in the time of his successor David I., when a community of canons-regular, under the rule of the order of St. Augustine, was finally established.

David, in dealing with the Culdees of St. Andrews, was in some respects less peremptory than the English reformers were with the canon-clerics at Durham, Winchester, and elsewhere.

He empowered the canons-regular to receive into their body the Culdees of Kilrimont if they consented to become canons; if

sunt ad regularem conversationem."—(Annal. de Wint. in Mr. Luard's Annal. Monast. vol. ii. p. 12.) At Durham, A.D. 1083, William the Conqueror ordained "ut canonici seculares de ecclesia beati Cuthberti amoveantur."—(Hist. Dunelm. Script. Tres, App. p. 5); and when the bishop inquired of them whether they would become canons-regulars or monks, they refused to become either,—"alloquitur primo illos quos in ecclesia invenerat ut vel clerici regulares vel monachi fierent, ut quovis ordine disciplinati vitam ducerent. Sed quoniam durum eis erat assueta relinquere, et in veteri mente nova meditari, neutrum admiserunt." On their refusal, an appeal was made to the king and the pope, and all agreed that they must be removed, but they were still permitted to remain if they became monks, an option of which only one availed himself.—(Sim. Dunelm. de Dunelmen. Eccles. pref. p. 2; Hist. de Dunelm. Eccles. lib. iv. cap. iii. ap. Twysden, Decem Scriptores.)

they should decline, they were to be permitted the enjoyment of their possessions during their lives, and on their death, regular canons were to be instituted in their place.[1]

The same monarch conferred on the canons of St. Andrews the island of Lochleven, that they might there institute their order in the ancient monastery of St. Serf. To the Culdees who might be in the latter he offered, that if they would live canonically, they might remain in peace, while those who resisted were at once to be ejected.[2]

A few years later, Pope Eugenius III. decreed that vacancies among the Culdees should be filled up by the appointment of regular canons.[3]

Their subsequent history consists of their struggles to resist the new order of things, and of the controversies arising out of them.

In 1147, Pope Eugenius had vested the election of the bishops of St. Andrews exclusively in the canons-regular, but it was not till the year 1273 that the Culdees were formally debarred from their prescriptive right to take part in the election. In 1332, when William Bell was elected to the see, the Culdees were absolutely excluded from any voice in the election, nor was their claim revived. But they continued their corporate existence, under another name, in the church of St. Mary de Rupe, with an establishment of a provost and ten prebendaries. After the Reformation the provostry became vested in the crown, and in 1616 was annexed to the See of St. Andrews.[4]

The history of the Culdees of Monymusk, a house of early

[1] Registr. Priorat. S. Andree, p. 186.
[2] Idem, p. 188.
[3] Idem, p. 49.
[4] Reeves' Culdees of the British Islands, pp. 40-41.

but uncertain date, affords some useful information on the condition of these ecclesiastics. This house of early origin, placed on the fertile banks of the river Don, in Aberdeenshire, comes to light in record towards the end of the twelfth century, when it received grants from Duncan Earl of Mar, and Roger Earl of Buchan.[1] In the year 1211 a complaint was made to the Pope by William, Bishop of St. Andrews, setting forth that "quidam qui se canonicos gerunt, et quidam alii Aberdonensis dyocesis infra villam de Munimusc pertinentem ad ipsum," were endeavouring to establish a regular canonry, contrary to his will, and in great prejudice of his church. A commission was accordingly issued to investigate and settle the question, and the decision was to the effect that the Culdees in future should have one refectory and one dormitory in common, and one oratory without a cemetery, and that the bodies of the Culdees, or of clerks or laymen living with them, should receive ecclesiastical burial in the cemetery of the parish of Monymusk; that there should be twelve Culdees, with a thirteenth, to be presented by them to the Bishop of St. Andrews to be their master or prior. On the death of Brice, the existing prior, the Culdees should of common consent select from their own number three, to be presented to the Bishop of St Andrews, for his selection of one as prior. It was declared unlawful for the Culdees to profess the order or life of monks or canons-regular, without the bishop's consent, or to exceed the number of their body before prescribed; that when a Culdee died or withdrew, those who remained should fill up the vacancy. They resigned into the bishop's hands the lands which they had received from Gilchrist, Earl of Mar, without his episcopal consent, so that hereafter they should pretend no right to

[1] Registr. Priorat. S. Andree, pp. 362, 370.

them which might prejudice the dignity of the bishop, the liberty of the church of St. Andrews, or the parish church of Monymusk. When the bishop should happen to visit Monymusk, he was to be received with due solemnity, and with a procession; and, on the other hand, the bishop promised to cherish and protect the said Culdees as his own.[1]

Between this date and the year 1245, the house of Monymusk received grants from the crown, the Earl of Mar, and the Bishops of Aberdeen and St. Andrews, the first of which is in favour of "St. Mary of Monymusk and the Culdees, or canons there serving God;" while, in the others, they simply appear as "canons." In 1245 a papal confirmation was granted in favour of "the prior and convent of Monymusk of the order of St. Augustine;"[2] showing that the change from the ancient character of the house had now been formally completed.

There were Culdees at Brechin. David I. granted a charter of certain rights to the bishops and Keledei of Brechin;[3] and down to the early part of the thirteenth century they were members of the Episcopal Chapter. Soon after this they disappear as Culdees, and were absorbed in the reconstructed corporation.[4]

According to an authority of the latter part of the thirteenth century,[5] Culdees formed the cathedral body at Dunblane, at Rosmarkie, at Dornoch, at Lismore, and at Dunkeld. Mylne, in his History of the Bishops of Dunkeld, speaks of a change in the constitution of the monastery of Dunkeld having been made by

[1] Registr. Priorat. S. Andree, p. 370.

[2] Idem, pp. 363, 367, 368, 372.

[3] Regist. Episcopat. Brechinen. p. 3.

[4] Regist. Vet. de Aberbrothoc, pp. 175, 179. Regist. Episcopat. Brechinen. p. 262.

[5] Catalogue of Monasteries annexed to Henry of Silgrave's Chronicle, MS. Cott., printed in Scalacronica, p. 241; and Reeves' Culdees, p. 32.

David I. when it was erected into a cathedral church, the Culdees having been superseded about the year 1127, and a bishop and canons coming in their place. The first bishop on this foundation was for a time abbot of the monastery, and subsequently a counsellor of the king. On this statement Dr. Reeves remarks, "In the concluding passage the writer seems to imply that the Kelledei who occupied the monastery which was attached to the mother church, were removed from this position, and constituted a college of secular clergy; while their former place was assigned to a society of regular canons, with the bishop, now made diocesan instead of abbot, at their head. These two corporations co-existed for nearly two centuries; and as at St. Andrews, so at Dunkeld, Silgrave's Catalogue notices the collateral societies of *canonici nigri* and *Keldei*."[1]

There were Culdees at Abernethy, who appear in records down to the early part of the thirteenth century.[2] In 1272 their establishment was converted into a society of canons-regular.[3]

We hear also of Culdees at Iona,[4] at Muthil,[5] and at Monifeith,[6] —all places of early ecclesiastical settlement.

From the records now referred to, it seems plain that the term *Culdee* was a popular designation of the members of various monastic bodies of early foundation in Scotland.[7] When they appear

[1] Reeves' Culdees of the British Islands, p. 42. Mylne's Vitæ Episcop. Dunkelden. pp. 4, 5.

[2] Registr. Vet. de Aberbrothoc, pp. 25, 26.

[3] Fordun, Scotichronicon, vol. ii. p. 120.

[4] Annals of Ulster, A.D. 1164, in Chron. of Picts and Scots, p. 372.

[5] Charters of Cambuskeneth, in the Culdees of the British Islands, pp. 140, 141.

[6] Registr. Vet. de Aberbrothoc, p. 82.

[7] About the middle of the tenth century the officiating clergy of St. Peter's at York were called *Colidei*.—(Dugdale, Monasticon Anglicanum, vol. vi. pt. ii.

with greater definiteness in records of the twelfth century, their character and position are the same with those of the monastic "families" in England, Ireland, and the Continent. They were monks living without rule, but with no obstacle in their position to their being received as members of the new foundations of regular canons, if they would agree to live canonically.[1]

At Monymusk, it would seem that the old body made an attempt at self-reformation, and wished to be regarded as canons without being subject to the ecclesiastical rule thus involved. The attempt indicates the strength of the current which had set in for the new institutions, and the slightness of the external difference which kept the bodies asunder.[2]

p. 607). Towards the end of the twelfth century Giraldus Cambrensis applies the same term to the monks of Bardsey island.—(Itinerar. Kambriæ, p. 124. Lond. 1868.) In Ireland the term cele-de was used by the Annalists to designate ecclesiastics at Armagh, at Clonmacnois, at Devenish, and at other monastic seats. The earliest notice is dated A.D. 811.—(Reeves' Culdees of the British Islands, pp. 6, 25.)

[1] It has been supposed by some that the Culdees were not monks but canons-secular. In our records, however, it appears that the communities of Culdees at St. Andrews and Lochleven were governed by *abbots*.—(Chron. of Picts and Scots, p. 174. Registr. Priorat. S. Andree, p. 118.) It is plain also that they differed in their mode of life from the secular canons under the rule of St. Chrodegang, "non communiter viventes" (Registr. Priorat. S. Andree, p. 145); in the hereditary character of their corporation; in their mode of administering the property and revenues of the church; and in their manner of performing the offices of divine service.—(Registr. Priorat. S. Andree, p. 370.)

[2] There is no reason for thinking that the Culdees differed in their doctrinal views from those which prevailed in the church around them. The library of the Culdees of St. Serf's Inch in Lochleven was given to the canons-regular of St. Andrews on the foundation of their house. The character of the books of which it was composed, says Dr. Reeves, "is just what might be expected in a small monastic establishment of that date, and the ritual works are those which were in general use."—(Reeves' Culdees, p. 131, *note*.) These consisted of a pastorale, a gradual, a missal, the works of Origen, the Sentences of St. Bernard, a treatise on the

The influences which gradually reversed this order in things ecclesiastical, were not the result of natural progress in the Celtic polity, but of foreign ideas and principles introduced from without, which ended also in the destruction of the civil institutions on which that polity rested.

Some of these are shadowed forth in a remarkable passage from a Chronicle of Durham, quoted by Selden, which has sometimes been regarded as meaningless and untrue, where, after recording the election of Turgot to be Bishop of St. Andrews in the year 1008, the chronicler proceeds: "*In diebus illis, jus Keledeorum per totum regnum Scotiæ transivit in Episcopatum Sancti Andreæ.*"[1] This is obviously an inexact statement, but it points to the completion of a great ecclesiastical revolution—viz. the change from abbatial to episcopal jurisdiction.[2]

In the beginning of the tenth century we find for the first time in our annals mention of a bishop whose seat was at St. Andrews. This was soon after the translation of the primacy from the abbey of St. Columba, at Dunkeld, to that of St. Rule, at Kilrimont. There can be little doubt that the bishop was an inmate of the

Sacraments, a portion of the Bible, a Lectionary, the Acts of the Apostles, the Gospels, the works of Prosper, the Books of Proverbs, Ecclesiastes, and Canticles, a Gloss on the Canticles, a book called "Interpretationes Dictionum," a collection of sentences, a commentary on Genesis, and selections of ecclesiastical rules.—(Registr. Priorat. S. Andree, p. 43.) These works were suitable for any religious community in Western Europe, and were accordingly transferred to the canons-regular for their use—a tolerably sure token that the differences between the bodies were less doctrinal ones, than on points of rule and discipline.

[1] Chronicon Dunelmense, in Selden's Introduction to Twysden's Hist. Angl. Scriptores X., p. vi.

[2] This has no connection with the episcopal *order*, which was always regarded as superior to that of the abbot.

monastery, and that he was elected by the Culdee monks out of their own number, receiving his share of the altar-oblations.[1]

For two succeeding centuries, the names of the bishops prove their native Celtic origin, and lead us to infer the continuance of the Celtic polity which made the abbot the centre of jurisdiction. During this period, however, the primacy of the bishop was taking shape and growing in prominence. Kellach, the first recorded bishop, took part with the king and the people at a council at Scone, where all swore to observe the laws and discipline of the faith.[2] His successor, Fothad, received possession of the Culdee monastery of St. Serf, in Lochleven, on undertaking the maintenance of the brethren of that house. In the first quarter of the eleventh century, Bishop Malduin granted the church of Markinch to the Culdees of Lochleven. His successor, Tuathal, gave them the church of Scoonie,[3] and from a second Fothad, who came next to the see, they got Auchterderran.[4] Events these, which not only indicated an improvement in the episcopal position, but also other changes of ecclesiastical polity; for we may discover in these grants of churches the first symptoms of parochial institutions. Still, all these native bishops were so far bound up with the effete and corrupt monastic system then existing, as to be unable or unwilling to check its evils; for, as the "History of the Foundation of St. Andrew" proceeds, after describing the corrupted state of the clerics there, "Nor could this monstrous abuse be corrected before the time of Alexander [the First] of happy memory,[5] who, besides enriching the church of St.

[1] Robertson's Scotland under her Early Kings, vol. i. p. 338.

[2] Chronicles of the Picts and Scots, p. 9. This was in the year 909.

[3] Registr. Priorat. S. Andree, p. 116.

[4] Idem, p. 117.

[5] Chronicles of the Picts and Scots, p. 189.

Andrews with many and valuable gifts, restored to it the lands called the Boar's Chase, with the professed object and understanding that a religious society should be established in that church for the maintenance of divine worship." Another indication of the growth of the episcopal power, is the fact that after the usurped ecclesiastical possessions had been recovered from their lay holders, they are found in the hands of *the bishop,* who was inclined to regard the whole as belonging to his see, and at last yielded up rather ungracefully to the newly-established canons, the portion of the lands which had fallen in through the deaths of the "personæ."[1]

But the evil continued to linger, for although Turgot, a prelate foreign in blood and in polity, was elected to be bishop in the time of King Alexander, yet, as we have seen, a fresh house of religion was not established till nearly forty years after, and both agencies were required to overpower the earlier abbatial system and its clan corruptions. Still, the first step may be said to have involved all that followed, so that the statement quoted by Selden from the ancient chronicler of Durham has much of substantial truth in it.

[1] Chronicles of the Picts and Scots, p. 193.

THE EARLY SCOTTISH CHURCH—*Continued.*

II. Of the Origin of Parishes and Dioceses.

DIOCESES AND PARISHES UNKNOWN IN THE EARLY SCOTTISH CHURCH—PREVALENCE OF THE MONASTIC SYSTEM IN IT—CLAN BISHOPS AND MONASTERIES—THE PLOU OF BRITTANY—THE SAXON PARISH—CHANGE OF THE CLAN TERRITORY INTO A PARISH.

The system of the Celtic Church of Alba is represented with tolerable accuracy in the following statement of Hector Boece:—"Nondum enim Scotorum regnum, uti nunc, in diœceses diuisum erat; sed quivis episcoporum, quos ea ætate vitæ sanctimonia cunctis reverendos fecerat, quocunque fuisset loco, sine discrimine pontificia munera obibat."[1]

Neither dioceses nor parishes, in the sense now attached to them, can be traced further back than to the time of Alexander I.

The patriarchal idea which pervaded all the arrangements of our Celtic forefathers, led them to mould their ecclesiastical polity on the divisions of tribes and families, involving a *personal* basis of arrangement.

The monastery founded by their spiritual ancestor became the religious centre of the tribe or clan.[2] It was endowed with tributes

[1] Scotorum Historiæ, Paris, 1527, fol. ccviii.

[2] An apt illustration of what is here said of clan-monasteries occurs in Colgan's Life of St. Boedan, abbot of Kill Boedain, from which it appears that the saint, in his journeyings in the remote parts of Ulster, was "a nobili stirpe Sodani Fiaco Aradio nati in partibus Dalaradiæ tunc rerum potiente honorifice et devote susceptus." Here

and lands by its members, while the religious sway of the abbot extended over the territories of the tribe, as was afterwards the case with the bishops when dioceses came to be formed, so that it has been said, "every Irish seignory had its own [cathedral], whose diocess runned with the seignory bound."[1] And as there were clan-monasteries, so it naturally followed that the *personal* relationship resulted also in clan-bishops, who were thus primarily bishops of a people, and not of a district. At times the early Irish bishops are described as bishops merely of a Dun or Rath, which, as being the seat of the chief and the centre of the clan, is used in speaking of the whole. Thus, A.D. 618, Tighernach records the death of Eoganus Episcopus Rath-sith-ensis (*i.e.* Munimenti Lemurum, O'Conor, vol. ii. p. 184).[2] Dr. Reeves quotes a passage from the tripartite life

---

he built a church, from him called Kill-Boedain, "quam agris et possessionibus dotarunt posteri Sodani, et precipue nobiles familiæ de Kinel-Decill, Clann-Scoba et Sil-noiridhin, quæ se, suosque posteros ei ut patrono in devotos clientes consecrarunt."—(Acta SS., p. 728, col. 2; p. 753, col. 2.)

[1] O'Flaherty's "Description of West Connaught," p. 1 (in Dr. Reeves' Eccles. Antiq. of Down, Connor, and Dromore, p. 303).

[2] It is in harmony with this state of things that our early chroniclers tell us that the bishops of St. Andrews were styled *chief bishops of the Scots*, that is, of the people who at its foundation, or by conquest of the Ardrigh of Alba, were subject to the monastery of S. Andrews, "in scriptis tam antiquis quam modernis inveniuntur dicti summi Archiepiscopi sive Summi Episcopi Scotorum." And the history of the foundation of St. Andrews, written soon after the introduction of diocesan arrangements, further informs us that in common parlance they were still called *Escop Alban*, *i.e.* Episcopi Albaniæ, which style they also received, by way of eminence, from all the other bishops of Scotland, "qui a locis quibus præsunt appellantur."—(Chronicles of the Picts and Scots, p. 191.)

On this subject Mr. Skene remarks:—"The territory forming the diocese of St. Andrews would almost seem to point out the limits of the Scottish population, and the districts actually occupied by them as a people. North of the Firth of Forth it comprised the whole of Fife, Kinross, and Gowrie—what may be called the central portion of the Scottish kingdom, which was peculiarly the kingdom of Scone. In

of St. Patrick,[1] to show that St. Cethecus, the bishop, had under his jurisdiction places in separate districts, among which were two, one in his father's country, the other in that of his mother, from which it appears that the *personal* connection of Cethecus with these places led to his being employed in them for the celebration of such offices as might be looked for from an Irish bishop of these times by their inhabitants, thereby giving him a claim to the customary rights and tributes.[2]

The incessant warfare in which the people lived, resulting in the subjection of one tribe to another, sometimes temporary, and at others permanent, must have thus led to frequent changes in the area of the jurisdiction of clan-monasteries.

Angus and Mearns it shared the churches with the diocese of Brechin in a manner so irregular and unsystematic, as to point to a mixed population, of which some of the villages were Scottish and some Pictish." —(Chronicles of the Picts and Scots, Pref., p. clxiv.)

[1] Eccl. Antiq. of Down, Connor, and Dromore, p. 137.

[2] This peculiarity in the constitution of the Celtic Church has been discussed, with his usual exhaustiveness and candour, by my friend, the learned Jesuit Father, Victor de Buck, in his Annotations on the Life of St. Colman Mac Duach (Acta Sanctorum, Octobris, Tom. xii. pp. 888, *et seq.*)

Quoting from an Irish life of St. Colman the following account of the origin of the see of Kill mac duach, "Fundata itaque est in hoc loco Kill-mic-Duach, ita ut omnis Aidhne regio et gens Guarii filii Colmani in perpetuum ad eum (S. Colmanum mac Duach) pertineant," the Father adds, "Quæ episcopalis sedis fundatio, plane diversa est a similibus per reliquum patriarchatum Romanum, et per Orientem institutionibus."

He afterwards thus explains these words —"id est, fundato templo Kill-mac-Duach, cum aliis necessariis ædibus, sedes constituta est capitis novæ progeniei ecclesiasticæ: quæ progenies iisdem constet hominibus (nempe Fiacriis meridionalibus) easdemque terras occupet, ac progenies sæcularis cujus caput est Guarius; ita ut S. Colmanus, per suos hæredes perpetuo dominetur in progenie ecclesiastica, quemadmodum Guarius per suos hæredes in progenie sæculari Fiacriorum meridionalium. Neque hoc singulare exemplum est: diœceses Enach Duin seu Annadown, Cill-

The district occupied by a tribe came to be distinguished as their "country" or portion; the "Dal" or territory of the children sprung from the original settler or founder, as Dalriada, the *Dal* of Riada, son of Conaire, King of Ireland; but the primary signification of the word is that of *descendants*, and only secondarily their territory.[1]

In the same way, the prefix *Hi*, so common in Irish names, is the plural of Hua, or O, "a grandson," and denotes *posterity*,—but it also secondarily designates the country occupied by them.[2]

The *Plou* of Brittany, in the same way, signified a people and a territory; but its original signification was that of the descendants of one of the first settlers, and secondarily the territory which they came to occupy.

According to the learned editor of the Chartulary of Redon, the word "plebs" in other countries meant a baptismal parish. In Brittany it had a peculiarity. Among the ancient Britons, the word *plouef* meant a cultivated territory—an organised colony—a parish. The British fugitives of the fifth century transported

Finnabrach seu Kilfenora, Ossoriensis et Corca-Laidhe ex gentibus seu progeniebus quoque ortæ sunt earumque finibus circumscriptæ. Plus mirabilitatis hæc non habent quam ecclesiæ in tentoriis et curribus apud populos scenitas et nomades in Oriente. Aidhne itaque regio quasi diœcesis facta est S. Colmani."

And again—"Parum itaque aut nihil intelligebant Hiberni, eorumque cognati Britones, Wallenses et Scoti de jurisdictione territorii finibus circumscripta; jurisdictio seu auctoritas personalis aut gentilis, quam patriarchalem dixeris, hæc una erat eis nota, probe intelligentibus patrem filiorum, avum nepotum et sic deinceps esse dominum, atque hanc dominationem, generatione ortam, intra consanguineos consistere, sed plane non capientibus quare quis alteri obnoxius fiat quia pedem aut sedem in ejus terras intulerit."

[1] Ecclesiastical Antiquities of Down, Connor, and Dromore, by Dr. Reeves, p. 320.

[2] Idem, p. 82.

naturally the word and the institution to the soil on which they came to settle. The chief of the *plou*, princeps plebis, tyrannus, tyern, mactyern, was ordinarily the son, the nephew, the parent of some expatriated *brenin*, around whom was grouped a certain number of compatriot fugitives like him. Debarking in Armorica with his companions, the Mactyern became the sovereign of a little people, over which he exercised such an authority as the chief of a clan in ancient times had. The Life of St. Guenole, written in the ninth century by Gurdestin, Abbot of Landevenech, contains a curious passage, which paints to the life the situation just indicated. Fracan, a fugitive, is here said to have established himself with his followers on a territory rendered fertile by the overflowing of the river. The district, thus settled on in the fifth century by Fracan, is to this day called *Plou-Fracan*; that is to say, the tribe, the territory, the parish of Fracan. This may indicate the origin of the *Plou* of Armorican Brittany.[1] It would seem that the parish of Kirkmichael, in Ayrshire, originally formed the territory of a clan, which appears in our records under the title of Muntir[2]duffy[3] and Muntircasduff.[4] The parish is described as parochia de Kyremychel Muntirduffy.

The Saxon parish was a district or division of land, shired or

[1] Chartular. Redon, Pref. lxxxiii.

[2] Muintir is the Gaelic word for a clan or tribe.

[3] Malcolm, son of Roland of Carric, by his charter (said to be dated in 1370), granted to John Kennedy, lord of Donnowyr, the lands of Freuchane and Kenethane, lying within the parish of Kyremychel Muntirduffy, in the earldom of Carric and shire of Are, with all the right which Murdach, son of Sowerli, had . . . paying on the feast of St. Michael Archangel, at Kyremychel Muntirduffy, in Carric, a pair of silver spurs.—(Note of the original among the Cassilis papers.)

[4] Among the missing charters of King David II. is one "anent the Clan of Muntircasduff, John M'Kennedy Captain thereof."—(Robertson's Index to the Charters, p. 57.)

cut off, and made subject in spiritual things to a church erected on it. In the early annals of the Saxon Church, the monastic system is as prominent as it was among the Celts; and the gospel was preached by itinerating monks, who went out from their monasteries among the surrounding tribes, the people assembling in convenient places to be taught;[1] but from some of the enactments of a provincial synod, held at Calcuith under Archbishop Cuthbert, A.D. 747, it would seem that already the monastic bodies had found it necessary to erect district churches on their lands, which were served by priests under them. It also appears that the lands of laymen had been divided into districts by the bishops, and placed under the charge of presbyters, and that these divisions in many cases coincided with the boundaries of the manor on which the church was built, while the priest ministering within their bounds was invested with exclusive right to their tithes and dues.[2] It is plain, however, that in Alba its monastic system, which was founded on the ecclesiastical subjection of certain tribes to their clan-monastery, and not on the idea of a defined territory with exclusive spiritual rights, continued to flourish down to the reign of David I., and that the changes which were begun in his mother's time, and were carried on by her sons, were the results of influences foreign to the Celtic polity which had hitherto prevailed.

It would seem that then the lesser district monasteries of Alba came to be superseded by churches, which were frequently erected on the site of these earlier foundations. It does not appear, how-

[1] Bede, H. E. c. 19, vol. i.

[2] Spelman's Concilia, pp. 247-8. Lingard's History of the Anglo-Saxon Church, vol. i. pp. 157-8. Thorpe's Ancient Laws and Institutes of England, vol. ii. p. 411.

ever, that the districts subjected to the churches depended directly on the manorial distribution; and there are circumstances in their history which rather indicate that, in some cases at least, the divisions depended on an earlier and different arrangement.[1]

The Pictish monasteries being the nuclei of clans or families, scattered over the country in the same way as the monastic bodies in Ireland, it is easy to understand that when the parochial divisions emerged, the territories in the occupation of these clans would be adopted as a natural field for the energies of permanent priests; while yet the primary consideration related to *the people* on the land, and not (in the outset at least) to the shire or district cut off. The divisions which came to be known as shires or parishes, were of very varying extent. Some of them were of great size, and would seem to have been the territories belonging to the chief monasteries, so that in later times two or three parishes were carved out of them; while others of less extent, probably represent the district monasteries of smaller importance, and their lands.

The boundaries of parishes often appear to be arbitrary, not coinciding with any known manorial distribution, and this probably arose from the grafting of the parochial or territorial arrangement on one where the subject of spiritual oversight *primarily* consisted of groups of families or clans of various size, and *secondarily* of

[1] The exclusive spiritual rights among the Celts were exercised over the *people* of the clan as descended from a common ancestor; and we find an instance of the system in operation in a tract in the Book of Lecan (fol. 92) treating of O'Kelly and his people of Hy-Many, where it appears that all the Hy-Many were bound to be baptized at the church of Camma, in the barony of Athlone and county of Roscommon, dedicated to St. Bridget: "St. Bridget has the baptism of the race of Mainé; and although the children may not (always) be brought to her church to be baptized, her Coarb has the power to collect the baptism penny from these tribes."—(O'Donovan's Annals of the Four Masters, vol. iii. p. 258.)

town-lands, also of varying size, which formed their settlement.

As an apt illustration of what is here said, I may adduce the account of the parish of Shilvodan, in Ulster, which sprang out of the earlier clan-arrangement. Its nucleus was the monastic church already referred to, built by St. Boedan, and from him called Kill-Boedain, which was enriched by gifts of lands from Sodan, son of the King of Ulster, and mainly from the families of Kinel-Decil, the Clann Scoba, and Sil-noiridhin, all of whom devoted themselves and their posterity as devout followers of St. Boedan, their patron saint. The people of these clans were called Siol-Bhaodain (*Progenies Boydani*), and their territories were formed into *a parish* when the time for parochial arrangements arrived.[1]

On the other hand, the primary idea of a parish, where we can trace its formation, in those parts of Scotland where Saxon influences were first developed, depended on that of a defined *territory*, within which the ministering priest had exclusive right. This may be illustrated by the case of Ednam or Ednaham, which Edgar, King of the Scots, bestowed on one of his Saxon followers, Thor the Long, when it was a wild and uninhabited district. Thor, having brought the land into cultivation, and settled his people upon it, at last erected a church in honour of St. Cuthbert, and conveyed it to the monks of Durham, in whose hands the district soon came to be the *parish* of Ednaham.[2]

[1] Reeves' Eccl. Antiq. of Down, Connor, and Dromore, p. 303.

[2] Dr. Raine's North Durham, Appendix, p. 38.

VI.

Celtic Monastery at Turriff.

NOTICE OF IT IN THE BOOK OF DEER—ITS FERLEGINN, OR MAN OF LEARNING—HIS DUTIES—THE SCOLOCS OF SCOTTISH RECORD—LATER ECCLESIASTICAL HISTORY OF TURRIFF—REMAINS OF EARLY ART IN THE CHOIR OF THE OLD CHURCH.

THE Book of Deer incidentally makes us acquainted for the first time with another of our early Celtic monasteries. In the grant by Gartnait the mormaer, and Ete his wife, of which the date is A.D. 1132 (p. liv.), we find among the witnesses, "Domongart ferleginn Turbruad," or ferleginn of Turriff; and that of Colban the mormaer, and Eva his wife, dated somewhat later, is witnessed by "Cormac abb. Turbruad," or Abbot of Turriff, who appears with the nobles or proprietary of Buchan, at Helan [Ellon], and is also a witness, with the king's earls and bishops, to the charter of immunity granted at Aberdeen by David I. to the clerics of Deer.

The monastery of Turriff,[1] of which we thus hear for the first time, is associated with St. Congan, one of the many Irish followers of St. Columba, who continued the great work of Christian illumination among the Northern Picts begun by the Abbot of Hy

[1] The word which in the Book of Deer appears as Turbruad, assumes, in later records, the following forms:—Turuered, Turuereth, Turfred, Turfered, Turreth, Turraf, Turef, Turreff. In the ordinary pronunciation, still in use, the place is called Turra.

St. Congan, who flourished in the beginning of the eighth century, was, according to the traditions of the Scottish Church, the son of a provincial chief of Leinster, to whose rule he succeeded. Afterwards forsaking his patrimony, he devoted himself to a religious life, and leaving Ireland with his sister Kentigerna, and her sons, St. Felan, St. Fursey, and St. Ultan, with seven other clerics, he settled at Lochalsh, in northern Argyle, where he spent a solitary and ascetic life, and, on his death, was buried at Iona or Hy. A church was built in his honour at the place, where he had spent his days, by his nephew St. Felan, and in the beginning of the sixteenth century the name of St. Congan continued to be held in reverence by the inhabitants of the district.[1]

It does not appear whether the monastery at Turriff was founded by St. Congan himself, or dedicated to his memory by another founder; but the neighbouring parishes on the Deveron are also associated with Irish missionaries, indicating the influence to which the introduction of the faith in the district is to be ascribed. Forglen was dedicated to St. Adamnan, Alvah to St. Columba, and Inverboyndie to St. Brandan.

The site of Turriff is a commanding one, and suggestive of its occupation by some of the early tribes as a rath. The church was placed on the summit of a lofty bank, sloping down rapidly on the west to the burn of Colp, which soon after joins the Deveron on its eastward course to the sea.

The *fer leginn*, or man of learning, was a prominent officer in the monasteries of Ireland, and he doubtless occupied a like position in the kindred institutions of Alba.[2]

[1] Breviar. Aberd. Part. Estival. fol. cxxvi.

[2] Eccl. Antiq. of Down and Connor, by Reeves, p. 145, *note;* and his edition of Adamnan's Columba, p. 365.

Colgan describes the office as it obtained in Ireland, first under the name of "scribnidh" or "scribhneoir"—that is, "scribe or writer;" and subsequently, from about the middle of the tenth century, when instruction in literature was added to the practice and teaching of penmanship, more commonly under the name of "ferleiginn," "lecturer," or "scholastic,"—literally "man of learning."[1]

The duty of this officer was the transcription of manuscripts and copying of deeds, and the rule of the schools. The Irish Annals abound in notices of these scribes or lecturers. Not the least famous of their number was the monk whom Alcuin addresses as "Colcus *lector* in Scotia," and whose death is thus recorded by the Four Masters under the year 789: "Colgu ua Duineacda ferleigind Cluana-mac-nois"—Colgu O'Donoghoe, lecturer of Clonmacnois.[2]

Turriff has thus to be regarded not only as a college of ecclesiastics, but as one of the schools of the day; and it is a matter of great interest to find it possessed of an officer so prominent in the sister establishments of Ireland, indicating the conformity which no doubt pervaded the ecclesiastical arrangements of both countries.[3]

[1] In 1164 we find a notice of the ferleiginn of Iona, who at that time was named Dubsidi.—(Annals of Ulster, in Chron. of Picts and Scots, p. 372.)

[2] See an exhaustive paper by my late friend, Joseph Robertson, LL.D., on Scholastic Offices in the Scotican Church, (Miscellany of the Spalding Club, vol. v.), where he quotes Colgan's Trias Thaumaturga, pp. 631, 632. See also Eccles. Antiq. of Down and Connor, p. 146, *note.*

[3] I have already referred to the right which the Bishops of St. Andrews possessed of demanding refection from the men of the Kirktown of Arbuthnott in illustration of the Celtic terms "can" and "cunveth," which so frequently occur in our early charters (p. lxxxviii.) The source from which our information on the subject is drawn, is the decreet of a synod of the clergy of the Archdeaconry of St. Andrews, held at Perth on the 11th of April 1206,

I have previously made some remarks on the transition from the monastic to the parochial system, the period of which had

in a case disputed between the Bishop of St. Andrews and the Lord of Arbuthnott as to their respective rights in the Kirk-town.—(Miscellany of the Spalding Club, vol. v. pp. 209-213.) In this record, the evidence of many witnesses is engrossed, and the details are highly instructive, not only in regard to the point for which I have already quoted it, but as throwing light on the condition of the "Scolocs," who figure in our chronicles and charters of the twelfth and thirteenth centuries, and who have been supposed to be the scholars or clerks of Pictish times. The state of the case between the disputants will be best understood from the following remarks of Dr. Joseph Robertson, in his valuable paper just referred to on "Scholastic Offices in the Scotican Church" (Idem, Appendix to the Preface, p. 63):—"When the light of record first breaks on the banks of the Bervie water in the last days of St. David, or in the following reign of his grandson, the maiden king, the manor of Arbuthnott is seen divided between the church and the crown. The primatial See of Albany, 'the bishopric of the Scots,' as it still wrote its titles, had the advowson of the church, with the church-land or 'Kirk-town.' This ecclesiastical territory was held of the bishop by certain tenants called parsons (*tenentes qui dicebantur personæ*), laymen, it would seem, who had the name and revenues of the parson, but did not possess the sacerdotal function, and who had sub-tenants under them, having houses of their own, and cattle which they pastured on the common. The fixed rent or 'conveth' due to the see would seem to have been two or three cows; and, small as the tribute was, the poverty of the occupants was such, that the bishop did not always enforce its payment. He appears, like the Irish prelates of more recent times, to have found his chief profit in the right of hospitality, or refection, lodging, and attendance, which he exacted for himself and for his servants whenever they visited the neighbourhood. Such was the tenure of the church-land. The lay manor of Arbuthnott was farmed from the crown by a steward or thane, until King Malcolm bestowed it in property upon Osbert Olifard, the crusader. He, too, possessed by a steward or thane. His successor Walter gave the land to Hugh of Swinton, the progenitor of all the Arbuthnotts. These occupied the manor themselves, and, although they were its lords, seem to have been styled in common speech its thanes. Their claims soon began to clash with those of the bishop. Although the church-land and its inhabitants belonged to the See of St. Andrews, the lay lord of Arbuthnott had certain rights over them. Every house in the 'Kirk-town' was bound to give him yearly ten cheeses, made of the whole milk at midsummer, and to furnish three men for gathering his corns in harvest. The bishop

almost arrived when we first become acquainted with the monastery of St. Congan. It probably involved the resumption of the monastic

seems also to have paid him a certain 'cane' or rent. He had besides an equal share with the bishop in the 'merchets' and 'bloodwits,' the fines for marriage and bloodshed, levied from the men of the lands, although these were amenable only to the bishop's courts. Not content with these dues, the new Lords of Arbuthnott began to remove the old occupants, and to till the lands themselves. The usurpation was resisted, although somewhat tardily it would seem, and became the subject of an inquest before a synod of the Scottish Church, which found for the bishop. It is in the evidence which was adduced on this occasion that we meet with the Scolocs."

The first witness was John of Hastings, who had been sheriff and forester of the Mearns in the time of Bishop Richard (A.D. 1163—A.D. 1178). He declared that in the time of that prelate there was a multitude of Scolocs in the Kirktown, and that the men of that land were subject to the court of the bishop as his men. Ysaac of Banevin swore that the steward of the bishop and his own followers, clerical and lay, received lodging in that land, and from the men upon it, as "his own men;" but that after the death of Bishop Hugh, and of Gillandres, one of the men who had resisted any invasion of their rights, Hugh of Swinton removed several of the Scolocs from the Kirktown one after another; also that Duncan, the son of Hugh, turned out all the Scolocs whom he found on the land after his father's death, and on their removal he began to till it.

Felix, another witness, declared that he had frequently seen the bishops lodged in his father's house, who held from the bishops, and ministered to their necessities with the Scolocs of the said land who then belonged to it ("cum Scoloccis ejusdem terræ qui tum pertinebant ad terram illam," and that Duncan had removed "nativos et Scolocos de terra."

The Scolocs of Arbuthnott appear here as the *nativi* of the bishop, holding the kirklands, apparently under the eight tenants called parsons. That this was their position farther appears from the case of their champion Gillandres; for the thane, in the belief that if he could effect *his* removal, there would be little difficulty in getting rid of the others, proposed to give to Bishop Hugh a horse worth five marks, on condition of his turning out Gillandres, but the bishop, hearing that he was native of the land, declared that he would on no account consent to such a step. The Scolocs "belonged to the land," were the "men of the bishop," possessing his lands of the Kirktown, and it was only after they were finally removed that the thane of the baron began to till the lands.

Mr. Robertson, in the paper from which I have just quoted, has illustrated the position of several bodies of Scolocs in Scotland. The records there cited are

lands of Buchan by the chiefs, as well as the endowment of the church of the district with a revenue from the tithes of lands within it.

This church was granted before 1214[1] by Marjory, Countess of Buchan,[2] to the monks of Arbroath.

especially full regarding the Scolocs of Ellon, the church of which place also belonged to the See of St. Andrews, and had an endowment of certain lands in the possession of Scolocs, called the scolog or scholar lands. These lands were held by them in such wise, that from them were to be provided for the parish church of Ellon four clerks, with copes and surplices, able to read and sing sufficiently.

The Scolocs of Ellon evidently occupied a very different position from their brethren of Arbuthnott. The latter could be turned out of their possessions by the Baron of Arbuthnott, the only right alleged on their behalf being that inherent in them as *nativi* of the Bishop of St. Andrews. The Scologs of Ellon were hereditary occupants or tenants of the scolog or scholar lands, so that, on the death of a Scolog, his heir, whether male or female, was entitled to be entered to his or her heritage, either by the bailie of the lands, without letter of inquest from the overlord, or by inquest and seisin thereupon following, after the manner and common use of the realm; while the tenure by which they held the lands was that of maintaining four clerks for the parish church of Ellon, of providing a certain number of wax candles for the "park" before the high altar, and of finding a smithy at Ellon.—(Miscell. Sp. Club, vol. v. Appendix to the Preface, pp. 58-59.)

It may be doubted whether sufficient evidence has been adduced for holding that all the persons called Scolocs or Scologs in our early records were of the same character, or were in all cases, as has been assumed, scolastics, or the lowest members of the clerical order; but, on the contrary, were in some cases simply the husbandmen or tenants of the land. What we know of the Scolocs of Arbuthnott and Ellon seems irreconcilable with such an idea. The former were many in number, and cultivated the soil of the Kirktown under the tenants called "parsons;" while the Scologs of Ellon were hereditary occupants of certain lands which descended to sons and daughters, with the burden of maintaining from the lands four clerks for the parish church of Ellon, besides the additional burdens above specified; the title of Scholar Lands, applied to them in later times, having arisen apparently from the tenure by which the tenants were bound to maintain four clerks in the parish church of Ellon.

[1] Registr. de Aberbroth. p. 6.

[2] Daughter and heiress of Fergus, the mormaer or earl of Buchan.

In the year 1273, her son William Cumyn, Earl of Buchan, founded at Turriff an almshouse for a master, six chaplains, and thirteen poor husbandmen of Buchan, by a charter dated at his house of Kelly, and witnessed, among others, by King Alexander III.[1]

To this foundation he granted a tract of ground around the town of Turriff, which he describes as "terre ecclesiastice ville de Turreff," being probably what had formed the territory of St. Congan's monastery.

It extended from Kinermit, on the west side of the town of Turriff, towards Delgaty on the east, and one of the boundaries expressed in the charter serves to connect it with the earlier establishment. The march is said to run by the standing stone of Balmaly and Kokuki, and so from that stone to the monks' gate (et sic ab illo lapide usque *ad uiam monachorum*),[2] an expression which seemed without meaning till the Book of Deer made us acquainted with the monks of St. Congan settled there.

The gift of the church of Turriff to the monks of Arbroath by the Countess Marjory appears to have been revoked by her, and it was included in the grant by her son to the hospital founded by him in honour of St. Congan.

In the year 1412, the church of Turriff was erected into a prebend of the cathedral of Saint Machar at Aberdeen, and the whole fruits of the benefice, in which the hospital

[1] One of the witnesses was the writer of the charter, who had added to his name the soubriquet of "Pater Noster."—(Collections on the Shires of Aberdeen and Banff, p. 470; Registrum Aberdonense, vol. i. p. 30.)

[2] Registrum Aberdonense, vol. i. p. 31.

of St. Congan seems to have merged, were assigned to the prebendary.[1]

In the year 1512, King James IV. erected the ecclesiastical lands of the church of Turriff, with its town and glebe, into a burgh of barony, with the privilege of a Sunday market and two fairs, one of which was to be held (and till lately continued to be held) on the 13th of October, being the feast of St. Congan.

In the year 1588, the church-lands conferred on the hospital of St. Congan in the thirteenth century, and probably granted to St. Congan himself five centuries earlier, were alienated to Francis, Earl of Erroll, by Mr. John Philp, parson of Turriff.[2]

The old parish church of St. Congan was a long narrow structure, 120 feet in length by 18 feet in width, without any architectural features suggestive of its date. When the new church was erected in 1794, the earlier building was left to decay, and the eastern end, still known as "the quire," is the only part now remaining.

The erection of the quire can be satisfactorily assigned to the first part of the sixteenth century, when it was built by Mr. Alexander Lyon, Chanter of Murray, and a son of John, fourth Lord Glamis. Of this man we read in an unprinted pedigree of the house that "he was a singular scholar in these tymes, and was tutor to his brother's sones, and lyeth buried in the quire of Turreffe, which he built; of whom, being a churchman and unmarryed,

[1] Illustrations of the Antiqs. of the Shires of Aberdeen and Banff, vol. ii. p. 337.

[2] The charter, dated 14th May 1588, describes the lands as the Kirk lands of Turreff, Knockiemiln, Miln of Turreff, and Mill lands.—(Erroll Writs.)

came no laufull succession. He dyed in the year of God 1541."[1]

In December 1861 portions of the choir were taken away, and on removing the stones from a window in the south wall, which had been built up, there appeared on the splay of one of the sides a human figure painted on the plaster in bright colours. Another similar painting was on the other splay of the window, but unfortunately it was destroyed before any drawing could be obtained.

Of the first, sketches and photographs were secured before the plaster was broken up, showing it to be the figure of a bishop fully habited—the right hand raised in benediction, with the pastoral staff in his left. The background was painted in large lozenge patterns, and an inscription in Gothic letters above—S. NIN IANUS.

There is reason to believe that there was a series of similar pictures round the church, and as the choir was erected in the first half of the sixteenth century, we might, perhaps, have inferred that fresco-painting was then in use for the decoration of parish churches in Scotland.

A curious passage, however, in the History of the Abbots of Kinloss, by Ferrerius, affords evidence that this was really the case. In describing the many beneficent works of Abbot Robert Reid, we are told that in the year 1538 he engaged a painter, Andrew Bairhum, whom he retained at Kinloss for three years, during which time this artist painted three pictures on panel for adorning the chapels of the Magdalene, of St. John the Evangelist, and St.

[1] See Illustr. of Antiqs. of the Shires of Aberdeen and Banff, vol. ii. p. 388.

Thomas of Canterbury. It is added that he painted, but in the lighter style now so fashionable throughout Scotland (" sed pictura leviore quæ nunc est per Scotiam receptissima"),[1] the chamber and oratory of the abbot, as well as another large room adjoining.[2]

There can be little doubt that the style of art thus indicated was that of fresco-painting, but so complete has been the destruction of our old ecclesiastical buildings in Scotland, that the figure of St. Ninian at Turriff is almost the only example of which we can speak with certainty.

As an interesting relic of Scottish art, and as associated with the church of St. Congan, I have thought it permissible to introduce a drawing of the fresco, from sketches made by Mr. Gibb at the time of the discovery.

In the north wall of the choir, and near to the east end, there is inserted an ambry of decorated work, and from the letters A L, which appear at the bottom, we may infer that it was erected by Alexander Lyon, the builder of the choir.[3]

In its gable there is built an ornamented stone which has

---

[1] Hist. Abbat. Monasterii de Kynlos, p. 51 (Ban. Club.)

[2] From the same author we derive an account of the ornaments with which Abbot Thomas Crystall of Kinloss enriched the parish church of Ellon a few years earlier. Of him he writes—" Nec minus accuratus fuit in ornanda ecclesia sua de Ellone, cui parem tabulam pictoria et statuaria arte deauratam cum illa Beatae Matris et Virginis apud Kynloss de qua paulo ante sumus locuti, contulit. Restituit quoque illic majus altare tabulato ubi et divae Annae statuam erexit; paravitque nova in choro subsellia; et vestes ad rem sacram faciendam tres, casulam videlicet ex bysso palmata, duas dalmaticas, cum albis, et id genus reliquis, liberalissime coemptas, tradidit."—(Idem, p. 76.)

[3] Similar ambries of the same period occur in the ruined churches of Kinkell and Auchindoir, and a third, which was placed in the old church of Kintore, is now built into the west gable of the parish kirk.

formed part of a structure of earlier date, besides other sculptured fragments, which have been used for building materials in the church which succeeded the monastery of St. Congan. Of these, and the ambry just described, drawings by Mr. Gibb are given in a separate plate.

PLATE 3.

AMBRY AT TURRIFF.

VII.

Early Buildings in Scotland.

I. "Towns" of Aberdour and Deer.

CATHAIRS—KAERS—OPPIDA—BRITISH DWELLINGS—DUNS—RATHS.

The Celtic word *cathair* in the Legend of St. Columbkille and Drostan, which is translated "town" or "city," was applied primarily by the ancient Irish to denote a class of their forts formed of circular uncemented stone walls. Dr. Petrie informs us that this is the strict meaning of the word, and that it is applied only in a secondary and figurative sense to "a city," adding that it appears to be one of a class of Irish words (of which he gives examples) descriptive of circular erections, and the same as the British *Kaer*.[1]

This last word, which enters so largely into the composition of the names of places in Brittany, was there originally applied to a fortified dwelling, and secondarily to a farm and manor-house.[2] In the Chartulary of the monastery of Redon we have instances of the synonymous use of the words "Kaer" and "Villa," as in the confirmation to the abbey, A.D. 1037, of the island of St. Guitual, with its lands and pertinents, and seven "villas in Plochidinuc id est

[1] Ordnance Survey of the County of Londonderry, vol. i. p. 213. Parish of Templemore, "Townlands."

[2] Chartular. de Redon, Pref. p. ccc.

Kaer en Treth, Kaer Guiscoiarn, Kaer Gleuhirian, Kaer Kerveneac, Kaer en Mostoer, Kaer Euen, and Kaer Caradoc."[1]

The "oppida" of the Armorican tribes in the time of Cæsar consisted of the fortresses to which the inhabitants retreated for safety. They were mostly situated on the coast, at the extremities of tongues of land or promontories, and appear to have been numerous, for we learn that although the Romans were able to take some of these "oppida," yet all their labour was thrown away, for as soon as the Veneti thought themselves no longer safe, they evacuated the *oppidum* which was attacked, embarked with all their goods on board their numerous vessels, and withdrew to the neighbouring "oppida," the situations of which offered the same advantages for a new resistance.[2] Of the "oppida" of the Britons, Cæsar writes, "Oppidum autem Britanni vocant, quum sylvas impeditas vallo atque fossa munierunt, quo, incursionis hostium vitandæ causa convenire consuerunt."[3]

The earthen wall and ditch were in other circumstances represented by ramparts of great stones on the tops of hills, as we learn from Tacitus, in the case of Caractacus.[4]

The dwelling-houses of the Britons appear to have been of the slightest construction. In one of Cæsar's references to them, he calls them "Casas, quæ more Gallico stramentis erant tectæ."[5] Diodorus Siculus speaks of them as mean habitations, constructed for the most part of reeds or of wood.[6] Strabo (in the Latin version of Xylander) says of the Gauls and Britons, "Domos e tabulis et cratibus construunt rotundos magno imposito fas-

[1] Chartular. de Redon, pp. 327-8.

[2] De Bell. Gall. iii. xii.

[3] De Bell. Gall. v. xxi.

[4] Annal. lib. xii. cc. 33-36.

[5] De Bello Gallico, lib. v. cap. 43.

[6] Biblioth. Histor. lib. v. ap. Monum. Hist. Brit. p. ii.

tigio.[1] Jornandes, a writer of the sixth century, says of the Caledonians "virgeas habitant casas."[2]

In many of the hill-forts and raths, both of England, Scotland, and Wales, vestiges of circular foundations may yet be seen, as at Caerby, Ingleborough, Yevering, Dunpelder, the Caterthuns, and the Barmekyn on Dunecht.

On very many of our uncultivated moors and hill-sides also, groups of similar circular foundations (the remains of villages) are yet to be seen, of which good examples are at Greaves Ash among the Cheviots, and at Balnabroch on the Ardle, in Perthshire.

When St. Columba first visited Brude, the Pictish King, he was residing in his dun,[3] on the banks of the Ness; and it is plain, from the description of Adamnan, that there were buildings within the circuit of the walls.[4]

It is probable that the abodes of the Pictish kings resembled the royal residences of the Irish at Tara, Aileach, and Emania—viz. raths and cathairs, within which were circular houses of wood or hurdle-work.[5] It would seem that one such residence of the Pictish kings was placed at the confluence of the Almond with the Tay, and is referred to in our annals as Rath-inueramon.[6]

[1] Strabo, Geogr. Gallia Britannia, lib. v. p. 136, ed. 1587.

[2] Monum. Hist. Brit. p. lxxxiii.

[3] The word "munitio" is used by Adamnan to describe the circular stone forts of Ireland, within which were wooden houses.

[4] Reeves' Adamnan's St. Columba, p. 151.

[5] A.D. 1014, in the account of a foray by the Osraighi and the men of East Munster, as far as Dun-na-sgiath, we read that they burned the dun, and seized some small spoils.—(O'Donovan's Annals of the Four Masters, vol. ii. p. 845.) Here the reference must be to the wooden structure within the dun. Another foray is noted in A.D. 1052, in which Dun-Feich was demolished (ibid. p. 861), where the wall seems to have been thrown down; and a few years later we read of the "burning" of three duns (ibid. p. 873).

[6] Chronicles of the Picts and Scots, p. 151.

The topography of Scotland preserves the memory of these duns and raths in many districts; but the progress of cultivation has obliterated many of the structures themselves, except those placed on hills, as at Dunecht, Caterthun, Barra, Craigphadric, and the like.[1]

It is plain, from numerous entries in the Annals of the Four Masters, that in Ireland the raths and duns continued in many cases to be occupied by the chieftains down to a comparatively recent period;[2] and it seems probable that they continued to be used in Scotland till towards the end of the Celtic period.

The words "civitas" and "urbs" were also applied to the early monastic establishments in Britain and Ireland, which, as in the case of St. Columba's monastery of Hy, consisted of a church, with groups of circular huts within an enclosing wall.[3]

[1] The rath in Athol, which, as we learn, was the capital of the earldom in the twelfth century (Liber de Scon, p. 35), was doubtless the residence of the earlier chiefs or mormaers of the district. The Lord of Badenoch in 1380 held a court at the standing-stones of the Rath of Kyngucy.—(Chartul. Morav. p. 184.) The moat of Ruthven, on which the Cummings erected their great castle, in its name perpetuates the memory of a still earlier structure or rath. At Rattray in Gowrie there is a remarkable fortified site; and at Rattray in Buchan there is another of the same character. We hear of the Rath of Katerlin in the twelfth century (Registr. Vet. de Aberbroth. pp. 88, 89), and the place is still called Rathfield. On the Kaims Hill at Ratho is a rath, with remains of enclosed hut-circles. The parishes of Rathen in Buchan in the county of Aberdeen, of Ruthven on the Deveron in the same county, and Rathven in the Enzie in Banffshire, were all probably the sites of the raths of district chieftains, and got their names by association with these structures. Rathelpie at St. Andrews, in the same way, may preserve the memory of King Alpin's Rath.

[2] Rathmore, which in the sixth century was a residence of the Dalaradian princes, appears to have been a place of habitation and importance so late as 1315, when it was burned by Edward Bruce.—(Reeves' Eccl. Antiq. of Down and Connor, pp. 69, 70.)

[3] Reeves' Adamnan, add. notes, p. 357 While the early monasteries were placed within circular walls resembling that of

The word *lis* or *les*, which also signifies a circular earthen fort, is often translated "civitas."[1]

When, therefore, we read of the "towns" or "cities" of Abbordobhoir and Deer, which the mormaer granted to the clerics, it seems probable that we are to understand the surrender of two of his fortified places, round which a population of the district tribes were clustered in their frail huts.

II. Opus Scoticum. Wooden Buildings.

The custom of the Irish to use wood as materials for their buildings, obtained for it in the middle ages the title of the Scots' style,[2]

---

the raths, duns, and cathairs of Pagan times, it frequently happened that these fortified sites were surrendered to the missionaries by the converted chiefs as sites of monasteries and churches.

Thus, "the church of Cill Benen was erected within the *arx* or fortress called Dun Lughaidh, from a lord of the country, who, with his father and four brothers, having been baptized by the Saints Patrick and Benen, gave up their dun or fortress for the purpose." Again, "the chief of the country of Briefny, Aodh Finn, the son of Feargna, on his conversion to Christianity by St. Caillin, gave up to him his cathair or stone fortress, in order that he might erect his monastic buildings within it."—(Petrie's Round Towers, p. 444.) The church at Nendrum stood within a cashel of three oval walls.—(Reeves' Eccles. Antiqs. p. 10.) The monarch Daire gave to St. Patrick a rath, within which he erected his first ecclesiastical establishment at Armagh.—(Todd's Life of St Patrick, p. 476.) At Derry, St. Columba got from Aodh, son of Ainmire, who was King of Erin at the time, his royal fort, within which he founded a church.—(Reeves' Adamnan, p. 160.) It would seem that some of our early Scottish churches were founded within duns—such as Dunkeld, Dunblane, and Dunfermline.

[1] Dr. Todd's St. Patrick, p. 479.

[2] Our own records have many examples of the use of the term Scotic as equivalent to Gaelic, and opposed to English, as in a deed dated in 1253 relating to the boundaries of Kingoldrum. One of these

"mos Scottorum," although, as will be seen, it was far from being peculiar to that people.

The distinction first appears in the History of Venerable Bede, when he describes the church erected by St. Finan in A.D. 662 at Lindisfarne, "quam more Scottorum non de lapide sed de robore secto totam composuit atque harundine texit."[1] It appears from many passages in the Lives of the Irish Saints that churches of wood or hurdle-work continued to be erected in Ireland in subsequent times, and it is plain that in the twelfth century the custom was still regarded as "Scotic," as we learn from St. Bernard's description of the oratory at Bangor, built by St. Malachy, "de lignis quidem lævigatis," which he styled "opus Scoticum pulchrum satis;"[2] and somewhat later, when St. Malachy began to build an oratory of stone at Bangor, "instar eorum quæ in aliis regionibus extructa conspexerat," the native objections took the shape of resentment against stone buildings as a novelty, "quid tibi visum est nostris hanc inducere regionibus novitatem? Scoti sumus non Galli."[3]

The wooden church erected by St. Finan at Lindisfarne was on the Scotic model of that at Iona, and there can be no reasonable doubt that the churches of St. Columba throughout the territory of the Picts were built of similar materials.[4]

was a marsh "que Scotice dicitur Moynebuche," while another boundary with the name of Hachethunethoner is translated into English as Midfield (quod *Anglice* dicitur *Midfield*).—(Registr. Vetus de Aberbroth. p. 228.) We have an earlier instance in the same register, where the lands of the abbey of Old Montrose are conveyed, with the addition, "que Scotice abthan vocatur."—(Idem, p. 4.)

[1] Hist. Eccl. iii. 25.

[2] St. Bernardi Vita, S. Malachiæ, ap. Migne, S. Bernardi Opera, Tom i. col. 1083.

[3] Idem, col. 1109.

[4] See Reeves' Adamnan, *notes*, pp. 106, 177.

This indeed is implied in the request made by the Pictish ruler Nectan to the Abbot Benedict Biscop, that he would send him masons who could build him a church *of stone*, "juxta morem Romanorum."

While the churches both in Ireland and Alba were probably in general formed of beams of sawn timber, it would seem that the houses were of wattle.[1] Adamnan notices the gathering "virgarum fasciculos ad hospitium construendum." St. Woloc, who laboured

[1] H. E. v. c. 21. Reeves' Adamnan's St. Columba, p. 106, *note*. In charters of burghal properties of the thirteenth and fourteenth centuries, stone houses are sometimes mentioned in a way which shows their rarity, and it is plain that most of the houses of our Scotch towns were wooden fabrics resting on foundations of stone, down to a comparatively recent period.—(Liber de Scon, p. 49.) A stone house was enough at times to give its name to the barony on which it was placed, and it would appear that the lands now called Stenhouse, in Stirlingshire, derived their name from the remarkable stone building called "Arthur's Oven," which stood on them till the time of its barbarous demolition before the middle of last century. In a charter dated in 1461, the granter is styled "Alexander de Broys de Stanehouse."—(Charters of Holyrood, p. 150.) In other cases, however, the term "domus Scoticana" is used for the sake of distinction, as in the case of one erected by the king within the castle of Inverness in 1263.—(Chamberlain Rolls, vol. i. p. *23.) We learn from a "Briefe Description of the Barony of Fort" [or Forth], in the county of Wexford, that "they greatlie sow Fyrse seeds, or plant the same in rowes some few ridges distant, which ordinarily in a few years grow 8 or 10 feet in height, and to that bigness and strength that (better timber being there deficient) dwelling-houses are therewith all roofed" [note]. Furze wood was used for the watlin (little wood) or wicker work, to which the thatch was fastened. Until the close of the last century, almost every dwelling-house was so roofed."—(Proceedings of Kilkenny Arch. Soc. vol. iv. p. 60, 1862.

Wattled houses were erected in some parts of the Highlands till recent times. Lachlan M'Pherson, a second son of the Laird of Cluny, and who ultimately succeeded to the chiefship, married Jean, second daughter of Sir Ewen Cameron of Locheil, and brought her home to a wattled house at Nuid, near Kingussie, about the end of the eighteenth century. Wattled huts were to be seen in many parts of the Highlands towards the end of last century, and some of them probably remain to the present day.

on the banks of the Deveron, built as his abode "casam calamis viminibusque contextam."[1] Adamnan notices in one case the parts of a house which formed the skeleton on which the hurdles were placed, and which remained after the destruction of the more perishable materials by fire.[2]

In the year 1233, we have a notice of a guest-house near the church of Kilpatrick, "fabricata de virgis," built on ground which Earl Alwine of Lennox granted to St. Patrick, on condition that the tenant should receive as guests pilgrims coming to the church.[3]

The custom of building houses and churches of wood prevailed also among the Britons. When St. Ninian erected a church of stone on the rugged shores of Galloway, we are told by Bede that it was "insolito Brittonibus more."[4] When St. Kentigern founded

---

[1] Breviar. Aberd. Part. Hyemal. fol. 45.

[2] Reeves' Adamnan's St. Columba, p. 114.

[3] Registr. de Passelet, p. 166. Mac Firbis of Lecan, in a topographical poem of the early part of the fifteenth century, sings of—

"A white wattled edifice of noble polish,
Habitation of the sweet-scented branches."

—(The Genealogies, Tribes, and Customs of Hy Fiachrach, Irish Arch. Soc., p. 265.)

[4] H. E. iii. 4. Ailred, the biographer of St. Ninian, tells us that the saint brought with him from Gaul workmen who could erect a church after the Roman fashion.

Besides the "White Church" of St. Ninian on the shore of the Solway Firth, we had other "White Churches" in Scotland.

In East Lothian was the church of Hamer or "Whitekirk," one of the foundations of St. Baldred; and in Aberdeenshire was "The White Church" of Buchan.

All of these churches were much resorted to by pilgrims, probably from feelings associated with their early foundation, and reverence for their founders.

The church at Durham, in which the body of St. Cuthbert reposed for three years, during the erection of the greater church to which it was translated in A.D. 999, was called *alba ecclesia*.—(Simeonis Dunelm. Hist. lib. iii. cap. ii.) A church was erected in honour of St Oswald near the place where he fell, "que Candida dicitur."—(Lelandi Collect. vol. i. p. 366.) See a notice of Temple-finn or White-church in the Diocese of Down, (Reeves' Eccles. Antiqs. p. 26.)

his monastery of St. Asaph in Wales, he built the church and other offices, of dressed wood, "more Britonum," "quum de lapide nondum construere poterant nec usum habebant."[1]

St. Gwynllyw, towards the end of the sixth century, "signavit cimiterium, et in medio tabulis et virgis fundavit templum."[2] About the same time St. Cadoc erected "insigne monasteriolum ex lignorum materie."[3]

Before the middle of the ninth century, Ronwallon, a man of power, conveyed to the Abbot of Redon his house made "ex tabulis ligneis."[4]

The use of wooden materials in buildings was also common among the Saxons.

Venerable Bede notices many instances of the erection of stone churches on sites previously occupied by wooden structures, and in describing the conversion of Northumbria, and the numbers baptized in streams by Paulinus, he adds—"Nondum enim oratoria vel baptisteria in ipso exordio nascentis ibi ecclesiæ poterant edificare."[5] To the same effect William of Malmesbury writes, "Neque ante Benedictum [Biscop] lapidei tabulatus domus in Britannia nisi per raro videbatur."[6]

In King Edgar's charter to the Abbey of Malmesbury, dated A.D. 974, he describes the state of the monasteries in his kingdom, "quæ velut muscivis scindulis cariosisque tabulis tigno tenus visibiliter diruta."[7]

---

[1] Vita Kentigerni ap. Pinkerton's Vitæ Sanctor. Scotiæ, p. 248.

[2] Lives of the Cambro-British Saints, Vita S. Gundleii, p. 148.

[3] Idem, p. 34.

[4] Chart. de Redon, p. 443.

[5] H. E. lib. ii. cap. xiv.

[6] Hist., vol. i. p. 82.

[7] Gesta Regum Anglorum, lib. ii. § 153, vol. ii. p. 247 (Eng. Hist. Soc.)

Bede describes a wooden dwelling-house in 654. The occupants were engaged in feasting at night, and having kindled a great fire in the middle, it happened that the sparks flying up set on fire the roof, which was made of wattles and thatched with hay.[1]

It was after their visits to the imperial city that Benedict Biscop, and his friend Wilfrid, were incited to erect their monasteries at Wearmouth and Hexham "Romano opere," and by means of tradesmen brought from abroad,—as at a later period, we have seen the Irish Malachi desirous of erecting a stone church like those which he had seen on his journey to Rome.[2]

[1] H. E. lib. iii. c. x.

[2] As ideas of Roman art were diffused by the pilgrims to the Holy City, on their return to their own homes, so it is interesting to notice, on the other hand, how the Irish ecclesiastics clung to their own customs. Thus, when the great Irish missionary, St. Columbanus, received from the King of Lombardy a site for his monastery at Bobbio in A.D. 615, he erected "ecclesiam in honore almæ genitricis semperque virginis Mariæ *ex lignis*." Towards the end of the ninth century, the erection of a church of stone, by the Abbot Agilulf, is recorded: "ecclesiam *ex lapidibus* construxit, turremque super eam edificavit et campanas fecit in ea pendere sicut nunc cernitur."—(Vita S. Columbani Abbatis, ap. Mabillon, Acta SS. Ord. Ben. Tom. ii. p. 37.) Another Irish custom is recorded in this life:—The saint erected a cross near to his church for his devotions, "consuetudo est enim hominibus hujus gentis unumquemque per diem centies et eo plus genuflectere."—(Idem, p. 38.)

The conflict of Roman with Scotic customs appears under other aspects in an ordinance of Louis le Debonnaire, in which, after reciting that the monastery of Landevennec, in Brittany, continued to follow the tonsure and other customs which had *been received from the Scots*, he enjoined the adoption of the rule of St. Benedict.—(Cartul. Landev. ap Morice, Memoires pour servir de Preuves a l'Histoire Ecclesiastique et Civile de Bretagne, vol. i. col. 228. Paris, 1742.)

We can trace the Scotic feeling of strangeness to stone churches so late as the thirteenth century, in the same country where the stone church of St. Ninian had been erected in the fifth. In the year 1164 Ailred of Rievaux went on a visit into Galloway, and was present at Kirkcudbright on the festival of its patron, St. Cuthbert. A bull was brought to the church as an oblation, which the clerics of the place baited in the churchyard. The more aged remonstrated against such a profanation, but one of the clerics mocked and

Contact with Roman art was followed in other countries by a like result. Thus, of St. Josse, a Breton saint who lived in the middle of the seventh century, we read that on his withdrawing to a retired life, "oratoria duo manibus suis nitebatur construere, unum videlicet B. Petri principis Apostolorum, aliud Sancti Pauli doctoris gentium venerationi deputans, *et utrumque ex lignis.*" Afterwards he went to Rome, and on his return it is said, "Habebat enim jam tunc ecclesiam novam *ex petris constructam,* quæ mox, postquam Dei famulus Roma veniens in eam patrocinia multa detulerat, dedicata est in honore Sancti Martini."[1]

The "mos Romanus," introduced into Northumbria by Benedict Biscop and Wilfrid, co-existed for a long time with the earlier custom of wooden buildings, just as the introduction of glass-making by these ardent improvers did not for a long time lead to a general knowledge or use of it, or to the extinction of the earlier modes of giving light.[2]

No doubt the use of stone in buildings came to be predominant in Northumbria at an earlier period than in Alba; but at the time when the use of wood in building is spoken of as a Scotic custom, it was in reality common to the Irish with many other people.

The wooden cathedral at Chester-le-Street, which had sheltered the body of St. Cuthbert in its wanderings, remained till about A.D. 1042, when Egelric, who became Bishop of Durham in that

said, "Nec Cuthberti hujus adesse presentia, nec huic loco talis ei probatur inesse potentia, *licet hujus ipsius sit petrosa et de lapidibus compacta ecclesiola.*"—(Reginaldi Dunelmensis Libellus de Admir. B. Cuthberti Virtutibus, p. 179. Surtees Soc.)

[1] Morice, Memoires pour servir de Preuves a l'Histoire de Bretagne, col. 210.

[2] See Sculptured Stones of Scotland, vol. ii. pref. p. 12, and *note*.

year, destroyed the ancient fabric, and in its place erected one of stone, "pro eo quod aliquando beati Cuthberti corpus ibidem quieverat."[1]

In some cases, however, the wooden erections were succeeded by others of stone at a much earlier period, as at Tynemouth, where King Edwin [616-633] "sacellum erexit ex ligno;" and his successor Oswald "monasteriolum de Tinemuthe ex ligno lapideum fecit."[2]

In the same way, the buildings of wooden materials in France were described as of "opus Gallicum."[3]

[1] Simeon, Hist. de Dunelm. Eccles. col. 34. Ap. Twysden, Decem Scriptores.

[2] Lelandi Collect. vol. iv. p. 43.

[3] At the end of an edict of Liutprand, the Lombard King, dated A.D. 735, are seven chapters, in the same corrupt Latin as the charters in the first volume of the great work of the Sardinian government, "Monumenta Historiae Patriae," where these documents are printed. The volume of the series from which I quote is entitled "Edicta Regum Langobardorum," and the chapters are headed—1. De Sala; 2. De Muro; 3. De Annonam Comacinorum; 4. De Opera; 5. De Caminata; 6. De Marmorarios; 7. De furnum, De puteum. That "de muro" contains some notices of "Gallican work" and "Roman work." It is as follows:—Si vero murum fecerit qui usque ad pedem unum sit grossus dupplicentur mercedes et usque ad quinque pedes subquinetur; et de ipso muro vadat per solidum unum pedes ducenti viginti quinque; si vero macinam mutaverit, det pedes centum octoginta in solidum unum usque ad pedes quinque sursum, in longitudinem vero ter quinos per tremisse. Similiter et si murum dealbaverit, sexcenti pedes vadat per solidum unum. Et si cum axes clauserit et opera gallica fecerit, mille quingenti pedes in solido vestito vadant. Et si arcum volserit, pedes duodecim vadat in solido uno. Si vero materias capelaverit majores minores, capita viginti per tremisse; armaturas vero et brachiolas quinque ponantur pro uno materio. 4. De opera. Similiter romanense si fecerit, sic repotet sicut gallica opera, mille quingentos pedes in solidos uno. Et scias quia ubi una tegula ponitur quindecim scindolas lebant; quia centum quinquaginta tegulas duo milia quingentas scindolas lebant. Et si massa fundederit, sexcenti pedes per solido uno.

The expressions, "Opus Gallicum" and "Opus Romanense" are thus commented on in certain "Adnotationes Caroli Promis," Appendix, xi. of the same volume, p. 245.

"Opera gallica, seu opus gallicum, nova

It will thus be seen that the custom, which has been termed a *Scotic* one, was, in so far as the materials of their buildings is

sane vox et glossatoribus ignota, videtur mihi fuisse illa ætate denominatio tabulatorum, sive parietum, ex asseribus ædes sepientium vel cellas dividentium, illo enim tempore plurimae struebantur ligneae aedes, uti apud Gallos (et hodie quoque generatim extra Italiam) mos adhuc viget, qui extructis in oppidis muris exterioribus ex lateribus vel saxis, intus dividunt per tabulata, in pagis vero et rure saepissime omnia lignea sunt. Nec carent codd. ferentes "*et opera cum alliga fecerit*," ubi nulla vocum significatio. Gallico vero operi respondent opus romaniense de quo inferius, opus saracenicum paulo post temporis vulgatum apud inferiores Italos, opus signinum iamdiu Romanis notum, necnon et alia quae nomen a gentibus vel oppidis acceperunt. Artificum vero stipendium alteri ex codicibus ferunt unius solidi pro pedibus D (de superficie semper habendum est) alteri idem obferunt pretium pro MD: hanc igitur lectionem rationi magis consentaneam, accepimus, alteram reiicimus, quippe quæ pretiorum proportioni haud aeque respondeat. Dubitavimus etiam, utrum, intelligendum esset de opere fornaceo (Gallis *pisé* Italis fortasse *pigiato*, idem referente voce) de quo abunde Plinius (Hist. Nat. xxxv. 48, 44, cf. etiam Palladium, i. 34) iamdiu in Africa et Hispania vulgatissimum quoque nostra etiam aetate magnopere utuntur Galli, Sardi et inter Subalpinos Italos praecipue Alexandrini rustici: hoc opus vero sollicitum sane, sed habita pretii ratione a nostra lege relati, plenum quidem laboris quodque non sine multis comparatis perficiendum est, vectibus scilicet et machinis et asseribus ad instruendas formas. Qua de causa mihi iudicium erit opus gallicum intelligendum esse non de formaceo sed de tabulato ligneo. Conferantur etiam § CLX. et adnotationes nostrae, ubi evidenter liquebit, gallicum opus ligneum fuisse, sive ex asseribus, vel magnis vel parvis, constasse."

IIII. "De opera. Titulus *de opera* referendus est ad omnem tecti materiationem.

"'Similiter romanense si fecerit, sic repotet sicut gallica opera mille quingentos pedes in solidos uno.' Vocabulum *romanense* adjectivum est *tecti*, intelligendumque tectum romano more structum (scilicet ex tegulis planis et testaceis pro nostratium antiqua et hodierna consuetudine) aestimandum esse ad idem pretium ac si gallico more seu ex ligneis asseribus." "Gallicum opus vidimus superius idem esse ac ligneum opus seu tabulatum. Tabulatum vero tectis struendis aptum, constat ex asseribus exilibus *scindulae* vel *scandulae* dictis (accepta antiquitus a Germanis voce *Schindel*) testibus Vitruvio (ii. 1), Plinio (xvi. 10. 15), Palladio (i. 22), aliisque non paucis ex veteribus scriptoribus; una autem et altera vox habetur in legibus nostris, ubi Liutprandus scindulas appellat, quas Rotharis (§ 282) Scandulas.

concerned, common to the Scots with the Britons, Saxons, and Franks, and that the terms applied to it were always intended to distinguish it from the Roman fashion of building with dressed stones.

In conclusion, I have to state that the Book of Deer was first brought to light in the year 1860, through the research of Mr. Henry Bradshaw, the librarian of the University Library, Cambridge; and it was at one time hoped that the Club might have had the benefit of the services of this accomplished scholar as editor of the work.

When it was found that Mr. Bradshaw's engagements rendered this impossible, the Council prevailed on Joseph Robertson, LL.D., to undertake the work; but after making a careful transcript of the text, he also was compelled to abandon the design from the pressure of his official duties.

The charge of editing the volume then devolved on me, and the work has been in progress during the last three years.

The plan adopted has already been incidentally referred to. It led me to give such a copy of the Book as represents all its peculiarities of text, orthography, and punctuation.

With the view of exhibiting the relation of the Deer Gospels to the Vulgate, a collation of them was made with the Codex Amiatinus, of which the results will be found at the bottom of each page; and a separate collation was also made of the fourth chapter

Pretium gallici operis (cf. adnot. 158) fuit ergo aequum sive ex parvis sive ex magnis asseribus ductum esset, habita ratione minoris impensae parvis asseribus (seu scindulis) comparandis auctaque opera in illis collocandis tum maioris impensae, minutaeque operae pro asseribus maioribus.

of St. John's Gospel, as in the Book of Deer, with the versions in the Codex Brixianus (Italic recension), the Vulgate, and the Celtic Gospels, known as the Book of Kells, the Book of Dimma, the Book of Moling, the Book of Armagh, the Lindisfarne Gospels, and an early fragment of the Gospels at Durham. The results are given in a tabular form at page xxxiv. of the Preface.

The plates of Facsimiles contain all the illuminations in the volume, and are exact representations of their present appearance.[1] The worn and stained condition of some of them would suggest that the volume had at times been carried about by those who used it. The figures on Plates XXI. and XXII. occur on the margins and open spaces throughout the Book, and appear to have been dashed off by the scribe in the course of his writing.

The editor cannot conclude these remarks without acknowledging the obligations under which he has been laid in the progress of his work.

Mr. Bradshaw's discovery of the volume (one only of the many happy results which have crowned his researches in the course of the last ten years) has already been referred to, but I must add that when engaged in the collation of the printed sheets with the original MS. at Cambridge, I received from Mr. Bradshaw much kindness and ready aid.

[1] Some pages of the Book of Deer have been reproduced by the process of photozincography in the first part of the volume of the National MSS. of Scotland, published under the directions of the Lord Clerk Register of Scotland. Drawings of many of the figures and borders have been given in "The Sculptured Stones of Scotland," volume second, and in Mr. Westwood's great work, "The Miniatures and Ornaments of Anglo-Saxon and Irish MSS.," but without any attempt to represent the colours of the illuminations, or the worn condition of the pages.

By the kind permission of the University authorities, the volume was sent for a time to the General Register House, Edinburgh, when a transcript was made of it by Mr. Robertson, and the drawings in facsimile were prepared by Mr. Gibb.

I thankfully bear my testimony to the care with which Mr. Gibb has completed his work. The plates are such as might have been expected from the artist of the "Sculptured Stones of Scotland," and have been pronounced by competent judges to equal any facsimiles of faded illuminations yet produced.

For collating the text with the Gospels in Trinity College, Dublin, and in the Chapter Library, Durham, I am indebted to the ready aid of Mr. Hennessy and Mr. Greenwell; and in the collations with the Vulgate, I have been much assisted by Mr. Macleod.

The valuable services of my old and valued friend Dr. Reeves, in reading the proofs of the prefatory chapters at a time when he had many other claims on his attention, require my special acknowledgments.

From Mr. James Peter, the minister of the parish of Deer, I have received much useful aid in my attempts to identify on the spot the names of the lands conveyed in the Celtic grants with those still applied to places in the district.

The translations of the Gaelic legend and grants in the volume have been given from the version of Mr. Whitley Stokes, the most accomplished Celtic scholar of the day. These curious memoranda formed the subject of a paper by Mr. Stokes, in the "Saturday Review" of 8th December 1860, where translations for the first time were given; and they appeared afterwards, accompanied by critical notes and a glossary, in his "Goidilica, or Notes on the

Gaelic Manuscripts, preserved at Turin, Milan, Berne, Leyden, the monastery of St. Paul's, Carinthia, and Cambridge, with eight hymns from the Liber Hymnorum, and the old-Irish notes in the Book of Armagh," pp. 47-63; a volume privately printed for the editor, at Calcutta, in the year 1866.

JOHN STUART.

EDINBURGH, *November* 1869.

INDEX.

Plate I

Fol. 1a

A. [illegible]

[illegible] lith.

Liber generationis ihu
xpi filii dauid filii abra
cham · abracham genuit isac
issac h genuit iacob · iacob h
genuit iudam · iudam ⁊ fratres eius
iudas h genuit pharis ⁊ zara
de thamar · pharis h genuit es
rom · esrom h genuit aram ·
aram h genuit aminadab · ami
nadab h genuit naason · naason
h genuit salmon · salmon h genuit
booz de rachab · booz h genuit
obeth ex ruth · obeth h genuit iesse
iesse h genuit dauid regem · dauid
h rex genuit salomonem ex ea quae
fuit uriae · salamon h genuit
roboam · roboam h genuit abiud ·
abiud h genuit asaph ⁊

The Book of Deer.

[Cap. I.] (1) **Liber** generationis ihesu[1] christi filii dauid[2] filii abracham[3]· Fol. 2.
(2) abracham[3] genuit issác[4]·Issác[4] autem genuit iacob·Iacob autem
genuit iudam·iudam[5] et fratres eius·(3) Iudas autem genuit phares et
zaram[6] dethamár[7]··phares autem genuit essrom[8]·essrom[8] autem genuit
aram··(4) Aram autem genuit aminadáb··aminadáb autem genuit naasón[9]··
naasón[9] autem genuit solmón[10]··(5) solmon[10] autem genuit boos[11] de-
ráchab[12]··Boos[11] autem genuit obéth exruth[13]··obéth autem genuit iesse·
iesse autem genuit dauid[2] regem··(6) Dauid[2] autem rex genuit salmonem[14]
exea[15] que[16] fuit urie[17]··(7) salamón[18] autem genuit roboam··roboas[19]
autem genuit abiúd[20]·abiud[21] autem genuit asaph[22]····7
(8) Asaphath[22] autem genuit iosapath[23]·iosapath[23] autem genuit Fol. 2 b.
ioram·ioras[24] autem genuit iozam[25]·(9) iozias[26] autem genuit ioatham·
iothas[27] autem genuit achaz·achaz autem genuit ezechiam··(10) ezechias
autem genuit mannassén[28]·mannasses[29] autem genuit amon·amos[30] autem
genuit iosiam·(11) iosias autem genuit iechoniam et fratres eius intrans-
migratione[31] babilonis[32] (12) etpost transmigrationem babilonis[32]·iechonias
genuit salathiel·salathiel autem genuit zorobbobel[33]·(13) zorobbabel[33] autem
genuit abiud·abiud autem genuit aliachim[34]·eliachim autem genuit azor··

---

1 Iesu.
2 David.
3 Abraham.
4 Isaac.
5 V. om.
6 Zarad.
7 de Thamar.
8 Esrom.
9 Naasson.
10 Salmon.
11 Booz.
12 de Racab.
13 ex Ruth.
14 Salomonem.
15 ex ea.
16 quae.
17 Uriae.
18 Salomon.
19 Roboam.
20 Abiam.
21 Abia.
22 Asa.
23 Iosaphat.
24 Ioram.
25 Oziam.
26 Ozias.
27 Ioatham.
28 Manassem.
29 Manasses.
30 Amon.
31 in transmigrationem.
32 Babylonis.
33 Zorobabel.
34 Eliachim.

(14) azor autem genuit saddoc·saddoc autem genuit achim·achim autem genuit eliud··(15) eliud autem genuit eleazar·eleazar autem genuit mathán[1]·mathán[1] autem genuit iacob·(16) iacob autem genuit ioseph uirum mariæ dequa natusest ihesus[2] qui uocatur Christus··7

Fol. 3. (17) Omnes igitur[3] generationes ababracham[4] usque adauid[5] generationes·xiiii[6]··et adauid[7] usque adtransmigrationem[8] babilonis[9] generationes·xiiii[6]··etadtransmigratione[10] babilonis[9] usque adchristum generationes·xiiii[6]····7

Finit prologus·Item incipit nunc euangelium secundum matheum··7··7

[1] Matthan.
[2] Iesus.
[3] ergo.
[4] ab Abraham.
[5] ad David.
[6] quattuordecim.
[7] a David.
[8] usque transmigrationem.
[9] Babylonis.
[10] a transmigratione.

7 blien acc ichodo ... ar ... 7 ar
chrostan ... chomall ... 7 ... daniel

Donchad mc mec
bead mec hidid
dorat acchad
madchor do crist
7 do drostan 7
do cholum cille
insore gobrath ma
lechi 7 comgell 7
gille crist mc fingun
inalnaidnaisi intesst 7
malcoluim mc
molini. Cormac
mc cinaeda do
rat gonige ...
li mhilsc. Com
gell mc caennai
g taisech clan
de canan do
rat do crist 7
do drostan 7
do cholum cille
gonige igort
he mor ...

...ar ... dom ... do dubacin ... 7 acchad.
... cholum cille ...
... ...

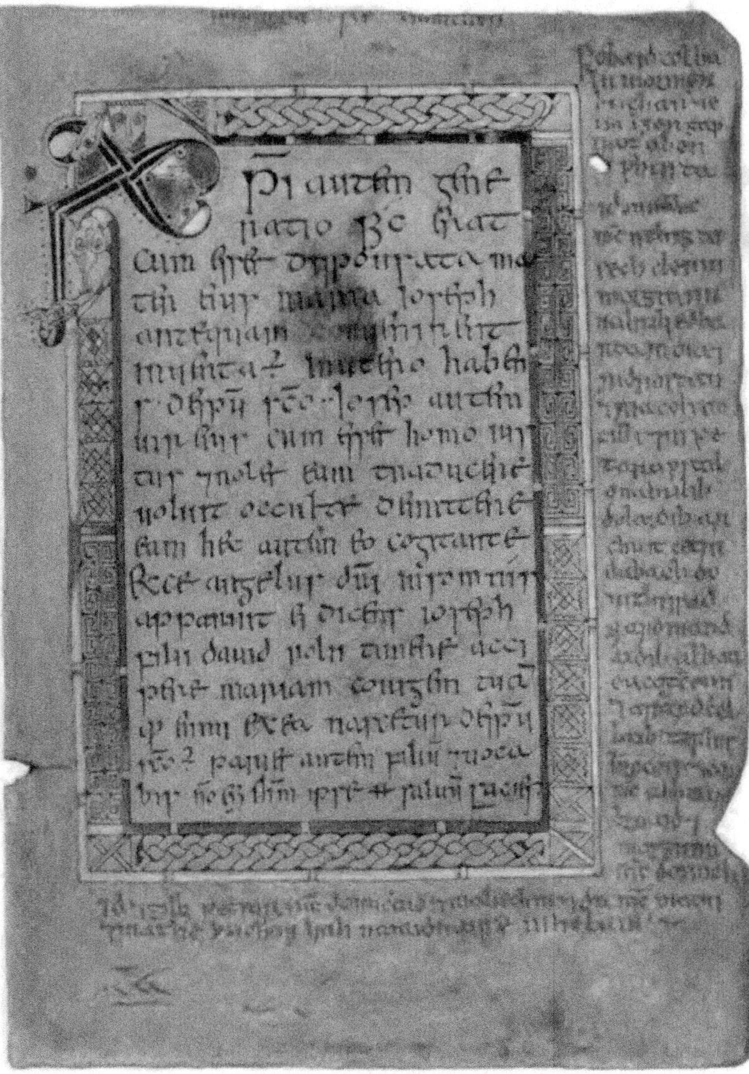

(18) **Christi** autem generatio sic erat Cum esset disponsata[1] Fol. 5.
mater eius maria ioseph antequam uenirent inuentaest inutero habens
despiritu sancto··(19) Iosep[2] autem uir eius cum esset homo[3] iustus et
nolet[4] eam traducere uoluit occulte demittere[5] eam (20) hec autem eo
cogitante Ecce angelus domini insomnís apparuit[6] ei dicens ioseph filii
dauid nolii[7] timere accipere mariam coiugem[8] tuam quod enim exea[9]
nascetur[10] despiritusanctoest (21) pariet autem filium etuocabis nomen
eius ihesum[11] ipse enim saluum faciet populum suum apeccatis eorum··7 Fol. 5 b.
(22) Hoc autem totum factum est vtadinpleretur[12] quod[13] dictum
est adomino per issiam[14] prophetam dicentem (23) ecce uirgo inutero
habebit etpariet filium etuocabunt nomen eius emanúel[15] quodest interpretatum nobiscum deus··7
(24) Exsurgens autem ioseph asomno fecit sicut preciperat[16] ei angelus
domini et accepit coiugem[17] suam (25) etnoncognoscebat eam donec peperit
filium suum primogenitum etuocauit nomen eius ihesum[18]··7

[Cap. II.] (1) Cum ergo natus esset[19] inbethlem[20] iuda[21] indiebus erodis[22] regis
ecce magi aboriente uenerunt inhierusolimam[23] (2) dicentes ubiest qui
natusest réx iudeorum[24] uidemus[25] enim stellam eius inoriente etuenimus
adorare[26]··7
(3) Audiens autem herodis[27] rex turbatusest etomnis hierusolima[28] Fol. 6.
cum eo[29] (4) etcongregans omnes principes sacerdotum etscribas populi
sciscitabatur abeis ubi christus nasceretur··7
(5) At illi dixerunt[30] inbethlem[20] iuda[21] sicenim scriptumest[31] (6) et tu

---

1 desponsata.
2 Ioseph.
3 V. om.
4 nollet.
5 dimittere.
6 paruit.
7 noli.
8 coniugem.
9 in ea.
10 natum est.
11 Iesum.
12 ut adimpleretur.
13 id quod.
14 V. om.
15 Emmanuhel.
16 praecepit.
17 coniugem.
18 Iesum.
19 V. adds Iesus.
20 Bethleem.
21 Iudeae.
22 Herodis.
23 Hierosolymam.
24 Iudaeorum?
25 Vidimus.
26 V. adds eum.
27 Herodes.
28 Hierosolyma.
29 illo.
30 V. adds ei.
31 V. adds per prophetam.

bethlem[1] terra iuda nequaquam minima es inprincipibus iuda exte enim-exiat[2] dux **qui regat**[3] populum meum israhél··7

(7) Hunc herodis[4] clam uocatis magís diligenter dedicit[5] abéis tempus **stelle que** apparuit éis (8) etmittens eos[6] in bethlem[1] dixit ite[7] interrogate diligenter depuero etcum inueneritis renuntiate mihi[8] et ego ueniens adorem eum (9) quicum audisent[9] regem abierunt··

Et ecce stella quam uiderant inhoriente[10] antecedebat eos usque dum ueniens staret supra ubi erat puer (10) uidentes autem stellam gauissi[11]·sunt· gaudio magno·ualde (11) etintrantes domum inuenerunt puerum cum maria
Fol. 6 b. matre eius etprocedentes[12] adorauerunt eum etapertis thesauris suis··7

Obtullerunt[13] ei munera aurum tús et mirram[14] (12) **et responso** accepto insomnís ne redirent adherodem sed[15] peraliam uiam reuersi sunt insuam[16] regionem (13) quicum **reg** [17]

Ecce angelus domini apparuit **insomnis**[18] Ioseph dicens surge et-accipe puerum etmatrem eius. **etfuge** inegiptum[19] etesto ibi usque[20] dicam tibi futurumestenim vtherodis[21] querat puerum adperdendum eum (14) **qui** consurgens accepit puerum etmatrem eius nocte etaccessit[22] in-egiptum[19] **(15) eterat** ibi usque adobitum hirodis[23] vtadinpleretur[24] quod dictumest adomino per prophetam dicentem exegipto uocaui filium meum (16) tunc herodis[21] uidens quoniam dilussus[25] esset amagis iratusest ualde etmittens occidit omnes pueros qui erat[26] inbethlem etinomnibus finibus[27] abimatu etinfra secundum tempus quod exquissierat[28] amagís (17) tunc et-inpletumest[29] quod dictumest perhieremiam prophetam dicentem (18) vox
Fol. 7. inrama audita est plorans[30] etululatus multus rachiel[31] ploratus filios suos et noluit consularii[32] quia nonsunt··

(19) Defuncto autem herode ecce apparuit angelus domini in-

[1] **Bethleem.**
[2] **exiet.**
[3] **reget.**
[4] **Herodes.**
[5] **didicit.**
[6] **illos.**
[7] **V. adds et.**
[8] **V. adds ut.**
[9] **audissent.**
[10] **oriente.**
[11] gavisi.
[12] procidentes.
[13] obtulerunt.
[14] murram.
[15] V. om.
[16] regionem suam.
[17] recessissent.
[18] somnio.
[19] Aegyptum.
[20] V. adds dum.
[21] Herodes.
[22] recessit.
[23] Herodis.
[24] adimpleretur.
[25] inlusus.
[26] erant.
[27] V. adds eius.
[28] exquisierat.
[29] adimpletum.
[30] ploratus.
[31] Rachel.
[32] consolari.

somnís ioseph inegipto (20) dicens surge etaccipe puerum etmatrem eius
etuade interram israhel defuncti sunt enim qui querebant animam pueri
(21) qui consurgens[1] accipit[2] puerum etmatrem eius etuenit interram
israhel (22) audiens autem quod[3] archilaus[4] regnaret iniudea proherode
patre suo timuit illúc ire etadmonitus insomnís secessit in partes galiliæ[5]
(23) etueniens habitauit inciuitate queuocatur nazaréth vtadinpleretur[6] quod
dictumest adomino[7] per prophetas quoniam nazareus uocabitur··7

[Cap. III.] (1) Indiebus autem illis uenit iohannis[8] babtista[9] predicans indeserto
iudae[10] (2) [11]dicens penitentiam agite adpropincauit[12] enim regnum celorum··
(3) Hic[13] enim quidictusest perissaiam[14] prophetam dicentem uóx
clamantis indeserto parate uiam domini rectas facite semitas eius···7
(4) Ipse autem iohannis[7] **habebat** uestimentum tuum[7] deillis[15] *Fol. 7 b.*
camellorum[16] etzonam pelliciam circa lumbos suos[17] esca autem eius erat
locuste[18] etmel siluestre··(5) tunc exieat[19] adeum hierusolima[20] etomnis
iudea etomnis **regio circa**[21] **iordanén (6) etbabtizabantur**[22] iniordanén[23]
abeo confitentes peccata sua··7
(7) Uidens autem multos phariseorum et saduceorum[24] uenientes
adbabtismum[25] suum dixit eis progenies uiperarum quis demonstrauit
uobis fugere afutura ira··(8) facite ergo fructum dignum penitentiæ (9) et-
ne uellitis[26] dicere interuos[27] patrem habeamus[28] abracham dico enim
uobis quia[29] potest deus exlapedibus[30] istis suscitare filios abrache[31] (10)
iam enim securís adradices[32] arborum possita[33]est omnis arbor[34] ergo qui[35]
non facit fructum bonum excidetur etinignem mittetur··7
(11) Ego quidem uos babtizo[36] inaqua et[7] inpenitentiam qui autem

[1] surgens.
[2] accepit.
[3] quia.
[4] Archelaus.
[5] Galilaeae.
[6] adimpleretur.
[7] V. om.
[8] Iohannes.
[9] baptista.
[10] Iudaeae.
[11] V. adds et.
[12] adpropinquavit.
[13] V. adds est.
[14] Esaiam.
[15] de pilis.
[16] camelorum.
[17] eius.
[18] lucustæ.
[19] exiebat.
[20] Hierosolyma.
[21] circum.
[22] baptizabantur.
[23] Iordane.
[24] Sadducaeorum.
[25] baptismum.
[26] velitis.
[27] intra vos.
[28] habemus.
[29] quoniam.
[30] de lapidibus.
[31] Abraham.
[32] radicem.
[33] posita.
[34] ergo arbor.
[35] quae.
[36] baptizo.

post me uenturusest fortior meest cuius nonsum dignus calciamenta portare··7

Ipse babtizauit uos[1] inspiritu sancto etigni (12) cuius uentilabrum

Fol. 8. inmanu sua etmundauit[2] aream suam·etcongregauit[3] tricum[4] inorreum[5] suum[6] phaleas[7] autem conburet[8] igni inextinguibili (13) tunc uenit ihesus agalilea iniordinén[9] adiohannem vtbabtizaretur abeo (14) iohannis[10] autem prohibebat eum dicens Ego adte[11] debeo babtizarí ettu uenis adme (15) respondit[12] autem ihesus dixit ei sine modo síc enim decet nós inplere[13] omnem iustitiam tunc demisit[14] eum (16) babtizatus autem ihesus[6] confestim ascendit deaqua etecce aperti sunt ei celi etuidit spiritum dei discendentem[15] decelo[6] sicut columbam uenientem super sé (17) etecce uox decelis dicens hicest filius meus dilectus inquo mihi bene[6] conplacui·

[Cap. IV.] (1) tunc ihesus ductusest indesertum aspiritu[16] uttemptaretur[17] addiabulo[18]··7

(2) Et cum ieiunasset·xl[19]·diebus·et lx[19] [20]·postea essurit[21] (3) et accedens adeum[22] temptator[23] dixit ei sí filius dei es·díc vtlapides panes isti[24] fiant (4) qui respondens dixit scriptumest enim[6]·

Noninpane solo uiuit homo sed inomni uerbo dei[25] quod procedit deore dei (5) tunc adsumsit[26] eum zabulus[27] insanctam ciuitatem et statuit

Fol. 8 b. eum supra pinnaculum templi·(6) et dixit ei Sí filius dei es mitte te deorsum scriptumestenim quia angelís suis mandauit dete vtcustodiant te inomnibus uiis tuis[28] [29] inmanibus tollent te ne forte offendas adlapidem pedem tuum·(7) ait illi ihesus rursum scriptumest nontemptabis[30] dominum deum tuum (8) iterum adsumsit[31] eum zabulus[27] inmontem

---

1 vos baptizavit.
2 permundavit.
3 congregabit.
4 triticum suum.
5 horreum.
6 V. om.
7 paleas.
8 comburet.
9 Iordanen.
10 Iohannes.
11 a te.
12 respondens.
13 implere.
14 dimisit.
15 descendentem.
16 ab spiritu.
17 temtaretur.
18 a diabolo.
19 quadraginta.
20 V. adds noctibus.
21 esuriit.
22 V. om.
23 temtator.
24 itsi panes.
25 V. om.
26 assumsit.
27 diabolus.
28 V. om. this clause from *et*.
29 V. adds et.
30 temtabis.
31 assumit.

excelsum ualde etostendit ei omnia regna mundi etgloriam eorum (9) etdixit ei[1] hec tibi omnia dabo si cadens adoraueris me·
(10) Hunc dicit ei ihesus uade retro[2] satanas scriptumest enim[3] domi-
num deum tuum adorabis etilli soli serueis··(11) Tunc reliquit **cum**
zabulus[4] etecce angeli accesserunt etministrabant ei··7
(12) Et cum[5] audisset ihesus[6] quod iohannis[7] traditus esset secessit
ingalileam (13) etrelicta ciuitate nazareth··7

Uenit ethabitauit incapharnauum[8] maritimam infinibus zabulón
et neptalim[9] (14) vtinpleretur[10] quod dictumest peressaiam[11] prophetam
dicentem[12]··(15) Terra zabulon et terra[13] neptalim[9] uia maris trans
iordenen galileæ gentium (16) populus qui sedebat in tenebris uidit
lucem[14] magnam[15] etsedentibus inregione etinumbra[16] mortis lúx ortaest
eis··7
(17) Exinde coepit ihesus predicare etdicere penitentiam agite adpro- Fol. 9.
pinquauit enim regnum celorum··7
(18) Ambulans autem ihesus[17] iuxta mare galiliæ uidit duo[18] fratres
simonem qui uocatur petrus etandream fratrem eius mittens[19] retia[20] inmare erant enim piscatores··7
(19) Etait illis ihesus[21] uenite post me etfaciam uos fieri piscatores hominum (20) at illi continuo relictís retibus secuti sunt eum··(21) [22]procedens
inde uidit alios duos fratres iacobum zebedei et iohannem fratrem eius
innaui cum zebedeo patre eorum reficientes retia sua·etuocauit eos (22) illi
autem statim relictis retibus suis[2]·etpatre secuti sunt[23]··7
(23) Et circum ibat ihesus totam galileam docens insinagogis[24] eorum
etpredicans euangelium regni etsanans **omnem** langorem[25] etomnem in-
firmitatem inpopulo··(24) Et abiit opinio eius intotam siriam[26]··Et obtulle-

[1] illi.
[2] V. om.
[3] V. om.
[4] diabolus.
[5] cum autem.
[6] V. om.
[7] Iohannes
[8] Capharnaum.
[9] Nepthalim.
[10] impleretur.
[11] Esaiam.
[12] V. om.
[13] V. om.
[14] lumen vidit.
[15] magnum.
[16] et umbra.
[17] V. om.
[18] duos.
[19] mittentes.
[20] rete.
[21] V. om.
[22] V. adds Et.
[23] V. adds eum.
[24] Synagogis.
[25] languorem.
[26] Syriam.

runt[1] ei omnes male habentes uarís langoribus[2] ettormentis conprechensós[3] etqui demonía habent[4] etlunaticos etparaliticos[5] etcurauit eos (25) et secute sunt eum turbe multe·degalilea et decapoli[6] etdehierusolimís[7] et[8] iudea et detransiordanén··7

[CAP. V.] (1) Uidens autem ihesus[9] turbas ascendit inmontem etcum sedisset
Fol. 9 b. accesserunt adeum discipuli eius (2) etaperiens ós suum docebat eos·· dicens··7

(3) Beati pauperes spiritu quoniam ipsorumest regnum celorum·

(4) Beati mites quoniam ipsi possidebunt terram··7

(5) Beati qui lugent nunc[10]·quoniam ipsi consulabuntur[11]··

(6) Beati qui essuriunt[12] etsitiunt iustitiam quoniam ipsi saturabuntur···7

(7) Beati misericordes quoniam ipsi misericordiam consequentur··7

(8) Beati mundo corde quoniam ipsi deum uidebunt··7

(9) Beati pacifici quoniam[13] filii dei uocabuntur··

(10) Beati qui persecutionem patiuntur propter iustitiam quoniam ipsorumest regnum celorum··7

(11) Beati estis cum male dixerint uobís homines[14] etpersecuti uos
fierint[15] etdixerint omne malum aduersum uos mentientes propter me
(12) gaudete etexultate quoniam mercis[16] uestra copiosaest in celis··síc
enim persecuti sunt et[14] prophetís[17] qui fuerunt ante uós··

(13) Uós estis sál terre quod sí sál euanuerit inquo salietur[18] adnihilum ualebit[19] nisi vtmittatur foras etconculcetur abhominibus··7

Fol. 10. (14) Uos estis lux mundi nonpotest ciuitas abscondi supra montem
possita[20] (15) neque accendant[21] lucernam etponunt eam submodio sed

---

1 obtulerunt.
2 variis languoribus.
3 comprehensos.
4 habebant.
5 paralyticos.
6 Decapolim.
7 et Hierosolymis.
8 V. adds de.
9 V. om.
10 V. om.
11 consolabuntur.
12 esuriunt.
13 V. adds ipsi.
14 V. om.
15 fuerint.
16 merces.
17 prophetas.
18 sallietur?
19 valet ultra.
20 posita.
21 accendunt.

super candellabrum[1] vtluceat omnibus hominibus[2] qui indomu[3] sunt (16)
sic luceat lux uestra coram hominibus utuideant bona[4] opera uestra et-
glorificent patrem uestrum qui incelisest··

(17) Nolite putare quia[5] ueni soluere legem aut prophetas·nonueni
soluere legem[2] sed adinplere[6] (18) amen quippe dico uobis donec trans-
eat celum etterra iota unum aut unus apex nonpreteribit alege usquequo[7]
omnia fiant (19) qui autem[8] soluerit unum demandatis istis minimis et
docuerit sic homines minimus uocabitur inregna[9] celorum qui autem fecerit
etdocuerit hic magnus uocabitur inregno celorum·

(20) Dico enim uobis quia nisi habundauerit[10] iustitia uestra plus quam
scribarum et phariseorum nonintrabitis inregno[11] celorum (21) audistis·
quia dictumest antiquis nonoccides qui autem occiderit reus erit iudicio[12]
(22) qui autem dixerit fatuæ[13] reus erit gehenne ignis···7

(23) Si[14] offeres monus[15] tuum adaltare etibi recordatus fueris quia Fol. 10 b.
frater tuus habet aliquid aduersus[16] te (24) relinque ibi monus[15] tuum
ante[17] ante[17] altare etuade[18] reconciliare fratri tuo ettunc ueniens offeres[19]
monus[15] tuum··

(25) Esto consentiens aduersario tuo cito dum es inuia cum eo ne
forte tradat te aduersarius iudici et iudex tradat te ministro etincarcerem
mittaris··

(26) Amen dico tibi nonexies inde donec reddas nouissimum cadren-
tem[20]··

(27) Audistis quia dictum est antiquis nonmechaueris[21]·(28) Ego
autem dico uobis quia[22] omnis qui uiderit mulierem adconcupiscendum
eam iam mechatus[23] est[24] incorde suo (29) quod si occulus[25] tuus

---

1 candelabrum.
2 V. om.
3 domo.
4 vestra bona opera.
5 quoniam.
6 adimplere.
7 donec.
8 ergo.
9 regno.
10 abundaverit.
11 regnum.
12 V. adds Ego autem dico vobis quia omnis qui irascitur fratri suo, reus erit iudicio: qui autem dixerit fratri suo racha, reus erit concilio:
13 fatue.
14 V. adds ergo.
15 munus.
16 adversum.
17 V. om., and has ad altare.
18 V. adds prius.
19 offers.
20 quadrantem.
21 moechaveris.
22 quoniam.
23 moechatus.
24 V. adds—eam.
25 oculus.

dexter scandalizat te erue eum etproiece[1] absté expedit enim tibi ut periat[2] unum membrorum tuorum quam totum corpus tuum mittatur ingehenam[3]·

(30) Si[4] dextera manus tua scandalizat te abscide eam et proiece[1] abste expedit enim tibi vt periat[2] unum membrorum tuorum quam totum corpus tuum eat ingehennam··

Fol. 11. (31) Dictum est autem qui cumque dimissirit[5] uxorem suam det illi libellum repudi[6]

(32) Ego autem dico uobis quia omnis qui[7] uxorem suam excepta fornicationis causa fecit[8] eam moechari etqui dismissam[9] duxerit adulterat

(33) Iterum audistis quia dictum est antiquis nonperiurabis[10] reddes autem domino iuramenta tua·

(34) Ego autem dico uobis noniurare omnino neque percelum quia thronus domini[11] est (35) neque perterram quia scabillum[12] pedum eius neque perhierusolimam[13] quia ciuitas[14] magni regis·

(36) Neque percapud[15] tuum iuraueris quia non potes unum capillum tuum[16] facire[17] aut nigrum (37) sit autem sermo uester·est est non non quod autem hís habundantius[18] amalo est··7

(38) Audistis quia dictumest occulum[19] proocculo[20] dentem prodente·(39) Ego autem dico uobís nonresistere malo sed sí quis te percusserit indexteram[21] maxillam tuam preueni[22] illi etalteram (40) etei[23] qui uult tecum iudicio contendere ettonicam[24] tuam tollere dimitte[25] ei[26]

Fol. 11 b. etpallium (41) etqui[27] te angarizauerit[28] mille passus uade cum illo etalia[26] duo (42) qui petit adte[29] et[26] dá ei etuolenti motuarí[30] áte ne auertaris·(43) audistis quia dictum est diliges proximum tuum et odies[31] inimicum tuum··7

---

1 proice.
2 pereat.
3 Gehennam.
4 V. has Et si.
5 dimiserit.
6 repudii.
7 V. adds dimiserit.
8 facit.
9 dimissam.
10 peierabis.
11 dei.
12 scabellum est.
13 Hierosolymam.
14 V. adds est.
15 caput.
16 V. om. and has album.
17 facere.
18 abundantius est.
19 oculum.
20 oculo et.
21 dextera maxilla tua.
22 praebe.
23 illi.
24 tunicam.
25 remitte.
26 V. om.
27 quicumque.
28 angariaberit.
29 a te.
30 mutuari.
31 odio habebis.

(44) Ego autem dico uobis·Diligite inimicos uestros et[1] benefacite hís
qui oderunt uos et orate propersequentibus et calumniantibus uobís[2] (45)
vtsitis filii patris uestri qui incelisest qui solem suum oriri facit super bonos
et malos et pluit super iustos etiniustos (46) sicnim diligatis eos qui uos
dilegunt[3] quam mercidem[4] habebitis nonne[5] puplicani[6] hoc faciunt (47)
etsi salutaueritis fratres uestros tantum quidamplius facitis nonne et[1] ethnici
hoc faciunt·(48) estote ergo[7] perfecti sicut etpater uester celistis[8] perfectus
est

[Cap. VI.] (1) adtendite[9] ne iustitiam uestram faciatis coram hominibus vt uidiamini[10]
abeis alioquín mercidem[4] nonhabebitis apud patrem uestrum qui in-
celis est···7

(2) Cum ergo facies elimoysinam[11] nolii[12] tuba canere ante te sicut Fol. 12.
hiphoriti[13] faciunt insinagogís[14] et inuicís vthonorificentur abhominibus·
Amen dico uobís reciperunt[15] mercidem[4] suam·(3) te autem faciente
elimoysinam[16] nesciat sinistra tua quid faciat dextera tua (4) vtsit elimoy-
sina[17] tua inabsconso[18] et pater tuus qui uidet inabsconso[18] reddet tibi···7

(5) Et cum arabitis[19] nolite fieri[20] sicut hippocrite[13] qui amant insinagogís[14] et inangulis platearum stantes orare utuideantur abhomini-
bus···7

Amen dico uobís reciperunt[15] mercidem[4] suam (6) tu autem cum
orabis intra incubiculum tuum etcluso[21] hostio[22] tuo orá patrem tuum inabsconso[18] etpater tuus qui uidet inabsconso[18] reddet tibi (7) orantes
autem·Nolíi[23] multum loqui sicut ethinici putant enim quia inmultilaquio[24]
suo exaudiantur···7

(8) Nolite ergo adsimularii[25] eís·sic[26] pater uester quid[27] opus sit Fol. 12 b.
uobís antequam petatis eum (9) síc ergo úos orabitis··

1 V. om.
2 vos.
3 diligunt.
4 mercedem.
5 V. adds et.
6 publicani.
7 V. adds vos.
8 caelestis.
9 Attendite.
10 videamini.
11 elemosynam.
12 noli.
13 hypocritae.
14 synagogis.
15 receperunt.
16 elemosynam.
17 elemosyna.
18 abscondito.
19 oratis.
20 non eritis.
21 clauso.
22 ostio.
23 nolite.
24 multiloquio.
25 assimilari.
26 scit enim.
27 quibus.

Pater noster qui es incelis sanctificetur nomen tuum (10) adueniat regnum tuum fiat uoluntas tua sicut incelo etinterra (11) panem nostrum supersubstantialem dá nobis hodie (12) etdimitte nobis debita nostra sicut etnos demittimus[1] debitoribus nostris (13) et ne nós inducas[2] intemptationem[3] sed libera nos amalo··7

(14) Si enim remisseritis[4] hominibus peccata eorum remittit[5] et uobís pater[6] celistis···7

Delicta uestra (15) si autem[7] dimisseritis[4] hominibus nec pater uester cœlistis[8] dimittet uobis[5] peccata uestra··

(16) Cum autem ieiunatis nolite fieri sicut hippocrite[9] tristes exterminant enim facies suas utpateant[10] hominibus ieiunantes····7

Amén dico uobís[11] reciperent[12] mercidem[13] suam (17) tú autem cum autem[8] ieiunas unge capud[14] tuum etfaciem tuam laua (18) ne
Fol. 13. uidearis hominibus ieiunans·sed patri tuo qui est inabscondo[15] etpater tuus qui uidet inabsconso[15] reddet tibi··7

(19) Nolite thesaurizare uobis thesauros interra ubi crugo ettinea demoletur[16] et[8]ubi fures effodiunt etfurantur··

(20) Thesaurizate autem uobís thesauros incelo ubi neque crugo neque tinea demoletur[16] et ubi fures noneffodiunt nec furantur (21) ubi enim fuerit[17] thesaurus tuus ibi erit[18] etcor tuum (22) lucerna corporis tui[8] est occulus[19] tuus[8]·sí fuerit occulus[20] semplex[21] totum corpus tuum lucidum erit·(23) sí autem occulus[19] tuus nequam fuerit totum corpus tuum tenebrosus[22] erit··

Si ergolu men quod intcest tenebre sunt ipse[8] tenebre quam[23] te[8] erunt··

(24) Nemo potest duobus dominis seruire·aut enim unum odio

---

[1] dimittimus.
[2] inducas nos.
[3] temtationem.
[4] dimiseritis.
[5] dimittet.
[6] V. adds vester.
[7] V. adds non.
[8] V. om.
[9] hypocritae.
[10] pareant.
[11] V. adds quia.
[12] receperunt.
[13] mercedem.
[14] caput.
[15] abscondito.
[16] demolitur.
[17] est.
[18] est.
[19] oculus.
[20] oculus tuus.
[21] simplex.
[22] tenebrosum.
[23] quantae.

habebit etalterum dileget[1] aut unum sustinebit etalterum contempnet[2]
nonpotestis deo seruire·et mammóne[3]···7
(25) Ideo dico uobís ne solliciti sitis animæ uestræ quid manducetis Fol. 13 b.
neque corpori uestro quid induemini[4] nonne anima plus est quam esca et-
corpus[5] quam uestimentum (26) respicite uolatilia cœli[6] nonserunt neque
metunt neque congregant inhorrea etpater uester celistis[7] pascit illa nonne
uós magis plures estis illis (27) qui[8] autem uestrum cogitans potest addi-
cere[9] ad staturam suam cubitum unum (28) etdeuestimento quid solliciti
sitis[10] considerate lilia agri quomodo crescunt nonlaborant neque neunt[11]
(29) dico autem uobis quoniam nec salamón[12] in[13]gloria sua coopertus-
est sicut unum exeis[14] (30) sí autem foenum[15] agri quod hodieest et
crás incliuanum[16] mittitur deus sic uestit quantomogis[17] uos modice[18]
fidei···7
(31) Nolite ergo solliciti esse dicentes quid manducabimus aut quid
bibemus aut quo operiemur (32) hec enim omnia gentes inquirunt scit enim
pater uester quid horum[19] indigetis·7
(33) Querite ergo[20] primum regnum dei[21] etiustitiam eius etheeomnia[22] Fol. 14.
prestabuntur[23] uobis··7
(34) Nolite ergo solliciti esse[24] incrástinvm crastinus enim dies sollicitus
erit sibi ipse sufficit enim[21] diei malitia sua···7

[Cap. VII.] (1) Nolite iudicare vtnoniudicemini (2) inquo enim indicio iu-
dicaueritis iudicabitur[25] deuobís[26] (3) quid enim[27] uides fistucam[28] inocculo[29] fratris tui ettrabem inocculo[29] tuo nonuides·(4)[30] quomodo dicis
fratri tuo sine ciciam fistucam[28] deocculo[29] tuo etecce trabis[31]est inocculo[29]

---

1 diliget.
2 contemnet.
3 mamonæ.
4 induamini.
5 V. adds plus est.
6 V. adds quoniam.
7 caelestis.
8 Quis.
9 adicere.
10 estis?
11 nent.
12 Salomon.
13 V. adds omni.
14 istis.
15 faenum.
16 clibanum.
17 magis.
18 minimae.
19 quia his omnibus.
20 autem.
21 V. om.
22 omnia haec.
23 adicientur.
24 esse solliciti.
25 iudicabimini.
26 V. om. and adds et in qua mensura mensi fueritis, metietur vobis.
27 autem.
28 festucam.
29 oculo.
30 V. adds Aut.
31 trabes.

tuo (5) hippocrita[1] eiee primum trabem deoculo[2] tuo[3] tunc uidebis eicere fistucam[4] [5]fratris tui··

(6) Nolite dare sanctum canibus neque mittatis margaretas[6] uestrás ante porcas[7] ne forte conculcent eas pedibus suis et conuersi disrumpant uós··

(7) Petite etdabitur uobis querite etinuenietis pulsate etaperietur nobis (8) omnis enim qui petit accipit

Fol. 14 b. Et qui querit inuenit etpulsanti aperietur (9) ante[8] quis est ex-uobis homo quem si petierit filius suus panem numquid lapidem porriget ei[9] (11) sí ergo uós cum sitis mali nostis bona dare filiis uestris quanto magis pater uester qui incelis est dabit bona petentibus te[10]··

(12) Omnia ergo quecumque uultís vtfaciant uobis homines bona et-ita[11] etuos facite eís héc[12] enim lex etprofete[13]··7

(13) Intrate perangustam portam quam[14] lata porta etinspatiosa[15] uia que ducit adperditionem etmulti sunt qui intrant peream (14) quam angusta porta [16]etspatiosa uia que ducit adperditionem et multi sunt qui intrant peream quam angusta porta[16] et arta uia que ducit aduitam et-pauci sunt qui inueniunt eam··7

(15) Adtendite[17] uobís[11] afalsís profetís[18] qui ueniunt aduós inues-timentís··7

Fol. 15. Ouium intrinsecus autem sunt lupirapaces (16) afructibus eorum cognoscetis eos··7

Numquid colligunt despinís uuás aut detribulís[19] ficas[20] (17) síc omnes[21] arbor bona bonus fructus[22] facit·

Mala autem arbor malos fructus[23] facit·(18) Nonpotest arbor mala bonus fructus facire[24]·neque arbor bona malos fructus[25] facere·

---

[1] Hypocrita.
[2] oculo.
[3] V. adds et.
[4] festucam.
[5] V. adds de oculo.
[6] margaritas.
[7] porcos.
[8] Aut.
[9] V. adds Aut si piscem petet, numquid serpentem porriget ei?
[10] se.
[11] V. om.
[12] V adds est.
[13] prophetæ.
[14] quia.
[15] spatiosa.
[16] [16] This is a repetition.
[17] Attendite.
[18] prophetis.
[19] tribolis.
[20] ficus?
[21] omnis.
[22] fructus bonos.
[23] fructus malos.
[24] bona fructus malos facere.
[25] mala fructus bonos.

(19) Omnis arbor que nonfacit fructum bonvm excidetur[1] etmittetur inignem[2] ··· 7

(20) Igitur exfructibus eorum cognoscetis eos··

(21) Nonomnis qui dicit mihi domine domine intrauit[3] inregnum celorum **sed** qui facit uoluntatem patris mei quiincelisest ipse intrauit[3] inregnum cælorum··

(22) Multi **mihi**[4] dicent **inilla** die domine domine nonne intuo **nomine**[5] profetauimus etintuo **nomine**[6] demonia eicimus[7] etintuo nomine[6] uirtutes multas facimus[8] (23) et tunc confitebor illis quia nunquam[9] noui uós discedite áme qui operamini iniquitatem··7

---

[1] exciditur.
[2] in ignem mittitur.
[3] intrabit.
[4] dicent mihi.
[5] in nomine tuo.
[6] nomine tuo.
[7] eiecimus.
[8] fecimus?
[9] numquam.

[Cap. I.] Fol. 17. (1) Initium euangelii ihesu[1] christi fili[2] dei (2) sicut scriptum
est inessia[3] profeta[4]···7

Ecce ego[5] mitto angelum meum **ante** faciem tuam qui preparauit[6]
uiam tuam ante[5] te[5]··

(3) Vóx clamantis indeserto parate uiam domini rectas facite semitas[7]

Fol. 17 b. (4) Fuit iohannis[8] babtizans etpredicans babtismum
penitentiæ in remisionem[9] peccatorum··7

(5) Et egrediebatur adillum omnis iudæ[10] regio et hierusollimite[11]
uniuersi et babtizabantur abillo iniordiane[12] flumine confitentes peccata
sua···7

(6) Et erat iohannis[13] uestitus pilis camelli[14] etzona pellicia circa
lumbos **suos**[15] etlocustas[16] etmel siluestre edebat etpredicabat·dicens (7)
uenit fortior me post me cuius nonsumdignus procumbens soluere **corrigiam**
calciamentorum eius (8) ego babtizauí uós[17] in[5] spiritu sancto···7

Fol. 18. (9) Etfactumest indiebus illis uenit ihesus anazaréth galilie[18] et babtizatus **est inordane**[19] abiohanne (10) et statim ascendens deaqua uidit
apertos cælos etspiritum tamquam columbam discendentem[20] etmanentem
in ipso.(11) etuóx factaest decelís tu es filius meus dilectus inte con-
placui[21]··7

(12) Et statim spiritum[22] expellit eum indesertum (13) [23]erat in-
deserto·xl[24]·diebus·et·xl[24]·noctibus ettemptabatur[25] asatana··7

Eratque cum bestís[26] etangeli ministrabant illi··(14) Post[27] autem
quam traditusest iohannis[13] uenit ihesus ingalileam···7

---

1 Iesu.
2 filii.
3 Esaia.
4 propheta.
5 V. **om.**
6 praeparabit.
7 V. adds eius.
8 Iohannes in deserto.
9 remissionem.
10 Iudaeae.
11 Hierosolymitæ.
12 Iordane.
13 Iohannes.
14 cameli.
15 eius.
16 lucustas.
17 V. adds aqua, ille vero baptizabit vos.
18 Galilaeae.
19 in Jordane.
20 descendentem.
21 complacui.
22 spiritus.
23 V. adds Et.
24 quadraginta.
25 temtabatur.
26 bestiis.
27 postquam.

Plate VIII Fol. 16[a]

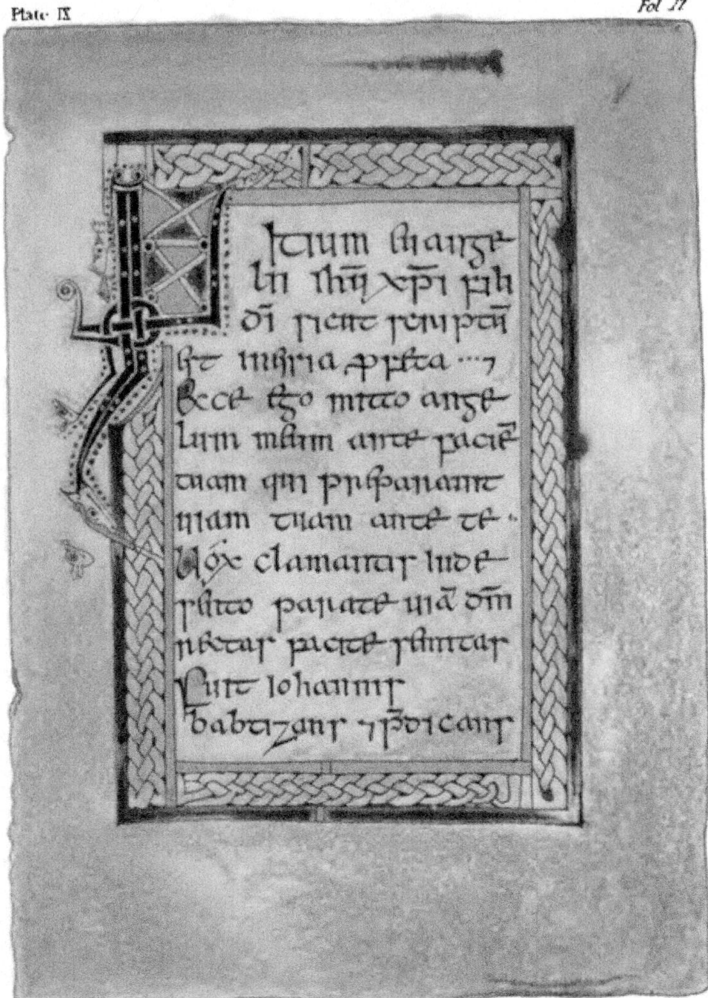
Initium euange
lii ihu xpi filii
di sicut scriptum
est in isaia propheta
Ecce ego mitto ange
lum meum ante faciem
tuam qui praeparauit
uiam tuam ante te
Uox clamantis in de
serto parate uiam dni
rectas facite semitas
Fuit iohannis
babtizans et praedicans

Predicans euangelium regni dei (15) etdicens quoniam inpletum[1]
est tempus etadpropincauit[2] regnum dei penitemini etcredite euangelio
(16) etpreteriens secus mare galilea[3] uidit simonem etandream fratrem
eius··7
mittentes retia inmare erant enim piscatores.. Fol. 18 b.
(17) Et dixit eis ihesus uenite post **me etfaciam uós** fieri piscatores
hominum (18) etprotinus relictís retibus secuti sunt eum··7
(19) Et progresus[4] inde pussillum[5] uidit iacobum zebedéi etiohannem
fratrem eius et ipsos innaui·conponentes[6] **retia** (20) etstatim uocauit illos
etrelicto patre suo zebedeo innaui cum mercinarís[7] secuti sunt eum··
(21) Et ingrediuntur capharnauum[8] etstatim sabbatis ingresus[9] in-[10]
sinagogam[11] docebat eos (22) etstupebant super doctrinam[12] eius·erant[13] enim
docens eos quasi potestatem habens[14] nonsicut scribæ··7
(23) Et erat insinagoga[15] eorum homo inspiritu inspiritu[10] inmundo **etex-**
clamauit·(24) dicens quid nobis ettibi ihesum[16] nazarene uenisti perdere
nós scio quis sis[17] sanctus dei··
(25) Et comminatus est ei ihesus dicens obmutesce etexí dehomine Fol. 19.
(26) spiritus[10] inmunde[10] etdiscerpens eum spiritus inmundus etexclamans
uoce magna exiuit abeo (27) etmirati sunt omnes ita vteonquerent[18] interse
dicentes **quid nam** est hóc **que** doctrina hec noua est[10] quia inpotestate
etspiritibus inmundís impereat[19] etobediunt[20] ei.(28) etprocessit rumor
eius statim inomnem regionem galiliæ[3]··7
(29) Et protinus egredientes disinagoga[21] uenerunt indomum simonis
etandrea[22] cum iacob[23] etioanne[24] (30) discumbebat[25] autem socrus simonis
febricgans[26] etstatim dicunt ei deilla (31) etaccedens eleuabit[27] eam et-[10]

[1] impletum.
[2] appropinquavit.
[3] Galilaeae.
[4] progressus.
[5] pusillum.
[6] componentes.
[7] mercennariis.
[8] **Capharnaum.**
[9] ingressus.
[10] V. om.
[11] synagogam.
[12] doctrina.
[13] erat.
[14] V. adds et.
[15] synagoga.
[16] Iesu.
[17] es.
[18] conquirerent.
[19] imperat.
[20] oboediunt.
[21] de synagoga.
[22] Andreae.
[23] Iacobo.
[24] Iohanne.
[25] Decumbebat.
[26] febricitans.
[27] elevavit.

adprechensa[1] manu eius etcontinuo dimisit eam febris etministrabat
eis···7
(32) Uespere autem facto cum occidisset sól adferebant[2] adeum omnes
male **habentes** etdemonia[3] (33) eterat omnis ciuitas **congregata adianuam**
Fol. 19 b. (34) **etcurauit multos qui** uexabatur[4] uarís[5] langoribus[6] etdemonia multa
eiciebat···7
Etnonsinebat ea loqui[7] quoniam sciebant[8]
(35) Etdeluculo[9] ualde surgens et[10]egressus abiit indesertum locum
ibique orabat (36) etpersecutus[11] est eum simón etqui cum illo erant (37)
etcum inuenisent[12] eum dixerunt ei **quia** omnes querunt te·(38) etait illis
ihesus[13] eamus inproximos uicos etciuitates vdet[14] ibi predicem et[10]adhóc
enim ueni (39) eterat predicans insinagogís[15] eorum etomni galilea etdemonia
eiciens··7
(40) Etuenit adeum leprossus[16] diprecans[17] eum etgenu flexo dixit
siuis potes **me** mundare (41) ihesus autem missertus[18] eius extendit
manuum[19] suam ettangens **eum** ait illi uolo mundare (42) etcum dixiset[20]
statim discessit abeo lepra etmundatusest (43) etcomminatusest[10] ei statim
et[10]eicit illum (44) etdicit ei uede mini[21] dixeris sed uade ostende te
principi sacerdotum etoffer proemundatione tua que precipit[22] moyses[23]
intestimonium illis···7
Fol. 20. (45) At ille egresus[24] coepit predicare etdefamare[25] sermonem ita
vtiam nonpossit[26] manifeste inciuitatem introíre sed foris indesertís locis
esse etconueniebant adeum undique···7

[Cap. II.] (1) Etiterum intrauit capharnauum[27] post dies (2) etauditumest quod
indomu[28] esset etconuenerunt multi ita vtnoncaperet neque adianuam

---

1 **adprehensa.**
2 **afferebant.**
3 **V. adds habentes.**
4 **vexabantur.**
5 **variis.**
6 **languoribus.**
7 **loqui ea.**
8 **V. adds eum.**
9 diluculo.
10 V. om.
11 secutus.
12 invenissent.
13 V. om.
14 **ut et.**
15 synagogis.
16 leprosus.
17 deprecans.
18 misertus.
19 manum.
20 dixisset.
21 Vide nemini.
22 praecepit.
23 Moses.
24 egressus.
25 diffamare.
26 posset.
27 Capharnaum.
28 domo.

etloquebatur eis uerbum (3) etuenerunt ferentes adeum paraliticum[1] qui aquatuor[2] portabatur (4) etcum non possent··

Offerre eum illi praeturba nundauerunt[3] tecum[4] ubi erat etpate facientes submisserunt[5] grabatum inquo paraliticus iacebat (5) cumuidisset autem ihesus fidem illorum ait paralitico filii demittuntur[6] tibi peccata (6) erant autem illíc quidam describís sedentes etcogitantes incordibus suis (7) quid híc sic loquitur blasfemat··[7]

Quis potest dimittere peccata nisi deus solus[8] (8) quo statim cognito ihesus spiritu suo··7

Quia sic cognitarent[9] intra[10] sé dicit illis quid ista cogitatis in- Fol. 20 b.
cordibus uestrís (9) quidestfacilius dicere paralitico dimittuntur tibi peccata
tua[11] án dicere surge ettolle grabatum[12] etambula··

(10) Ut autem sciretis[13] quia potestatem habet filius hominis interra dimittendi peccata ait paralitico (11) tibi dico surge et[14]tolle grabatum[15] tuum etuade indomum tuam (12) etstatim ille surrexit et[14]sublato grabatto abiit coram omnibus ita vtadmirarentur[16] omnes ethonorificent[17] deum dicentes quia nunquam[18] síc uidimus··7

(13) Et egresus[19] est rursus admare.omnisque turba ueniebat adeum et docebat eos (14) etcum preteriret uidit leui malphei[20] sedentem adte loneum[21] etait illi sequere me etsurgens secutusesteum··7

(15) Et factum est cum acumberet[22] indomu[23] illius multi puplicani[24] etpeccatores simul discumbebant cum ihesu etdiscipulis eius erant Fol. 21.
enim multi qui etsequebantur eum (16) etscribe etpharisaei uidentes qui[25]
manducaret·

Cum peccatoribus etpuplicanís diciebant[26] discipulis eius quare cum puplicanís etpeccatoribus manducat etbibit magister uester··7

---

1 paralyticum.
2 quattuor.
3 nudaverunt.
4 tectum.
5 summiserunt.
6 dimittuntur.
7 blasphemat.
8 solus deus?
9 cogitarent.
10 inter.
11 V. om.
12 grabattum tuum.
13 sciatis.
14 V. om.
15 grabattum.
16 ammirarentur.
17 honorificarent.
18 numquam.
19 egressus.
20 Levin Alphei.
21 teloneum.
22 accumberet.
23 domo.
24 publicani.
25 quia.
26 dicebant.

(17) Hoc audito ihesus ait illis nonnecesse habent sani medico[1] sed
qui male habent·Non enim ueni uocare iustos sed peccatores (18) et-
erant discipuli iohannis etpharisei ieunantes[2] etueniunt etdicunt illi cúr[3]
discipuli iohannis etphariseorum ieiunant tu[4] autem discipuli noniciunant
(19) etait illis ihesus numquid possunt filii nuptiarum quam diu [5]est cum
illis sponsus[5] ieiunare quanto tempore habent secum sponsum nonpossunt
ieiunare (20) uenient **autem dies cum** auferetur abeís[6] ettunc ieiunabunt
inilla die (21) nemo enim[7] adsumentum[8] pani[9] rudis adsuit[10] in[7]uestimento
ueteri···7

Fol. 21 b. Alioquín auferet supplimentum[11] nouum aueteri etmaior scissura
fit (22) etnemo mittit uinum nouum[12] in utres uetres[13] alioquín disrumpet
uinum utres etuinum effundetur[14] etvtres peribunt sed uinum nouum **in**-
utres nouos mitti debet etutraque[7] seruiantur[7]

(23) Etfactum est iterum cum sabbatis ambulet[15] ihesus[7] persata etdiscipuli **eius** ceperunt[16] pregredii[17] etuellere spicas (24) pharisei autem
dicebant ei ecce quid faciunt sabbatis quod nonlicet (25) etait illis numquam
legistis quid fecerit dauid quando necessitatem habuit etessuritur[18] ipse etqui cum eo erant (26) quando[19] introuit[20] in[21]domum dei suabithar[22] principe
sacerdotum etpanes propossitionis[23] manducauit quos nonlicet manducare
nisi solis[21] sacerdotibus etdedit eis qui cum eo erant···7

(27) Et dicebat illis[24] sabbatum propter hominem factumest etnon-
Fol. 22. homo propter sabbatum (28) itaque dominus est filius **hominis** etiam
sabbati···7

[Cap. III.] (1) Et introiuit[20] iterum sinagogam eterat[25] homo habens manum aridam
(2) etobseruabant eum si sabbatis curaret vtaccussarent[26] illum (3) etait
homini habenti manum aridam surge inmedivm (4) etdicit eis licet sabbatis

---

[1] medicum.
[2] ieiunantes.
[3] Quare.
[4] tui.
[5] **sponsus cum illis est.**
[6] **V. adds sponsus.**
[7] V. om.
[8] assumentum.
[9] panni.
[10] assuit.
[11] supplementum.
[12] novellum.
[13] **veteres.**
[14] effunditur.
[15] ambularet.
[16] coeperunt.
[17] praegredi.
[18] esuriit.
[19] quomodo.
[20] introiit.
[21] V. om.
[22] **sub** Abiathar.
[23] propositionis.
[24] eis.
[25] V. adds ibi.
[26] accusarent.

benefacere án male animam saluam facire[1] án perdere at illi tacebant (5)
etcircumspiciens eos cum ira··

Contristatus super cecitatem[2] cordis eorum dicit homini extende
manum tuam etextendit etresistuta[3] est manus illi···

(6) Exeuntes autem[4] pharisei cum herodianis consilium faciebant
aduersus eum quomodo eum perderent (7) etihesus cum discipulis suis
secessit admare··7

Et multa turba agalilia[5] etaciuda[6] secutaest eum·(8) et[7]abierusolimis[8]
et abidumea ettransiordanén etqui circa tirum[9] etsidonem multitudo magna
audientes que faciebat uenerunt adeum·7 (9) etdixit discipulis suis utin-[7] Fol. 22 b.
nauicula sibi deseruiret propter turbam ne conprimerent eum··

(10) Multos enim sanabat ita vtinruerent ineum[10] tangerent quotquot autem habebant plagas (11) etspiritus inmundos[11] cum illum uidebant
procidebant ei··

Et clamabant[12] (12) tues filius Dei etuechementer[13] comminabatur
eís ne manifestarent illum··

(13) Et ascendens inmontem uocauit adsé quos uoluit ipse aduenerunt[14]
ad eum (14) etfecit vtessent·xii[15]·cum illo etut mitteret eos predicare
euangelium (15) etdedit illis potestatem curandi[16] eteiciendi demonia··

(16) Et inpossuit[17] simoni nomen petrum[18] (17) etiacobum zebedei etiohannem fratrem iacobi etinpossuit[17] eis nomina boarnerges[19] quodest filii
tonitrui (18) etandream etphilippum etbartholomeum etmatheum[20] etthomam
etiacobum alphei etthadeum[21] etsimonem cannaneum[22] (19) etiudam
scaríoth[23] qui[24] tradit[25] illum····7

(20) Et ueniunt addomum etconuenit iterum turba ita vtnonpossent
neque panem manducare (21) etcum audissent sui discipuli[7] exierunt tenere Fol. 23.

---

[1] facere.
[2] caecitate.
[3] restituta.
[4] V. adds statim.
[5] Galilaea.
[6] et iudaea.
[7] V. om.
[8] Hierosolymis.
[9] Tyrum.
[10] V. adds ut illum.
[11] inmundi.
[12] V. adds dicentes.
[13] vehementer.
[14] et venerunt.
[15] duodecim.
[16] V. adds infirmitates.
[17] imposuit.
[18] Petrus.
[19] Boanerges.
[20] Mattheum.
[21] Taddeum.
[22] Cananaeum.
[23] Scariot.
[24] V. adds et.
[25] tradidit.

eum dicebant enim quoniam infurorem conuersus[1]est (22) etscribæ qui
abierusolimís[2] discenderant[3] dicebant quoniam belzebub[4] habet etquia inprincipe inprincipe[5] demonum eicit demonia··

(23) Et conuocatis éis inparabulís[6] dicebat illis quomodo potest satanas
satanán eicere (24) etsí regnvm inse diuidatur nonpotest stare regnum
illud[7] (25) etsí domus super semet ipsam·disperiatur[8] nonpoterit[9] domus
illa stare·(26) etsi satanas consurrexerit[10] insemet ipsum dispertitus[11] etnonpotest[12] stare sed finem habet (27) nemo potest uassa[13] fortis ingressus
in[5]domum diripere nisi prius alliget fortem[14] ettunc domus[15] eius diri-
piet[16]··7

(28) Amen dico uobís quoniam omnia dimittentur filiis hominum peccata
Fol. 23 b. et blasfemiæ[17] quibus blasphemauerint[18]···7 (29) inspiritum sanctum nonhabet remissionem inaeternum sed reus erit eterni delicti (30) quoniam
dicebant spiritum inmundum habet (31) etueniunt mater eius etfratres etforis
stantes misserunt[19] adeum uocantes eum (32) etsedebat circa eum turba etdicunt ei·

Ecce mater tua etfratres tui foris querunt te (33) etrespondens eis
ait que est mater mea etfratres mei (34) etcircum spiciens eos qui incircuitu
eius stabant[20] ait···7

Ecce mater mea etfratres mei (35) qui[21] faciunt[22] uoluntatem dei
qui enim fecerit uoluntatem dei híc frater meus etsorar[23] mea etmater est·
[Cap. IV.] (1) etiterum coepit docere admare.etcongregata est adeum turba multa[24]
vt[25]nauem ascendens sederet inmari etomnis turba circa mare super terram
erat (2) etdocebat illos, inparabulís[6] multa etdicebat illís indoctrína sua
(3) audite··7

Ecce exiit seminas[26] adseminandum (4) etcum[27] seminat illud[28]

[1] versus.
[2] Hierosolymia.
[3] descenderant.
[4] Beelzebub.
[5] V. om.
[6] parabolis.
[7] illius.
[8] dispertiatur.
[9] potest.
[10] consurrexit.
[11] V. adds est.
[12] poterit.
[13] vasa.
[14] fortem alliget.
[15] domum.
[16] deripiet.
[17] blasphemiae.
[18] V. adds qui autem blasphemaverit.
[19] miserunt.
[20] sedebant.
[21] V. adds enim.
[22] fecerit.
[23] soror.
[24] V. adds ita.
[25] V. adds in.
[26] seminans.
[27] dum.
[28] aliud.

decedit[1] circa uiam etuenerunt uolucres etcomederunt illud (5) aliud uero Fol. 24.
cecidit super petrosa ubi nonhabuit terra[2] etstatim exortum est quoniam
nonhabebat altitudinem terre (6)·etquando exortum[3] est sól exestuauit
et[4]eoquod nonhaberet radicem exaruit·(7) et aliud cecidit inspinas[5] etascenderunt spine etsoffocauerunt illut[6] etfructum nondedit (8) aliut
cecidit interram bonam etdabat fructum ascendentem etcrescentem et-
adferebat unum·xxxta[7]·etunum sexaginta·etunum centum·(9) etdicebat
qui habet aures audiendi audiet[8]···7

(10) Et cum esset singularis interrogauerunt eum hii[9] qui cum eo
erant cum duodecim parabulas[10] (11) etdicebat eis uobis autem[11] tatum[12]
est scribere[13] misterium[14] regni dei··7

Illis autem qui foris sunt inparabulís.[15]

Omnia fiunt (12) utuidentes uideant etnonuideant etaudientes
audiant etnonintellegant ne quando conuertantur etdemittantur[16] eis
peccata (13) etait illis nescitis parabulam[17] hanc etquomodo··7

Omnes parabulas[10] cognoscetis (14) qui seminat uerbum seminat (15) Fol. 24 b.
hii[18] autem sunt qui circa uiam ubi seminatur uerbum [19]etqui neglegentur
uerbum accipiunt[19] etcum audierint conuestim[20] uenit satanas etaufert[21]
quod seminatum est incorde[22] eorum (16) ethii[18] sunt qui[11] similiter qui
super petrosa.seminantur qui cum audierint uerbum statim cum gaudio
accipiunt illud (17) etnonhabent radicem insé sed temporales sunt deinde
orta tribulatione etpersecutione propter uerbum confestim scandalizantur
(18) etalii sunt[23] inspinís seminantur hii[9] sunt qui uerbum audiunt (19)
etherumnæ[24] seculi etdeceptio diuitiarum etcirca relinqua[25] concupiscentiæ
introeuntes sofficant[26] uerbum etsine fructu efficitur (20) ethii[9] sunt qui
supra[27] terram bonam seminati sunt

[1] cecidit.
[2] terram multam.
[3] exortus.
[4] V. om.
[5] spinis.
[6] illud.
[7] triginta.
[8] audiat.
[9] hi.
[10] parabolas.
[11] V. om.
[12] datum.
[13] scire.
[14] mysterium.
[15] parabolis.
[16] dimittantur.
[17] parabolam.
[18] hi.
[19] V. om. this clause.
[20] confestim.
[21] V. adds verbum.
[22] corda.
[23] V. adds qui.
[24] aerumnae.
[25] reliqua.
[26] suffocant.
[27] super.

Hii[1] sunt[1] qui audiunt uerbum etsuscipiunt etfructificant unum ·xxxmum[2]·etunum·lxxmum[3]·etunum centum···7

(21) Et dicebat illis numquid uenit lucerna vtsubmodio ponatur aut sub-lecto nonne vtsupra[4] candelabrum[5] (22) nonenim est aliquid absconditum quod nonmanifestetur nec factum est occultum sed utinpalam ueniat (23) sí quis habet aures audiendi audiat··7

(24) Et dicebat illis uidete quid audiatis inqua mensura mensi fueritis remittetur[6] uobis etaudicietur[7] **uobis** (25) quid[8] enim habet dabitur ei[9] et-qui nonhabet etiam quod habet auferetur abillo···7

(26) Et dicebat síc est regnum dei quem admodum sí faciat homo[10] iactet[1] semen[11] interra[12] (27) etdormiat etexsurgat nocte ac die etsemen germinat[13] etincrescat dum nescit ille (28) ultro enim terra fructificat primum herbam deinde spicam deinde plenum frumentum inspica (29) etcum sé produxerit fructus statim mittit falcem quoniam mesis adest[14]···7

Fol. 25 b. (30) **Et dicebat** cui adsimilabimus regnum dei aut cui parabulæ[15] con-parabimus **illud (31)** síc[16] est[1] vtgranum sinapis quod cum siminatum[17] fuerit interra **minimum**[18] est omnibus seminibus que sunt interra (32) et-cum seminatum fuerit ascendit etfit maius omnibus holeribus etfacit **ramos** magnos **ita** vtpossint subumbra eius aues celi habitare··

(33) Et **talibus** multis parabulís[19] loquebatur eís uerbum prout poterant audire (34) sine parabula autem nonloquebatur eís··7

Seorsum autem discipulis suis deserebat[20] omnia (35) etait illís die illa[21] cum sero esset factum transeamus contra (36) etdimittentes turbam adsumunt eum ita vterat[22] innaui·

Et aliæ naues erant cum illo (37) etfacta est procella magna uenti **etfluctus mittebat** innauem **ita** vtinpleretur[23] nauis (38) eterat ipse inpuppi
Fol. 26. supra ceruicel[24] dormiens et excitant eum··7

---

[1] V. om.
[2] triginta.
[3] sexaginta.
[4] super.
[5] V. adds ponatur.
[6] remetietur.
[7] adicietur.
[8] Qui.
[9] illi.
[10] homo iaciat.
[11] sementem.
[12] terram.
[13] germinet.
[14] adest messis.
[15] parabolae.
[16] sicut.
[17] seminatum.
[18] minus.
[19] parabolis.
[20] disserebat.
[21] illa die.
[22] erant.
[23] impleretur.
[24] cervical.

Et dicunt[1] magister nonadte pertinet quia perimus (39) etexsurgens
comminatus est uento etdixit marí tace[2] obmutesce etcessauit uentus
etfacta est tranquillitás magna (40) etait illis quid timidi estis needum
habitis[3] fidem ettimebunt[4] magno timore[5] etdicebant adalterutrum quis
[CAP. V.] putas est iste quia ad[6]uentus etmare obediunt[7] ei (1) et uenerunt transfretum maris in regionem gera senorum····7

(2) Et exeuntes[8] ei denaui statim occurrit ei demonumentis[9] inspiritu
inmundo (3) qui domicilium habebat inmonumentís et neque catenis iam
quisquam eum poterat ligáre (4) quoniam sepe pedibus[10] etcatenis uinctus
disrumpísset[11] catanas[12] etconpedes[13] conminuisset[14] etnemo poterat eum
domare (5) etsemper nocte ac die inmonumentís etinmontibus erat etclamans
etconcedens[15] selapedibus[16] (6) uidiens[17] autem ihesus[18] alongare[19] cucurit[20]
etadorauit eum··

(7) Et clamans uoce magna dixit[21] quid mihi ettibi ihesu filii dei Fol. 26 b.
summi adiuro te perdeum ne me torques[22] (8) dicebat enim illi exíi[23] spiritus
inmunde abhomine (9) etinterrogabat eum quod tibi nomen est etdicit ei
legio nomen mihi est quia multi sumus (10) etdeprecabatur eum multum
ne sé expelleret extra regionem (11) erat autem ibi circa montem grex
porcorum magnus pascens (12) etdeprecabantur eum spiritus dicentes mitte
nos inporcos utineos introeamus (13) etconcessit eís statim ihesus etex-
euntes spiritus inmundi introierunt inporcos etmagno inpetv grex precipit-
atus est inmare erant autem quassi[24] duo milia etsoffocati sunt inmare
(14) qui autem pascebant eos fugerunt etnuntiauerunt inciuitate[25] etin-
agros etegressi sunt uidere quid esset facti (15) etuenerunt[26] adihesum
etuident eum[27] qui ademonia[28] uexabatur sedentem uestitum etsanc mentis

1 V. adds ei.
2 V. adds et.
3 habetis.
4 timuerunt.
5 timore magno.
6 et.
7 oboediunt.
8 exeunti.
9 V. adds homo.
10 compedibus.
11 disrupisset.
12 catenas.
13 compedes.
14 comminuisset.
15 concidens.
16 lapidibus.
17 videns.
18 Iesum.
19 longe.
20 cucurrit.
21 dicit.
22 torqueas.
23 Exi.
24 V. om this clause, and has ad duo milia.
25 civitatem.
26 veniunt.
27 illum.
28 daemonio.

Fol. 27. ettimuerunt (16) etnarrauerunt illis qui uiderant qualiter factum esset ei
et[1]qui demonium habuerat etdeporcis (17) etrogare eum coeperunt vtdis-
cediret[2] afinibus eorum··

(18) Cumque ascenderet in[1]nauem cepit[3] illum deprecari quia[4] demonia[5]
uexatus fuerat vtesset cum illo (19) etnonadmissit[6] eum sed ait illi uade
indomum tuam adtuos etadnuntia illis quanta tibi dominus feerit et-
misertus est[1] sit tui (20) et[7]cepit[3] predicare indecapuli[8] quanta sibi
fecesset[9] dominus[1] ihesus etomnes mirabantur···7

(21) Et cum transcendisset ihesus innaui rursus transfretum conuenit
turba multa adillum eterat circa mare (22) etuenit[10] dearchi sinagogís[11]
nomine iairus etuidens eum procedit[12] adpedes eius (23) etdeprecatur[13]
eum multum dicens quoniam filia mea inextremís est ueni inpone manús
super eam··ut saluassit[14] etuiuat (24) ethabíit[15] cum illo etsequebatur
eum turba multa etconprimebant[16] illum (25) etmulier que erat inprofluio[17]
Fol. 27 b. sanguinis annis·xii[18]·(26) etfuerat multa perpessa aconplurimís[19] medici-
bus[20] eterogauerat omnia sua nec quicquam proficerat[21] sed[22] deterius
habebat (27) et[1]cum audisset deihesu uenit inturba retro ettetigit uestimentum eius (28) dicebat enim quia si uel uestimentum[23] tetigero[24 25] (29)
etconfestim siccatus est fons sanguinis eius etsensit corpore quod sanata
esset aplaga (30) etstatim ihesus cognoscens insemet ipso uirtutem que
exierat deo[26] conuersus adturbam aiebat quis tetigit uestimenta mea (31)
etdicebant ei discipuli sui uides turbam··7

Conprimentem te etdicis quis me tetigit (32) etcircumspiciebat
uidere eam que hoc fecerat (33) mulier autem timens ettremens sciens
quo[27] factum esset insé uenit etprocidit ante eum etdixit ei omnem
ueritatem (34) ille autem dixit[28] filia fides tua te saluam fecit uade inpace
etesto sana aplaga tua (35) adhúc eo loquente ueniunt abarchi sina-
gogo.[29]

[1] V. om.
[2] discederet.
[3] coepit.
[4] qui.
[5] daemonio.
[6] admisit.
[7] V. adds abiit et.
[8] Decapoli.
[9] fecisset.
[10] V. adds quidam.
[11] archesynagogis.
[12] procidit.
[13] deprecabatur.
[14] sit.
[15] abiit.
[16] comprimebant.
[17] profluvio.
[18] duodecim.
[19] compluribus.
[20] medicis.
[21] profecerat.
[22] V. adds magis.
[23] V. adds eius.
[24] tetigero.
[25] V. adds salva ero.
[26] de eo.
[27] quod.
[28] V. adds ei.
[29] archesynagogo.

Quoniam quidē
multi conati sᷓ
ordinare narra
tionem quæ in nobis c
plętae sunt rerum si
cut tradiderunt nobis
qui ab initio ipsi uide
runt ⁊ ministri fuerunt
sermonis uisum est ⁊ mihi
adsecuto principio omni
bus diligenter ex ordine
tibi scribere obtime
theophile ut cognos
cas uerum ..

[Cap. I.] (1) Quoniam quidem multi conati sunt ordinare narrationem Fol. 30.
que innobis completæ sunt rerum (2) sicut traderunt[1] nobis **qui** abinitio
ipsi uiderunt etmisnistri fuerunt sermonis (3) uisumest etmihi **adsecuto**[2]
principio[3] omnibus[4] diligenter exordine tibi scribere obtime[5] **theofile (4)**
vtcognoscas eorum··

Uerborum dequibus eruditus es ueritatem··7 Fol. 30 b.

(5) Fuit indiebus herodis regis iude[6] sacerdos quidam nomine zacharias
deuice abia et uxor illi defiliabus aarón etnonen[7] ei[8] elizabéth[9] (6) erant
autem iusti ambo ante deum INcendentes[10] inomnibus mandatís etiustifica-
tionibus domini sine querilla[11] (7) etnon erat illis filius eo quod esset
elizabéth[9] sterelis etambo processissent indiebus suis·(8) factum est autem
cum sacerdotio fungeretur inordine uicis sue ante deum (9) secundum consuetudinem sacerdoti sorte[12] exiit utincensum poneret ingresus[13] intemplum Fol. 31.
domini (10) etomnis multitudo erat populi orans foris hora incensi (11)
apparuit autem illi angelus domini adstans[14] adextrís altaris incensi (12)
etzacharias turbatus est uidens ettimor inruit super eum (13) ait autem
adillum angelus ne timeas zacharias quia[15] exaudita est deprecatio tua etuxor
tua elizabéth[9] pari [16] filium etuocabis nomen eius iohannem (14) eterit
gaudium tibi etexultatio etmulti innatiuitate eius gaudebunt (15) erit
enim magnus coram domino etuinum etsiceram[17] nonbibet etspiritu sancto
replebitur adhúc exutero matris sue (16) et multos filiorum israhel
conuertit[18] addominum deum ipsorum (17) etipse precidet[19] ante illum·
inspiritu etuirtute heliæ vtconuertat corda patruum[20] infilios etincredibiles
adprudentiam iustorum parare domino plebem perfectam (18) etdixit Fol. 31 b.
zacharias adangelum unde hóc sciam·Ego enim sum senex etuxor mea
precessit[21] indiebus suis··7

[1] tradiderunt.
[2] assecuto.
[3] a principio.
[4] omnia.
[5] optime.
[6] Iudaeae.
[7] nomen.
[8] eius.
[9] Elisabet.
[10] incedentes.
[11] querella.
[12] forte.
[13] ingressus.
[14] stans.
[15] quoniam.
[16] V. adds pariet and tibi.
[17] sicera.
[18] convertet.
[19] praecedet.
[20] patrum.
[21] processit.

(19) Et respondens angelus dixit ei·Ego sum gabriel[1] qui adsto ante
deum etmissus sum loqui adte et hæc tibi euangelizare··7
(20) Et ecce eris tacens nonpoteris loqui usque indiem quo hec fiant
proeoquod non credisti[2] uerbis meis que inplebuntur[3] intempore suo
(21) eterat plebs exspectans zachariam etmirabantur quod tardaret ipse
intemplo·(22) egressus autem nonpoteret[4] loqui adillos etcognouerunt
quod uisionem uidisset intemplo etipse erat innuens eis etpermansit mutus·
(23) etfactum est[5] utinpleti[6] sunt dies offici[7] eius abiit indomum suam: (24)
Fol. 32. post hos autem dies concepit elizabéth[8] uxor eius et occultababat[9] se
mensibus quinque dicens·
(25) Quia sic mihi fecit[10] dominus indiebus quibus respexit auferre
obprobrium meum interhomines (26) inmense autem sexto misus[11] est
angelus gabriel[12] adeo inciuitatem galile[13] cui nomen nazaréth (27)
aduirguinem[14] disponsatam[15] uiro cui nomen erat ioseph dedomo dauid
etnomen uirginis maria (28) etingressus angelus adeam dixit haue gratia
plena dominus tecum benedicta tu intermulieres[16] (29) que cum audisset
turbata est insermone eius etcogitabat qualis esset ista locutio[17] (30) etait
angelus ei ne timeas maria·INuenisti enim gratiam aput deum (31) ecce
concipies inutero etparies filium etuocabis nomen eius ihesum·(32) hic erit
magnus etfilius altissimi uocabitur etdabit illi dominus deus sedem dauid
patris eius (33) etregnauit[18] indomum[19] iacob inæternum etregni eius nonerit
Finis···7
Fol. 32 b. (34) Dixit autem maria adangelum quomodo fiat[20] istud quoniam
uirum noncognosco (35) etrespondens angelus dixit ei spiritus sanctus super
ueniat[21] inte etuirtus altissimi obumbrauit[22] tibi ideoque[23] quod nascetur
sanctum uocabitur filius dei···
(36) Ecce elizabéth[24] cognata tua etipsa concepit filium insenecta sua

[1] Gabrihel.
[2] credidisti.
[3] implebuntur.
[4] poterat.
[5] facti sunt.
[6] impleti.
[7] officii.
[8] Elisabet.
[9] occultabat.
[10] fecit mihi.
[11] missus.
[12] Gabrihel.
[13] Galilaeae.
[14] virginem.
[15] desponsatam.
[16] in mulieribus.
[17] salutatio.
[18] regnabit.
[19] in domo.
[20] fiet.
[21] superveniet.
[22] obumbrabit.
[23] V. adds et.
[24] Elisabet.

et hic mensis est sextus illi que uocatur sterilis[1] (37) quia nonerit inpos-
sibile aput[2] deum omne uerbum (38) dixit autem maria ecce ancella domini
fiat mihi secundum uerbum tuum et discessit abilla angelus (39) exsurgens
autem maria indiebus illis abiit inmontana conpestinatione[3] inciuitatem
iuda (40) et intrauit indomum zachariæ et salutauit elizabeth[4] (41) etfactum
est vtaudiuit salutationem mariæ elizabeth[4] exsultauit infans[5] inutero eius
etrepleta est spiritu sancto elizabeth[4] (42) etexclamauit uoce magna etdixit
benedicta tu inter mulieres

Et benedictus fructus uentris **tui** (43) etunde hóc **mihi** vtueniat Fol. 33.
mater domini[6] adme (44) ecce enim utfacta est uox salutationis tue
inauribus meis exultauit ingaudio infans inutero meo (45) etbeata que
credidit quoniam perficientur ea que dicta sunt ei adomino··7

(46) [7]Magnificat anima mea dominum (47) etexsultauit[8] spiritus
meus indeo salutari meo (48) quia respexit humilitatem ancille sue ecce
enim exhóc beatum[9] me dicent omnes generationes (49) qui[10] fecit mihi
magna qui potens est etsanctum nomen eius (50) etmissericordia[11] eius
inproginies[12] etproginies[12] timentibus eum (51) fecit potentiam inbrachio suo
dispersit superbos mente cordis sui (52) depossuit[13] potentes desede et-
altauit[14] humiles (53) essurientes[15] inpleuit bonis etdiuites dimissit[16] inanes
(54) suscepit israhel puerum suum memorari misericordie (55) sicut locutus
est adpatres Nostros abracham etsemini eius insecula··7 Fol. 33 b.

(56) Mansit autem maria cum illa quassi[17] mensibus tribus etreuersa
est indomum suam (57) elizabéth[18] autem inpletum[19] est tempus pariendi··7

Et peperit filium (58) etaudierunt uicini etcognati eius quia mag-
nificauit dominus misericordiam suam cum illa etcongratulabantur ei (59)
etfactum **est** indie octauo uenerunt circumcidere puerum etuocabant[20] eum
zachariam nomine patris eius[21] (60) etrespondens mater eius dixit nequaquam es[22] **sed uocabitur iohannes (61)** etdixerunt adillam quia nemo est

---

[1] sterelis.
[2] apud.
[3] cum festinatione.
[4] Elisabet.
[5] infans.
[6] V. adds mei.
[7] V. adds Et ait Maria.
[8] exultavit.
[9] beatam.
[10] quia.
[11] misericordia.
[12] progenies.
[13] deposuit.
[14] exaltavit.
[15] esurientes.
[16] dimisit.
[17] quasi.
[18] Elisabeth.
[19] impletum.
[20] vocant.
[21] nomine patris eius Zachariam.
[22] V. om.

incognitione tua qui uocetur hóc nomine (62) innuebant autem patri eius quem uellet uocari eum (63) etpostulans pugillarem[1] scripsit diciens[2] iohannes est nomen eius etmirati sunt uniuersi (64) apertum est autem ilico ós eius et lingua eius etloquebatur benedicens deum (65) etfactum est
Fol. 34. timor super omnes uicinos eorum etsuper omnia montana iudee Deuulgabantur omnia uerba hæc (66) etpossuerunt[3] omnes qui audierant incorde suo dicentes quid putatis[4] pueris[5] te[6] erit etenim manus domini erat cum illo (67) etzacharias **pater** eius inpletus[7] est spiritu sancto etprophetauit dicens····7

(68) Benedictus dominus[8] deus israhel quia uisitauit etfecit redemptionem[9] plebis[10] sue (69) eterexit cornu salutis nobis indomu[11] dauid **pueri** sui (70) sicut locutus est perós sanctorum quia[12] seculo sunt prophetarum eius (71) salutem eximicís[13] nostris etdemanu omnium qui nos oderunt (72) adfaciendum[14] misericordiam cum patribus nostris etmemorari testamenti sui sancti (73) ius iurandum quod iurauit adabracham patrem nostrum daturum sé nobis (74) vtsine timore demanibus[15] **inimicorum** nostrorum liberati seruiamus illi (75) insanctitate etiusticia coram ipso omnibus diebus nostris (76) ettu puer propheta altissimi uocaueris[16] preibis enim ante faciem domini parare uias eius··7
Fol. 34 b. (77) addandam scientiam salutis plebi eius inremisionem[17] peccatorum eorum (78) peruiscera misericordia[18] dei nostri inquibus uisitauit nos oriens exalto (79) et[19]inluminare hís qui intenebris et[20]umbra mortis sedent addirigendos pedes nostros inuiam pacis··7

(80) Puer autem crescebat etconfortebatur[21] in[19]spiritu eterat indesertis[22] usque indiem ostentionis[23] sue adisrahél··

[CAP. II.] (1) Factum est autem indiebus illis exiit edictum acessare[24] agusto[25]

1 pugilarem.
2 dicens.
3 posuerunt.
4 putas.
5 puer.
6 iste.
7 impletus.
8 V. om.
9 redemtionem.
10 plebi.
11 domo.
12 qui a.
13 ex inimicis.
14 faciendam.
15 de manu.
16 vocaberis.
17 remissionem.
18 misericordiae.
19 V. om.
20 V. adds in.
21 confortabatur.
22 deserto.
23 ostensionis.
24 Caesare.
25 Augusto.

vtdescriberetur uniuersus orbis (2) hæc descriptio prima factaest apreside[1]
siriæ[2] cirino[3] (3) etibant omnes utprofeterentur[4] singuli insuam ciuitatem··

(4) Ascendit autem ioseph agalilea deciuitate nazaréth iniudiam[5]
ciuitatem dauid que uocatur bethlem[6] eoquod esset de domo etfamilia
dauid (5) vtprofeteretur[7] cum maria disponsata[8] sibi uxore pregnante (6)
factumest[9] cum essent ibi inpleti[10] sunt dies vtpariret[11] (7) etpeperit filium
suum primogenitum etpannís eum··7
inuoluit etreclinauit eum inpresepio[12] quia noncrat ei[13] locus inde- Fol. 35.
uersorio[14]··7

(8) Et pastores erant inregione eadem uigilantes etcustodientes uigilias
noctis supra gregem suum.

(9) Et ecce angelus domini stetit iuxta illos etclaritás domini[15] circum-
fulsit illos ettimuerunt timore magno (10) et dixit illís angelus nolite timere
ecce enim euangelizo uobis gaudium magnum quod erit omni populo (11)
quia natusest uobís hodie saluator quiest christus dominus inciuitate dauid
(12) ethoc uobís signum inuenietis infantem pannís inuolutum etpossitum[16]
inpresepio.[12]

(13) Et subito factaest cum angelo multitudo exercitus[17] cælestis lau-
dantium deum etdicentium (14) gloria inaltissimis deo etinterra páx
hominibus bone uoluntatis···7

(15) Et factum est vtdescesserunt[18] abeis angeli incelum pastores
loquebantur adinuicem·Transeamus usque in[19]bethlem etuideamus hoc Fol. 35 b.
uerbum quod factum est··7

Quod[20] dominus[21] ostendit nobis (16) etuenerunt festinantes etinuenerunt mariam etioseph etinfantem possitum[22] inpresepio[12] (17) uidentes
autem cognouerunt deuerbo hoc[23] dictum est[24] illis depuero hoc (18)
etomnes qui audierunt mirati sunt etdehís que dicta erant apastoribus adipsos·

---

[1] V. om.
[2] Syriae.
[3] Cyrino.
[4] profiterentur.
[5] Iudaeam.
[6] Bethleem.
[7] profiteretur.
[8] desponsata.
[9] V. adds autem.
[10] impleti.
[11] pareret.
[12] praesipio.
[13] eis.
[14] diversorio.
[15] dei.
[16] positum.
[17] militiae.
[18] discesserunt.
[19] V. om.
[20] V. adds fecit.
[21] V. adds et.
[22] positum.
[23] V. om.
[24] erat.

(19) Maria autem conseruat[1] omnia uerba hec conferens incorde suo (20)
etreuersi sunt pastores glorificantes etlaudantes deum inomnibus que
audierunt etuiderunt sicut dictum est adillos··

(21) Et postquam consummati sunt dies octo vtcircumcideretur uocatumest nomen eius ihesus quod uocatumest abangelo prius quam inutero
conciperetur··

(22) Et postquam inpleti[2] sunt dies purgationis eius secundum legem
moysi[3] tullerunt[4] illum inhierusalem vtadsisterent[5] illum[6] domino (23)
Fol. 36. sicut scriptumest inlege domini quod[7] omne masculinum et[8] aperiens
uuluam sanctum domino uocabitur (24) etut darent hostias[9] secundum
quod dictum est inlege domini[10] pár turturum aut duos pullos colum-
barum··

(25) Etecce homo erat inhierusalem cui nomen erat[10] simeón ethomo
iste iustus ettimoratus expectans consulationem[11] israhel etspiritus sanctus
erant[12] inipso[13] (26) etresponsum acciperant[14] aspiritu[15] sancto nonuisurum
sé mortem nisi prius uideret christum dominum[16] (27) etuenit inspiritu intemplum etcum inducerent puerum ihesum parentes eius vtfacirent[17]
secundum consutudinem[18] legis proeo (28) etipse accipit[19] eum inulnas suas
etbenedixit deum etdixit···

(29) Nunc demitte[20] seruum tuum domine secundum uerbum tuum
inpace (30) quia uiderunt occuli[21] mei salutare tuum (31) quod preparasti[22]
ante faciem omnium populorum (32) lumen adreuelationem gentium
etgloriam plebis suæ[23] israhel··(33) et erat pater eius etmater mirantes
super hís que dicebantur deillo (34) etbenedixit illos siméon[24]·

Fol. 36 b. Et dixit admariam matrem eius ecce possitus[25] est híc inruinam et-
resurrectionem multorum inisrahel etinsignum cui contradicetur (35) ettuam
ipsius animam pertransiuit[26] gladius utreuelentur exmultís cordibus cogita-

[1] conservabat.
[2] impleti.
[3] Mosi.
[4] tulerunt.
[5] sisterent.
[6] eum.
[7] quia.
[8] adaperiens.
[9] hostiam.
[10] V. om.
[11] consolationem.
[12] erat.
[13] in eo.
[14] acceperat.
[15] ab Spiritu.
[16] domini.
[17] facerent.
[18] consuetudinem.
[19] accepit.
[20] dimittis.
[21] oculi.
[22] parasti.
[23] tuae.
[24] Symeon.
[25] positus.
[26] pertransibit.

tiones (36) eterat anna Prophetiza[1] filia panuel[2] detribu asér héc processerat indiebus multís etuixerat cum uiro suo annís·uii[3] auirginitate sua
(37) et hec uidua usque adannos·lxxxiiii[4]·que nondiscendebat[5] detemplo
ieiuniis etobsecrationibus seruiens deo[6] nocte ac die (38) ethec ipsa hora
superuiniens[7] confitebatur domino etloquebatur deillo omnibus qui ex-
pectabant redemptionem[8] hierusalem (39) etut perfecerunt omnia secundum
legem domini reuersi sunt ingalileam inciuitatem suam nazaréth···7
(40) Puer autem crescebat etconfortabatur plenus sapientia etgratia dei[9]
inillo (41) etibant parentes eius peromnes annos inhierusalem indie sol-
empni[10] pasce·[11]
(42) Et cum factus esset annorum·xii[12]·ascendentibus illis inhieru- Fol. 37.
solima[13] secundum consuetudinem dies[14] festi (43) consummatisque diebus
cum redirent remansit puerís[15] [16]inhierusalem etnoncognouerunt parentes
eius (44) existimantes autem illum esse incomitatu uenerunt inter[17]diei
etrequirebant eum intercognatos etnotos (45) etnoninuenientes regressi sunt
inhierusalem requirentes eum·(46) et factum est post triduum inuenerunt
eum[18] intemplo sedentem inmedio doctorum audientem illos etinterro-
gantem illos[6]···7
(47) Stupebant autem omnes qui eum audiebant super prudentia etres-
ponsiosis[19] eius (48) etuidentes admirati[20] sunt····7

Dixit[21] mater eius adillum filii quid fecisti nobis síc[6] ecce pater tuus
etego dolentes querebamus te (49) etait adillos quid est quod me queritis[22]
nesciebatis quoniam[23] inhís que patris mei sunt oportet me esse (50) etipsi Fol. 37 b.
nonintellexerunt uerbum quod locutus est adillos (51) etdiscendit cum eis
etuenit nazaréth et erat subditus illis etmater eius conseruat[24] omnia uerba
hæc incorde[25] (52) ethís[26] proficebat[27] sapientia et[6]ætates etgratia aput[28]
deum ethomines··7

[1] prophetissa.
[2] Phanuel.
[3] septem.
[4] octoginta quattuor.
[5] discedebat.
[6] V. om.
[7] superveniens.
[8] redemtionem.
[9] V. adds erat.
[10] sollemni.
[11] paschae.
[12] duodecim.
[13] Hierosolymam.
[14] diei.
[15] puer.
[16] V. adds Iesus.
[17] iter.
[18] illum.
[19] responsis.
[20] ammirati.
[21] V. adds et.
[22] quaerebatis.
[23] quia.
[24] conservabat.
[25] V. adds suo.
[26] Iesus.
[27] proficiebat.
[28] apud.

[CAP. III.] (1) Anno autem quinto decimo imperii tiberii cessaris[1] procurante
autem[2] pontio pilato iudeam tetracha autem galile[3] herode pilipho[4] autem
fratre eius detracha[5] iture[6] ettraconitidis[7] regionis etlisania[8] abiliane[9]
tetracha[5] (2) subprincipibus sacerdotum anna et caipha[10]··7

Factum est uerbum domini[11] super iohannem zachariæ filium indeserto (3) etuenit inomnem regionem iordanis predicans babtismum pene-
tentiæ inremisionem[12] pectorum[13] (4) sicut scriptum est inlibro sermonum
essaie[14] prophete·Uox clamantis indeserto parate uiam domini rectas facite
semitas eius (5) omnis uallis inplebitur[15] etomnis mons etcollis humiliabitur
Fol. 38. et erunt praua indirecta etaspera inuias planas (6) etuidebit omnis caro
salutare dei··

(7) Dicebat ergo adturbas que exiebant ut babtizarentur abipso geni-
mina uiperarum quis ostendit uobis fugere afutura[16] ira (8) facite ergo
fructus dignos penitentiæ etnecoperitis[17] dicere patrem habeamus[18] abracham
dico enim uobís quia potest deus delapedibus[19] istís suscitare filios abrache
(9) iamenim securís adradices[20] arborum possita[21] est omnis ergo arbor
nonfaciens fructum bonum[22] excidetur[23] etinignem[22] mittetur[24]···7

(10) Et interrogabant eum[25] turbae dicentes quid ergo faciemus
(11) respondens autem dicebat illis qui abet[26] duas tunicas det nonhabenti
etqui habet escas similiter faciat (12) uenerunt autem etpublicani vtbab-
tizarentur etdixerunt adillum magister quid faciemus (13) at ille dixit
adeos nihil amplius quam constitutum est uobís faciatis (14) interrogabant
autem eum etmilites dicentes quid faciemus etnós et ait illis neminem
concutiatis neque columniam[27] faciatis etcontienti[28] esttote[29] stipentís[30]
uestrís (15) existimante autem populo etcogitantibus omnibus incordibus suis

[1] Caesaris.
[2] V. om.
[3] Galilaeae.
[4] Philippo.
[5] tetrarcha.
[6] Itureae.
[7] Trachonitidis.
[8] Lysania.
[9] Abilinae.
[10] Caiapha.
[11] dei.
[12] remissionem.
[13] peccatorum.
[14] Esaiae.
[15] implebitur.
[16] ventura.
[17] coeperitis.
[18] habemus.
[19] lapidibus.
[20] radicem.
[21] posita.
[22] V. om.
[23] exciditur.
[24] mittitur.
[25] eum.
[26] habet.
[27] calumniam.
[28] contenti.
[29] estote.
[30] stipendiis.

deiohannén[1] eforte[2] ipse esset christus (16) respondit iohannes dicens
omnibus··7

Ego quidem baptizo uos aqua[3] uenit[4] autem fortior me·cuius
nonsum dignus soluere corrigiam calciamentorum eius ipse uós babtizauit[5]
inspiritu sancto.[6]

(17) Cuius uentilabrum inmanu eius[7] purgauit aream suam etcon-
gregauit[8] triticum inorreum[9] suum paleas autem conburet igni inextinguibili (18) multa quidem etalia exortans[10] euangelizabat populum··7

(19) Herodis[11] autem detracha[12] cumcorriperetur abillo deherodia de[13]
uxóre fratris sui etdeomnibus malís que fecit herodis[14] (20) adiecit ethoc Fol. 39.
supra omnia etinclusit iohannem incarcerem[15]··7

(21) Factum est autem cum babtizaretur omnis populus et ihesu
babtizato etorante apertum est celum (22) etdiscendit[16] spiritus sancti[17]
corporali specie sicut columba inipsum·etuóx decelo factaest tu es filius
meus[18] inte bene[19]conplacuit[20] mihi··7

(23) Et ipse ihesus erat incipiens quassi[21] annorum·xxxta[22] ut-
putabatur[23] filius ioseph···7

Qui fuit eli[24]
Qui fuit matthete[25]
(24) Qui fuit leui
Qui fuit melchi
Qui fuit ianne
Qui fuit ioseph
(25) Qui fuit matthatie[26]
Qui fuit amos
Qui fuit nauum[27]

Qui fuit esli
Qui fuit nagae[28]
(26) Qui fuit maata[29]
Qui fuit matthatiæ[25]
Qui fuit simei[30]
Qui fuit iosech[31]
Qui fuit iuda[32]
(27) Qui fuit iohanna
Qui fuit resa

[1] Iohanne.
[2] ne forte.
[3] aqua baptizo vos.
[4] veniet.
[5] baptizabit.
[6] V. adds et igni.
[7] V. adds et.
[8] congregabit.
[9] horreum.
[10] exhortans.
[11] Herodes.
[12] tetrarcha.
[13] Herodiade.
[14] Herodes.
[15] carcere.
[16] descendit.
[17] sanctus.
[18] V. adds dilectus.
[19] V. om.
[20] complacuit.
[21] quasi.
[22] triginta.
[23] putaretur
[24] Heli.
[25] Mattat.
[26] Matthathiae.
[27] Naum.
[28] Naggae.
[29] Maath.
[30] Semei.
[31] Iosec.
[32] Ioda.

Qui fuit iorobabel[1]
Qui fuit salathiel
Fol. 39 b. Qui fuit neri
(28) Qui fuit melchi
Qui fuit addi
Qui fuit chosam[2]
Qui fuit helmadam
Qui fuit er[3]
(29) Qui fuit iesu[4]
Qui fuit eliezer
Qui fuit zorum[5]
Qui fuit matthat[6]
Qui fuit leui
(30) Qui fuit simeón[7]
Qui fuit iuda
Qui fuit ioseph
Qui fuit iona
Qui fuit eliachim
(31) Qui fuit melcha[8]
Qui fuit menna
Qui fuit matthatia[9]
Qui fuit nathan
Qui fuit dauid
(32) Qui fuit iesse
Qui fuit obéth[10]
Qui fuit boos[11]
Qui fuit salmón

Qui fuit nassón[12]
(33) Qui fuit aminadab
Qui fuit aram[13]
Qui fuit esrom
Qui fuit phares
Qui fuit iudae
(34) Qui fuit iacob
Qui fuit isác[14]
Qui fuit abarcham[15]
Qui fuit thare
Qui fuit nachor
(35) Qui fuit seruch
Qui fuit ragau
Qui fuit phalec
Qui fuit eber
Qui fuit sale
(36) Qui fuit cainán[16]
Qui fuit arfaxat
Qui fuit sém
Qui fuit noe Fol. 40.
Qui fuit laméch
(37) Qui fuit mathusa[17]
Qui fuit enóc[18]
Qui fuit ioréd[19]
Qui fuit maleel[20]
(38) Qui fuit enos[21]
Qui fuit adam[22]

[1] Zorobabel.
[2] Cosam.
[3] Her.
[4] Ihesu.
[5] Iorim.
[6] Matthad.
[7] Symeon.
[8] Melea.
[9] Matthata.
[10] Obed.
[11] Booz.
[12] Naasson.
[13] Aran.
[14] Isaac.
[15] Abraham.
[16] Chainan.
[17] Matthusale.
[18] Enoch.
[19] Iared.
[20] Malelehel.
[21] Cainan.
[22] Enos.

Qui fuit cainán[1] Qui fuit dei····7·7
Qui fuit séth[2]

[CAP. IV.] (1) Ihs[3] autem plenus spiritu sancto regresus[4] est tum[5] abiordane etagebatur inspiritu indesertum[6] (2) ettemptabatur[7] adiabulo[8]···7

[1] Seth.
[2] Adam.
[3] Iesus.
[4] regressus.
[5] V. om.
[6] V. adds diebus quadraginta.
[7] temtabatur.
[8] diabolo.

[CAP. I.] (1) IN PRINCIPIO erat uerbum **etuerbum erat** aput[1] deum etdeus
Fol. 42. erat uerbum (2) hoc erat inprincipio aput[1] deum (3) omnia peripsum facta
sunt **etsinc** ipso factum est nihil quod factum est (4) inipso uita est[2] et
uita erat·lúx hominum (5) etlúx intenebrís **lucet** ettenebre eam noncon-
prehenderunt[3]···7

(6) Fuit homo misus[4] adeo cui **nomen** erat iohannes (7) **híc uenit**
Fol. 42 b. intestimonium vttestimonium perhiberet delumine vtomnes crederent **peril-
lum (8)** nonerat ille lux sed vttestimonium perhiberet delumine···7

(9) Erat lúx uera **que** inluminat **omnem** hominem uenientem **inmundum** (10) inmundo **erat etmundus peripsum factus est** etmundus **eum**
noncognouit···

(11) In propria **uenit** etsui eum **nonreceperunt (12)** quotquot autem
receperunt eum dedit **cis**[5] potestatem **filios dei fieri hís** qui credunt innomine **eius** (13) qui nonexsanguinibus neque **exuoluntate** carnem[6] neque
exuoluntate uiri sed exdeo nati **sunt·u**[7]·(14) etuerbum caro factum est
ethabitauit inuobís[8] etuidimus **gloriam eius** gloriam quassi[9] unigeniti apatre
plenum **gratiæ etueritatis··7**

(15) **Iohannes testimonium perhibet** deipso etclamat diciens **híc erat**
quem **dixi uobis qui post me** uenturus est ante **me factus est** quia **prior me**
erat···7

Fol. 43. (16) Et deplenitudine **eius nos omnes** accipimus[10] gratiam **progratia**
(17) quia léx permoysén[11] dataest gratia autem[7] etueritas perihesum
christum facta est···7

(18) Deum nemo uidit umquam nisi[7] **unigenitus** filius qui est insinu
patris **ipse enarrauit···**

(19) **Et hoc est testimonium iohannis quando** miserunt iudei abhieruso-

---

[1] apud.
[2] erat.
[3] comprehenderunt.
[4] missus.
[5] illis.
[6] carnis.
[7] V. om.
[8] nobis.
[9] quasi.
[10] accepimus.
[11] Mosen.

Plate XVI. Fol. 42

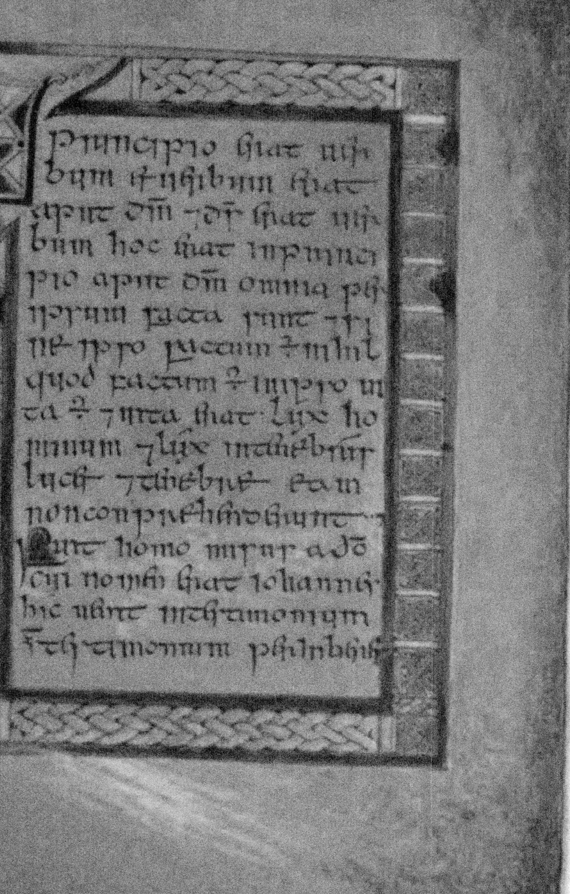

limis[1] sacerdotes etleuitás adeum utinterrogarent eum tu es quis[2]
(20) etconfessus est etnonnegauit etconfessus est quia nonsum ego christus
(21) et interrogauerunt eum quid ergo helias es tu etdicit nonsum propheta
es tu etrespondit non (22) dixerunt ergo et[3]quis es vtresponsum demus
híis[4] qui misserunt[5] nos quid dicis dete ipso··7
(23) Ait ego uox clamantes[6] indeserto dirigite uiam domini sic[7] dixit
issaias[8] propheta·
(24) Et qui missi fuerant[9] expharisceis (25) [10]interrogauerunt eum·et-
dixerunt ei[11]·quid ergo baptizas si tú nones christus···7
Neque helias neque propheta (26) respondit éis iohannes diciens Fol. 43 b.
ego babtizo inaqua medius autem uestrum stetit quem uos nescitis[12]
(27) ipse est qui post me uenturus est qui ante me factus est cuius ego
nonsum dignus vtsoluam eius corrigiam calciamenti eius[11]··7
(28) Haec inbethania facta sunt trans iordanén ubi erat iohannes babtizans (29) altera die uidit iohannes ihesum uenientem adse··7
Et ait ecce agnus dei ecce[11] qui tullit[13] peccatum mundi··7
(30) Hic est dequo dixi post me uenit uir qui ante me factus est quia
prior me erat·(31) et ego nesciebam cum sed vtmanifestaretur pleni[11]
[14]israhel et[11]propteria[15] ueni ego inaqua babtizans (32) ettestimonium
perhibuit iohannes diciens[16] quia uidi ipsum[17] discendentem[18] sicut[19]
columbam decelo etmansit super eum (33) etego nesciebam eum sed qui
missit[20] me babtizare inaqua ille mihi dixit super quem uideris spiritum Fol. 44.
discendentem[18] etmanentem super eum hicest qui babtizauit[21] inspiritu
sancto[22] (34) ego uidi ettestimonium perhibui quod hicest filius dei···7
(35) Altera die iterum stabat iohannes etexdiscipulis eius duo·(36) et-
respiciens ihesum ambulantem dicit·ecce agnus dei (37) etaudierunt eum
dúo discipuli loquentem etsecuti sunt ihesum (38) conuersus autem ihesus

[1] Hierosolymis.
[2] Tu quis es?
[3] ei.
[4] **his.**
[5] miserunt.
[6] clamantis.
[7] sicut.
[8] Esaias.
[9] V. adds erant.
[10] V. adds et.
[11] V. om.
[12] non scitis.
[13] **tollit.**
[14] **V. adds in.**
[15] **propterea.**
[16] **dicens.**
[17] **spiritum.**
[18] descendentem.
[19] quasi.
[20] misit.
[21] baptizat.
[22] V. adds et.

etuidens cos sequentes sé dicit eís quid queritis qui dixerunt ei rabbi quod
dicitur interpretatum magister ubi habitas··7

(39) Dicit eís uenite etuidete uenerunt etuiderunt ubi maneret **et-
aput**[1] cum manserunt die illo hora autem erat quassi[2]·x[3]·(40) erat autem
andreas frater simonis petri unus de[4]duobus qui audierant abiohanne
etsecuti fuerant eum··7

(41) Inuenit hic primum fratrem suum simonem **etdicit ei** inuenimus
messiam quodestinterpretatum christus (42) etadduxit **eum** adihesum
intuitus autem eum ihesus dixit tu es simón filius iohanna tu uocaueris
cefas[5] quod interpretatur petrus···7

Fol. 44 b. (43) Increastinum uoluit exire in galileam et inuenit philiphum[6] etdicit
ei ihesus[7] sequere me (44) erat autem philiphus[8] abethsaitha[9] ciuitate
andræ[10] etpetri (45) inuenit pilippus[11] nathanél[12] etdicit ei quem scripsit
moyses[13] inlege etprophete inuenimus ihesum filium ioseph·anazaréth[14]
(46) potest aliquid boni esse dicit ei pilippus[8] ueni etuide (47) uidit ihesus
nathanél[12] uenientem adsé etdicit deeo·ecce uere uir[7] israhel[15] ita inquo
nonestdolus[16] (48) dicit et[17]nathanél[12] unde me nosti·

Respondit ihesus etdixit ei priusquam te philippus uocaret **cum**
esses subarbore[7] ficu uidi té (49) et[7]respondit ei nathanél[12] etait[18] **rabbi tu**
es filius dei tu es rex israhel·(50) respondit **ihesus etdixit ei quia dixi tibi**
uidete[19] subficu credis·maius hís uidebis **(51) etdicit eis**[20]···7···7··7

Amen amén dico uobis uidi[21] celum apertum etangelos dei ascen-
dentes etdiscendentes[22] supra filium hominis··

[Cap. II.] (1) Et die tertio nuptiæ factæ sunt inchana[23] galilae[24]·et erat mater
Fol. 45. ihesu ibi (2) uocatus est autem ibi et[25]discipuli eius adnuptias (3) etdefi-
ciente uino··dicit mater ihesu adeum uinum nonhabent·(4) etdicit ei

1 apud.
2 quasi.
3 decima.
4 **ex.**
5 **Cephas.**
6 **Philippum.**
7 **V. om.**
8 **Philippus.**
9 **Bethsaida.**
10 **Andreae.**
11 **Philippus.**
12 **Nathánahel.**
13 **Moses.**
14 **V. adds Et dixit ei** Nathanahel **A** Nazareth.
15 Israhelita.
16 dolus non est.
17 ei.
18 **et ait.**
19 **vidi te**
20 ei.
21 videbitis.
22 descendentes.
23 Cana.
24 Galilaeae.
25 V. adds Iesus.

ihesus quid mihi ettibi[1] est mulier nondum uenit hora mea··(5) dicit
mater eius ministris quodcunque[2] dixerit uobis·[3]
(6) Erant autem ibi lapidæ[4] hidries[5] expossitæ[6] secundum purifica-
tionem iudeorum capientes singule metretas binas uel ternas··(7) et[7] dicit
eis ihesus inplete[8] idrias[9] aqua··etinpleuerunt[10] eas usque adsumum[11]··
(8) et dicit eis ihesus aurite[12] nunc etferte archiitriclino[13] ettullerunt[14] (9)
vtautem gustauit architriclinus[15] aquam uinum factum[16]·etnonsciebat
unde esset ministri autem sciebant qui aurierant[17] aquam··uocat sponsum
architriclinus[15] (10) et dicit ei·omnis homo primum bonum uinum ponit[18]
inebriati fuerint tunc id quod deterrius[19] est tú seruasti bonum uinum
usque adhúc (11) hóc fecit initium signorum ihesus in chana[20] galileæ··
etmanifestauit gloriam suam et crediderunt ineum discipuli eius···7
(12) Post hóc discendit[21] capharnaum··ipse etmater eius etfratres eius
etdisciupuli eius·etibi manserunt non multis diebus··· Fol. 45 b.
(13) Et proberabat phasca[22] iudiorum[23] etascendit hierusolima[24] ihesus··
(14) Et inuenit intemplo uendentes boues etoues etcolumbas etnum
mularios[25] sedentes (15) etcum fecisset quasi flagillum[26] defuniculís··omnes
eicit[27] detemplo··oues quoque etboues··etnum mulariorum effudit aés·
etmensas subuertit (16) ethís qui columbás uendebant dixit auferte ista
hinc··Nolite facire[28] domum patris mei··domum negotiationis··
(17) Recordati uero sunt discipuli eius··quia scriptum est zelus domús
tue comedit me·(18) responderunt ergo iudei·etdixerunt ei·quod signum
ostendis nobís quia hæc facis··
(19) Respondit ihesus etdixit illis[29] soluite templum hoc etintribus diebus
excitabo illut[30]··(20) dixerunt ei[31] ego[32] iudei·quadraginta etecx annis

[1] tibi et mihi.
[2] quodcumque.
[3] V. adds facite.
[4] lapideae.
[5] hydriae.
[6] sex positae.
[7] V. om.
[8] Implete.
[9] hydrias.
[10] impleverunt.
[11] summum.
[12] Haurite.
[13] archetriclino.
[14] tulerunt.
[15] archetriclinus.
[16] factam.
[17] hauserant.
[18] V. adds et cum.
[19] deterius.
[20] Cana.
[21] descendit.
[22] pascha.
[23] Iudæorum.
[24] Hierosolyma.
[25] nummularios.
[26] flagellum.
[27] eiecit.
[28] facere.
[29] eis.
[30] illud.
[31] V. om.
[32] ergo.

ædificatum est templum est[1] hoc··ettucribus[2] diebus excitabis illut[3]·· (21) ille autem dicebat detemplo corporis sui (22) cum ergo surrexísset[4] amortuis···7

Fol. 46. Recordati sunt discipuli eius·quia hoc dicebat etcrediderunt scripturæ·etsermoni quem dixit ihesus·(23) cum autem esset et[1]hierusolimís[5] inpascha indie festo multi crediderunt innomine eius·uidentes signa eius que faciebat··(24) ipse autem ihesus noncredebat semet ipsum eís·eoquod ipse nosset omnes··(25) et quia opus et[6]non erat vtquis testimonium perhiberet dehomine ipse enim sciebat quo[7] esset inhomine··7

[Cap. III.] (1) Erat autem[8] expharisefs nicodimus[9] nomine princeps iudeorum· (2) hic uenit adeum nocte·etdixit ei rabbi·scimus quia adeo uenisti magister nemo enim potest hec signa facire[10] que tu facis·nisi fuerit dominus[11] cum eo (3) respondit ihesus etdixit ei··

Amén amen dico tibi nisi quis natus fuerit denouo[12] nonpotest uidere regnum dei·(4) dicit adeum nicodemus quomodo potest homo nasci cum senex sit numquid potest inuentrem matris suæ rursus[13] introíre etnasci (5) respondit ihesus··

Amén amén dico tibi nisi quis renatus fuerit exaqua etspiritu nonpotest introire inregnum dei (6) quod natum est excarne caro est··et quod

Fol. 46 b. natum est exspiritu sanctus[14] est·(7) nonmireris quia dixi tibi··oportet uos nasci denouo[15]··(8) spiritus ubi uult spirat etuocem eius audis[16] non uos[17] unde ueniat etquo uadat··

Sic enim[18] omnis qui natus est exspiritu (9) respondit nicodimus[19] etdixit ei et[20] quomodo possunt hæc ex[20]fieri··(10) respondit ihesus etdixit ei tu es magister[21] israhel et héc ignoras··

(11) Amen amen dico tibi quia quod scimus loquimus[22] [23]testamur·et-

1 V. om.
2 tu tribus.
3 illud.
4 resurrexisset.
5 Hierosolymis.
6 ei.
7 quid.
8 V. adds homo.
9 Nicodemus.
10 facere.
11 deus.
12 denuo.
13 iterato.
14 spiritus.
15 denuo.
16 V. adds sed.
17 scis.
18 est.
19 Nicodemus.
20 V. om.
21 V. adds in.
22 loquimur.
23 V. adds et quod vidimus.

testimonium nostrum nonaccipitis (12) sí terréna dixi uobis etnoncredistis[1]
quomodo sídixero uobis celestia credistis[2]··

(13) Et nemo ascendit incælo[3] nisi qui discendit[4] decelo filius hominis
quiest incelo (14) etsicut moyses[5] exaltauit serpentem indeserto·ita
exaltari oportet filium hominis (15) vtomnis qui credit inipso nonperiat[6]
sed habeat uitam eternam··7

(16) Sic enim dilexit deus hunc[7] mundum vtfilium suum unigenitum
daret vtomnis qui credit ineum nonpereat sed habeat uitam æternam··7

(17) Non enim misit deus filium suum inmundum vtiudicet mundum sed
vt saluetur mundus peripsum·(18) qui credit ineum noniudicatur qui autem
noncredit iam iudicatus est quia noncredit[8] innomine unigeniti filii dei··7
(19) Hoc est autem iudicium·qui lúx uenit inmundum vtiudicet[7] **et-** Fol. 47
diléxerunt homines magis tenebras.quam lucem··erant enim eorum mala
opera·(20) Omnis enim qui male agit odit lucem etnonuenit adlucem
vtnonarguantur opera eius··(21) Qui autem[9] **ueritatem uenit** adlucem
vtmanifestantur[10] opera[11] eius·quia indeo **sunt** facta··7

(22) Post hæc uenit ihesus etdiscipuli eius inudeam terram·etillic
demorabatur[12] cum eís etbabtizabat···7

(23) Erat autem etiohannes babtizans inænón iuxta salim quia aquæ
multæ erant illi[13] etaduenichant multi[14] etbabtizabantur··7

(24) Non[15] enim misus[16] fuerat incarcerem iohannes··

(25) Facta[17] ergo quæstio exdicipulis iohannis cum iudeís depurificatione·
(26) etinuenerunt[18] adiohannem etdixerunt ei rabbi··qui erat tecum trans-
iordanén cui tu testimonium perhibuisti ecce[19] babtizat·etomnes ueniunt
adeum·(27) respondit iohannes·etdixit nonpotest homo accipere quicquam
··nisi fuerit ei[20] datum decelo··(28) Ipsi uos mihi testimonium perhibetis
quod dixirim[21] ego nonsum christus sed quia misus[16] sum ante illum····7··7

---

[1] creditis.
[2] credetis.
[3] caelum.
[4] descendit.
[5] Moses.
[6] pereat.
[7] V. om.
[8] credidit.
[9] V. adds facit.
[10] manifestentur.
[11] eius opera.
[12] morabatur.
[13] illic.
[14] V. om.
[15] nondum enim.
[16] missus.
[17] V. adds est.
[18] venerunt.
[19] V. adds hic.
[20] ei fuerit.
[21] dixerim.

Fol. 47 b. (29) Qui **habet** sponsam sponsus est·amicus autem sponsi qui stat etaudite[1] **cum**·cum[2] gaudio gaudet propter uocem sponsi hoc ergo gaudium meum inpletum[3] est·(30) illum oportet crescere me autem minuí·**(31) qui** desursum uenit supra omnes est qui est deterra··deterra est et[4]terra loquitur··Qui decelo uenit supra omnes est (32) **etquod** uidet **etaudit**[5] hóc testatur ettestimonium **eius** nemo accipit··(33) Qui accipit eum[6] testimonium signauit quia deus uerax est (34) quem enim misit deus·uerba dei loquitur nonenim admensuram dat deus spiritum··7

(35) Pater diligit filium etomnia dedit inmanus eius··(36) Qui credit infilium habet uitam æternam··qui autem incredulus est infilio[2] nonuidebit uitam sed ira dei manet super eum··

[Cap. IV.] (1) vtergo cognouit ihesus quia audierunt farisei[7]··quia ihesus plures discipulos facit etbaptizat[8] quam iohannes·(2) quamquam ihesus nonbaptizaret sed discipuli eius··7

(3) Relinquit[9] iudeam ethabít[10] iterum ingalileam··(4) Oportebat enim[11] transire persamariam (5) uenit ergo inciuitatem samariæ que dicitur sichár[12] **iuxta** predium quod dedit iacob ioseph filio suo·(6) erat **autem ibi** fons iacob···7···7

Fol. 48. IHESUS ergo fatigatus exitenere··sedebat síc super fontem hora erat quasi sexta (7) uenit mulier desamaria aurire[13] aquam dicit ei ihesus dá mihi bibere (8) disciputi enim eius abierant inciuitatem··vtcibos emerent·(9) dicit[14] ei mulier illa samaritana··Quomodo[15] iudaeus cum **sis** bibere ame poscis que sum mulier samaritana nonenim coutuntur iudei samaritanís···

(10) Respondit ihesus etdixit ei·si scires **donum dei etquis** est qui dicit tibi dá mihi bibere tú forsitán petisses abeo et dedisset tibi aquam uiuam·(11) **dicit ei mulier domine neque** inquo aurias[16] habes·etputeus **altus est**

---

1 audit.
2 V. om.
3 impletum.
4 V. adds de.
5 audivit.
6 eius.
7 Pharisaei.
8 V. adds magis.
9 reliquit.
10 abiit.
11 autem eum.
12 Sychar.
13 haurire.
14 V. adds ergo.
15 V. adds tu.
16 haurias.

unde ergo habes aquam uiuam (12) numquid tu maior es patre nostro iacob
quidedit nobis puteum et ipse exeo[1] bibit etfilii eius etpecora eius··
(13) Respondit ihesus etdixit ei omnis qui bibit exaqua hác sitiat[2]
iterum qui autem biberit exaqua quam ergo[3] dabo ei··Nonsitiet inæternum
(14) sed aqua quam ego dabo ei··Fiet ineo fons aque salientis inuitam
æternam··(15) Dicit ei[4] mulier domine dá mihi bibere[5] hanc aquam··
utnonsitiam neque ueniam húc aurire··(16) Dicit ei ihesus uade uoca
uirum tuum etuení húc[5]·(17) respondit mulier etdixit nonhabeo uirum dicit
ei ihesus benedixisti···7

Quia nonhabeo uirum·(18) quinque enim uirós habuisti etnunc Fol. 48 b.
quem habes nonest tuus uir hoc uere dixisti (19) dicit ei mulier domine··
uideo quia propheta es tu··(20) patres nostri inmonte hoc adorauerunt etuos
dicitis quia inhierusolimís[6] locus ubi adorare oportet·(21) dicit ei ihesus
mulier crede mihi quia uiniet hora quando neque inmonte hóc neque in-
hierusolimis[6] adorabitis patrem (22) uos adoratis quod nescitis··Nos
adoramus quod scimus quia salus exiudeis est (23) sed uenit hora etnunc
est quando ueri adoratores adorabunt patrem··INspiritu etueritate nam
etpater tales querit eos[5] qui adorent eum··(24) spiritus est deus eteos qui
adorent[7] eum inspiritu etueritate oportet adorare·(25) Dicit ei mulier scio
quia misias[8] qui dicitur christus··

Cum ergo uenit[9] ille nobis adnuntiauit[10] omnia (26) dicit **ei** ihesus
ego sum qui loquor tecum (27) etcontinuo uenerunt discipuli eius etmira-
bántur··quia cum muliere loqueretur[11] nemo tamen dixit ei[5] quid queris aut
quid loqueris cum ea (28) relinquit[12] ergo hidriam[13] suam mulier·ethabíit[14]
inciuitatem··et dicit illis hominibus·(29) uenite etuidete hominem·qui
dixit mihi omnia·que cumque feci··numquid ipseest christus (30) exierunt
Deciuitate etuinebant[15] adeum (31) interea rogabant eum discipuli eius[5] Fol. 49.
dicentes rabbi manduca··(32) ille autem dixit eis ego cibum[16] manducare

[1] ex eo ipse.
[2] sitiet.
[3] ego.
[4] ad eum.
[5] V. om.
[6] Hierosolymis est.
[7] adorant.
[8] Messias.
[9] venerit.
[10] adnuntiabit.
[11] loquebatur.
[12] reliquit.
[13] hydriam.
[14] abiit.
[15] veniebant.
[16] V. adds habeo.

quem uos nescitis[1] (33) dicebant ergo discipuli adinuicem numquid aliquis
attulit **ci** manducare·(34) dicit eis ihesus meus cibus est vtfaciam uoluntatem eius qui missit[2] me vtperficiam opus eius (35) nonne uós dicitis quod
adhúc quatuor[3] menses sunt·etmensis[4] uenit··Ecce dico uobis leuate
occulos[5] uestros etuidete regiones quia albí[6] sunt[7] admessem (36) etqui
mitit[8] mercidem[9] accipiet[10]··Etcongregat fructum inuitam æternam··ut
etqui seminat simul gaudeat etqui metit (37) inhóc enim est uerbum uerum··
quia alius est qui seminat[11] alius est qui mettit[8]··(38) Ego misi uós me[12]
tere quod uós nonlaborastis alii laborauerunt··etuós inlaborem eorum in-
troistis··(39) exciuitate autem illa multi crediderunt incum samaritanorum
propter uerbum mulieris testimonium perhibentis··quia dixit mihi omnia
que cumque feci··(40) Cum uenissent ergo adillum samaritani rogauerunt
eum utubi[13] maneret etmansit ibi duos dies[14] (41) multo plures crediderunt
Fol. 49 *b.* propter sermonem eius (42) etmulieri dicebant·Quia iam nonpropter tuam
loquellam credimus ipsi enim audiuimus etscimus quia híc est uere[15]
saluator mundi···

(43) **Post duos autem dies exiit inde et** habiit[16] in galileam··(44) Ipse
enim ihesus testimonium perhibuit qua propheta insua patria[17] nonhabet··
(45) CUM ergo uenisset ingalileam exceperunt eum galiliae cum omnia
uidissent que **fecerat** hierusolimís[18] indie festo etipsi enim uenerant indiem[19] festum·(46) uenit ergo iterum inchanna[20] galiliæ[21] ubi fecit aquam
uinum···7

Et erat quidam regulus cuius filius infirmabatur in[22]cafarnaum[23]
(47) hic cum audisset quia ihesus adueniret a iudea ingalileam··abiit adeum
etrogabat eum vt discenderet[24] etsanaret filium eius··INcipiebat enim mori
(48) dixit ergo ihesus adeum nisi signa adprodigia uideritis noncreditis (49)
dicit adeum regulus··domine discende[25] priusquam moriatur filius meus

[1] **non scitis.**
[2] **misit.**
[3] **quattuor.**
[4] **messis.**
[5] **oculos.**
[6] **albae.**
[7] **V. adds iam.**
[8] metit.
[9] **mercedem.**
[10] **accipit.**
[11] **V. adds et.**
[12] metere.
[13] ut ibi.
[14] V. adds et.
[15] vere hic est.
[16] abiit.
[17] V. adds honorem.
[18] Hierosolymis.
[19] ad diem.
[20] Cana.
[21] Galilaeae.
[22] V. om.
[23] Capharnaum.
[24] descenderet.
[25] descende.

(50) dicit ei ihesus uade filius tuus uidit[1] credidit homo sermoni quem
dixit ei ihesus etibat·(51) iam autem eo discendente[2] serui occurrerunt ei
adnuntiauerunt[3] ei[4] dicentes·quia filius eius uiueret (52) interrogabat ergo
horam ab eis inqua melius habuerit . et dixerunt ei quia heri hora septima
reliquit eum febris··7

(53) Cognouit ergo pater quia[5] illa hora erat inqua dixit ei ihesus·· Fol. 50.
filius tuus uidit[6]··etcredidit ipse etdomus eius tota (54) hoc iterum
secundum signum fecit ihesus cum uenisset aiudea ingaliliam[7]····7

[Cap. V.] (1) Post hæc erat dies festus iudeorum etascendit ihesus hierusolimís[8]··
(2) est[9] hierusolimís[8] super probatica piscina que cognominatur ebreice[10]
bedsaida[11]··quinque porticus habens (3) inhís iacebat multitudo magna
languentium··cecorum claudorum·aridorum··expectantium aque motum
(4) angelus autem domini secundum tempus discendebat[12] inpiscinam
etmouebat aquam quique[13] ergo primus discendisset[14] post motionem[15] aque
sanus fiebat··alanguore quo cumque[16] tenebatur··

(5) Erat autem ibi[17] homo quidam[18] annos habens ininfirmitate sua
(6) hunc cum uidisset ihesus iacentem et cognouisset quia multum iam
tempus habet dicit ei·uis sanus fieri··(7) respondit ei languidus·domine
hominem nonhabeo utcum turbata fuerit aqua mittat me inpiscinam dum
uenio enim ego··alius ante me discendit[19]··

(8) Dicit ei ihesus·surge **et[4] tolle** grabatum tuum·et ambula (9) Fol. 50 b.
etstatim sanus factus est homo··etsustulit grabatum[20] suum·et ambulabat
erat autem sabbatum inillo die (10) dicebant ivdei illi qui sanus[21] fuerat··
sabbatum est nonlicet tibi tollere grabatum[20] tuum··(11) respondit eís
qui me fecit sanum··ille mihi dixit tolle grabbatum[20] tuum etambula (12)
interrogauerunt ergo eum·quis est ille homo qui tibi dixit[22] tolle

---

[1] vivit.
[2] descendente.
[3] et nuntiaverunt.
[4] V. om.
[5] quod.
[6] vivit.
[7] Galilaeam.
[8] Hierosolymis.
[9] V. adds autem.
[10] hebraice.
[11] Bethsaida.
[12] descendebat.
[13] qui.
[14] descendisset.
[15] motum.
[16] a quocumque languore.
[17] quidam homo ibi.
[18] V. adds triginta octo.
[19] descendit.
[20] grabattum.
[21] sanatus.
[22] dixit tibi.

grabatum[1] tuum etambula·· (13) is autem qui sanus fuerat effectus
nesciebat quis esset··ihesus enim declinauit aturba constituta inlocum[2]
(14) postea inuenit eum ihesus intemplo··etdixit illi ecce sanus factus es
iam noli peccare ne deterius tibi aliquid continguat[3] (15) abiit ille homo··
ET nuntiauit iudeis quia ihesus esset qui eum[4] fecit sanum·(16) propteria[5]
persequebantur iudei ihesum quia hæc faciebat insabbato·ihesus autem
respondit eis pater meus usque modo operatur etego operior[6]··propteria[7]
ergo magis querebant eum iudei interficere·· Quia nonsolum soluebat
sabbatum sed ad[8]patrem suum dicebat deum æqualem sé faciens deo··7
Fol. 51. Respondit itaque ihesus etdixit eís··
(19) Amén amen dico uobis nonpotest filius[9] facire[10] quicquam nisi
quod uiderit patrem facientem que cumque enim ille fecerit hæc similiter
etfilius faciet[11] (20) pater enim diligit filium etomnia demonstruat[12] ei que
ipse facit··etmaiora híis[13] demonstrauit[14] et[15] opera·utuos miremini (21)
sicut enim pater suscitat mortuos etuiuificat··sic etfilius quos uult uiuificat
(22) neque enim pater iudicat quemquam·sed iudicio[16] omne dedit filio·
(23) vtomnes honorificent filium sicut honorificauit[17] patrem··7
Qui nonhonorificent[18] filium nonhonorificat patrem qui misit illum··
(24) Amén amén dico uobís qui uerbum meum audit etcredit ei·qui
missit[19] me habet uitam eternam··etiniudicium nonuenit[20] sed transit[21]
amorte·[22]
(25) Amén amén dico uobís quia uenit hora etnunc est quando mortui
audient uocem filii dei etqui audierint uiuent (26) sicut enim pater habet
uitam insemet ipso sic dedit etfilio uitam habere insemet ipso (27) etpotestatem dedit ei a[23]iudicium facere quia filius hominis est (28) nolite mirari
hoc quia uenit hora··7
Fol. 51 b. ENqua omnes qui inmonumentis sunt·audient uocem eius (29) et-

1 grabattum.
2 loco.
3 contingat.
4 fecit eum.
5 propterea.
6 operor.
7 propterea.
8 et.
9 V. adds a se.
10 facere.
11 et filius similiter facit.
12 demonstrat.
13 his.
14 demonstrabit.
15 ei.
16 iudicium.
17 honorificant.
18 honorificat.
19 misit.
20 veniet.
21 transiet.
22 V. adds in vitam.
23 et.

procedent **qui** bona fecerunt **inresurrectionem** uite qui vero mala egerunt
inresurrectionem iudicii (30) nonpossum ego ame ipso facire[1] quicquam
sicut·audio[2] iudicio etiudicum meum iustum est··7

Quia nonqua[3] ergo[4] uoluntatem meam **sed uoluntatem eius** qui
missit me[5]··

(31) Sí ego testimonium perhibeo deme testimonium meum nonestuerum··
(32) alius est qui testimonium perhibet deme etscio quia est **uerum**[6] testimonium quod peribet[7] deme··(33) uos misistis adiohannen··ettestimonium
perhibuit ueritati (34) ego autem **nonabomine**[8] testimonium accipio sed
hæc dico vtuós salui sitis (35) ille erat lucerna ardens et lucens uos autem
uoluisti[9] exsultare[10] adhoram inluce eius·(36) ego autem habeo testimonium
maius iohanne opera enim que dedit mihi pater vtperficiam ea··ipsa opera
que ego facio testimonium perhibent deme quia pater me misit·(37) et qui
misit me pater··ipse testimonium perhibuit deme··

Neque uocem eius audistis[11] umquam neque speciam eius uidistis·
(38) etuerbum eius nonhabetis inuobís manens quia quem misit ille huic Fol. 52.
uos non creditis··(39) Scrutamini scripturas quia uós putatis inipsis uitam
æternam habere etille sunt que testimoni perhibent deme (40) etnon-
uultís uenire adme utuitam habetis[12]··(41) Claritatis[13] abhominibus **non-**
accipio (42) sed cognoui uós **quia dilectionem dei nonhabetis inuobís**···7

(43) Ego ueni innomine patris mei **etnonaccipistis**[14] **me··Sí alius** uenerit
innomine suo illum accipietis[15]··(44) etgloriam que asolo **est deo** nonqueri-
tis··(45) Nolite putare quia ego accusaturus sim uos aput[16] patrem quia[17]
accuset[18] uos moyses[19] inquo uós speratis··(46) Sí enim crederitis[20] mosi
crederitis[20] forsitán etmihi deme enim[21] scripsit·(47) Si autem illius litterís
noncreditis quomodo meís uerbís creditis·[22]

[1] facere.
[2] iudico.
[3] non quaero.
[4] V. om.
[5] me misit.
[6] verum est.
[7] perhibet.
[8] ab homine.
[9] voluistis.
[10] exultare.
[11] unquam audistis.
[12] habeatis.
[13] claritatem.
[14] Accipitis.
[15] V. adds Quomodo potestis vos credere, qui gloriam ab invicem accipitia.
[16] apud.
[17] est qui.
[18] accusat.
[19] Moses.
[20] crederetis.
[21] V. adds ille.
[22] credetis?

H

[CAP VI.] (1) **Post** hæc habiit[1] ihesus transmare galiliæ[2] quodest tiberiades[3]
(2) adsequebatur[4] eum multitudo magna quia uidebant[5] signa·que facie-
bat super hiis[6] qui infirmabantur·(3) subiit[7] ergo inmontem[8] ihesus etibi
sedebat **cum discipulís suis···7···7**
Fol. 52 b. (4) Erat autem proximum pascha dies festus iudeorum··
(5) Cum subleuasset ergo occulos[9] ihesus·etuidisset quia multitudo
maxima uenit adeum dicit adphippum[10] unde ememus panes·vtmanducent
hii[11] (6) hóc **autem** dicebat **temptans**[12] eum ipse enim sciebat quid esset
futurus[13]·(7) respondit ei philippus **ducentorum** denariorum panes·Non-
sufficiunt eís vtunus quisque modicum·quid accipiat (8) dicit ei·unus
exdiscipulis eius·andreas simonis frater petri··(9) estpuer unus híc qui
·habet·u·[14]·panes ordiacios[15] etduos pisces·sed hec quid sunt intertantos·
(10) **dixit ergo ihesus** facite homines discumbere erat autem fenum multum
inloco **discuperunt**[16] **ergo** uiri numero quasi·u·[14]·milia··(11) accipit[17] ergo
panes ihesus etcum gratias egisset disbuit[18] discumbentibus similiter expis-
cibus quantum uolebant (12) vtautem inpleti[19] sunt dixit discipulis suis
colligite que superauerunt fragmenta[20] ne pereant (13) colligentur[21] ergo
etinpleuerunt[22]·xii[23]·cophinos fragmentorum··ex·u[14]·panibus hordiacís[24]
qui[25] superfuerunt hiis[26] qui manducauerunt··(14) illi ergo homines cum
uidissent quod fecerat signum··dicebant quia hic est uere propheta qui
Fol. 53. uenturus est inmundum··7(15) ihesus ergo cum cognouisset quia uenturi
essent utraperent eum etfacerent eum regem··
Fugit iterum inmontem ipse solus (16) vtautem sero factum est
discenderunt[27] discipuli eius admare·(17) Etcum ascendissent nauem··
uenerunt trans mare incafarnaum[28] ettenebre iam factæ erant etnonuenerat
adeos ihesus··(18) mare **autem uento magno flante** exsurgebat··(19) cum

[1] abiit.
[2] Galilaeae.
[3] Tiberiadis.
[4] et sequebatur.
[5] videbat.
[6] his.
[7] subit.
[8] in monte.
[9] oculos.
[10] ad Philippum.
[11] hi ?
[12] temtans.
[13] **facturus.**
[14] **quinque.**
[15] hordiacios.
[16] Discubuerunt.
[17] Accepit.
[18] distribuit.
[19] saturati.
[20] fragmentorum.
[21] collegerunt.
[22] impleverunt.
[23] duodecim.
[24] hordiaciis.
[25] quae.
[26] his.
[27] descenderunt.
[28] Capharnaum.

remigassent ergo quassi[1] stadia·xxu[2]·aut·xxxta[3]·uident ihesum ambulantem supra mare et proximum nauifieri··ettimuerunt (20) ille autem dixit[4] eís ego sum nolite timbre[5] (21) uoluerunt ergo accipere eum innaui[6]··etstatim fuit nauis adterram inaquam[7] ibant[8]··

(22) Altera die turba que stabat transmare uidit quia nauicula alia nonerat ibi nisi una··etquia nonintroisset cum discipulis suis[9] innaue[10] sed soli discipuli eius abissent··(23) Aliæ uero super uenerunt naues·atibriade[11] iuxta locum ubi manducauerunt panem··gratias **agentes dominum**[12] (24) cum ergo uidisset turba quia ihesus nonesset **ibi** neque discipuli eius [13]innauem sed soli discipuli eius abissent··

Aliæ vero super uenerunt naues·atiberiade iuxta locum ubi man- Fol. 53 b.
ducauerunt panem gratias agentes dominus cum ergo uidisset turba quia ihesus nonesset ibi discipuli eius[13] ascenderunt nauiculas etuenerunt cafarnaum[14] querentes ihesum (25) etcum inuenissent eum transmare dixerunt[15] rabi[16]··Quando húc uenisti (26) respondit eís ihesus·etdixit··7

Amén amén dico uobís queritis me nonquia uidistis signa sed quia manducastis expanibus etsaturati estis (27) operamini noncibum que periit[17] sed qui permanet inuitam æternam quem filius hominis uobis dabit··hunc enim pater signauit deus··(28) dixerunt ergo adeum quid faciemus vtoperemur pera[18] dei··

(29) Respondit ihesus etdixit eís hoc est opus dei·vteredatis ineum quem misit ille··(30) dixerunt ergo ei quod ergo tú facis signum vtuideamus etcredeamus[19] tibi quid operaris··(31) patres enim[20] manducauerunt indeserto·Sicut scriptum est panem decelo dedit eís mandveare·(32) dixit ergo eís ihesus··

Amén amén dico uobís nonmoyses[21] dedit uobís panem decelo sed pater meus dat uobís panem decelo uerum (33) panis enim dei est qui dis-

---

[1] quasi.
[2] viginti quinque.
[3] triginta.
[4] dicit.
[5] timere.
[6] in navem.
[7] **quam.**
[8] **ibat.**
[9] V. adds Iesus.
[10] navem.
[11] Tiberiade.
[12] domino.
[13] Thirty-two words are here repeated.
[14] Capharnaum.
[15] **V. adds ei.**
[16] **Rabbi.**
[17] **perit.**
[18] opera.
[19] credamus.
[20] V. om. and adds nostri mannam.
[21] Moses.

cendit[1] decelo·etdat uitam mundo (34) dixerunt ergo adeum domine semper nobis[2] dá panem hunc panem semper hunc[3]···7

Fol. 54. (35) Dixit autem eis ihesus ego sum panis uitæ··qui uenit[4] adme nonessuriet[5] et qui credit inme nonsitiet umquam (36) sed dixi uobís··quiaetuidistis me etnoncredistis[6]····7

(37) Omne quod dat mihi **pater admc ueniet**··

Etenim[7] qui uenit adme noneiciam foras (38) quia discendi[8] decelo nonut faciam uoluntatem meam **sed** uoluntatem eius qui misit me··7

(39) Hec est autem uoluntas eius **qui** missit **me** patris vtomne quod dedit mihi nonperdam exeo·quicquam[9] sed **resuscitem** illum in[9]nouissimo die (40) hæc[10] enim uoluntas patris mei qui misit me vtomnis[11] uidet filium etcredit ineum[12]··etresuscitabo ego eum **innouissimo die**····7

(41) Murmurabant ergo iudei deillo quia dixisset ego sum panis qui decelo discendi[13]·(42) etdicebant nonne hicest ihesus filius ioseph cuius[14] **nouimus patrem** et matrem quomodo ergo hic[15] dicit quia decelo discendi[13]··

(43) Respondit ergo ihesus etdixit eis nolite murmurare[16] inuicem·(44) nemo potest uenire adme nisi pater **qui misit me** traxerit eum etego resus-

Fol. 54 b. citabo **eum in[9]nouissimo** die···7 (45) est scriptum inprophetís **eterunt omnes** docebiles[17] **dei omnis qui audit[18] apatre[19]** uenit adme (46) nonquia **patrem** uidit quisquam **nisi his[20] quiest adeo hic uidit** patrem··

(47) Amén amén dico uobis qui credit inme habet uitam æternam··

(49) Ego sum panis uite··(49) patres uestri manducauerunt indeserto mannam etmortui sunt·(50) hic est panis decelo discendens[21] vtsí quis exipso manducauerit nonmoriatur··(51) Ego sum panis uiuus qui decelo discendi[22]·· **Sí** quis manducauerit exhoc pane uiuet inæternum etpanis quem ego dabo caro meaest promundi uita··7

(52) Litigabant ergo iudei **adinuicem** dicentes quomodo potest

---

[1] **descendit.**
[2] **da nobis.**
[3] **V. om. last three words.**
[4] **veniet.**
[5] **esuriet.**
[6] creditis.
[7] eum.
[8] descendi.
[9] V. om.
[10] V. adds est.
[11] V. adds qui.
[12] V. adds habeat vitam aeternam.
[13] descendi.
[14] V. adds nos.
[15] dicit hic.
[16] V adds in.
[17] docibiles.
[18] audivit.
[19] V. adds et didicit.
[20] is.
[21] descendens.
[22] descendi.

hic nobís carnem suam[1] dare admanducandum·(53) dixit ergo eis ihesus··

Amen ámen dico uobis nisi manducaueritis carnem filii hominis·· etbiberitis eius sanguinem nonhabebitis uitam inuobís (54) qui manducat meam carnem etbibit[2] meum sanguinem habeet[3] uitam eternam etego resuscitabo eum innouissimo die··7

(55) Caro enim mea uere est cibum[4]··etsangues[5] meus uereest potus··

(56) Qui manducat meam carnem·etbibit meum sanguinem inme manet etego inillo···7

(57) Sicut misit pater uiuiens[6] etego uiuo propter patrem etqui man- Fol. 55.
ducat me etipse uiuiens[7] propter me··(58) hic est panis qui decelo discendit[8]··Nonsicut manducauerunt patres uestri mannam etmortui sunt·qui manducat hunc panem uiuet inæternum··

(59) Hæc dixit insinagoga[9]··docens incapharnaum··(60) multi ergo audientes exdiscipulis eius dixerunt durus est hic sermo··quis potest eum audire··(61) sciens autem ihesus aput[10] semet ipsum quia murmurarent dehóc discipuli eius dixit eís hoc uós scandalizat··

(62) Si ergo uideritis filium hominis ascendentem ubi erat prius (63) spiritus est qui uiuificat caro nonprodest quicquam··

Uerba que ego locutus sum uobís spiritus etuita sunt[11] (64) quidam exuobis qui noncredunt··

Sciebat eum[12] abinitio ihesus qui essent credentes etcuius[13] traditurus esset eum··(65) Etdicebat propteria[14] dixi uobís quia nemo potest uenire adme nisi fuerit eidatum apatre meo·(66) Exhoc multi discipulorum eius abierunt retro etiam noncum illo ambulabant··(67) Dixit ergo ihesus·adxii[15] num[16] etuós multis[17] abire···7

(68) Respondit ergo ei simón petrus domine adquem ibimus uerba uite Fol. 55 b.

1 carnem suam nobis.
2 bibet.
3 habet.
4 cibus.
5 sanguis.
6 me vivens pater.
7 vivet.
8 descendit.
9 synagoga.
10 apud.
11 V. adds sed sunt.
12 enim.
13 quis.
14 Propterea.
15 duodecim.
16 numquid.
17 vultis.

æternæ habes (69) etnós credimus[1]··etcognouimus quia tu es christus filius dei···

(70) Respondit eis ihesus nonne ego uós·xii[2]·elegii[3]·etexuobís unus diabulus[4] est··(71) dicebat autem iudam simonem[5] sariothis[6] hic enim erat traditurus eum cum esset unus exduodecim··7

[CAP. VII.] (1) Post hec autem[7] ambulabat ihesus ingalilea[8] nonenim uolebat iniudeam ambulare··quia querebant eum iudei interficere·(2) erat autem inproximo dies festus iudeorum scenopigia[9]····7

(3) Dixerunt autem adeum fratres eius transí hinc etuade iniudeam vtdet[10] discipuli tui uideant opera[11] que facis··(4) nemo quippe[12] inocculto quid[13] facit··et querit ipse in palam esse sí hæc facis manifestate[14] ipsvm mundo (5) neque enim·fratres eius credebant ineum.

(6) Dicit ergo eis ihesus tempus meum nondum uenit··tempus autem uestrum semper[15] paratum (7) nonpotest mundus odísse uós me autem odit quia ego testimonium perhibeo deillo··Quia opera eius mala sunt (8) uós ascendite addiem festum hunc ego nonascendo addiem festum istum·quia meum tempus nondum inpletum[16] est··(9) hæc cum dixisset ipse[17] ingalilea··
Fol. 56. (10) vtautem ascenderunt fratres eius tunc etipse discendit[18] addiem festum nonmanifeste sed quassi[19] inocculto (11) iudei ergo querebant eum indie festo··etdicebant ubi est ille·(12) etmurmur multus [20]erat deeo inturba quidam enim dicebant quia bonus est··alii autem dicebant nonsed seducit turbas (13) nemo tamen palam loquebatur deillo··propter metum iudeorum·(14) iam autem die festo mediante ascendit ihesus intemplum·etdocebat (15) etmirabantur iudei dicentes quomodo hic literas[21] scit cum nondedicerit[22]··

(16) Respondit eís ihesus·etdixit mea doctrina nonest mea sed eius qui misit me (17) si quis uoluerit uoluntatem eius facire[23] cognoscit[24] doctrina

1 credidimus.
2 duodecim.
3 elegi.
4 diabolus.
5 Simonis.
6 Scariotis.
7 V. om.
8 Galilaeam.
9 scenopegia.
10 Vt et.
11 V. adds tua.
12 Enim.
13 aliquid.
14 manifesta te.
15 V. adds est.
16 impletum.
17 V. adds mansit.
18 ascendit.
19 quasi.
20 de eo erat.
21 litteras.
22 didicerit?
23 facere.
24 cognoscet de.

utrum exdeo sit án ego ame ipso loquar (18) quia[1] asemet ipso loquitur
gloriam propriam querit qui autem querit gloriam eius qui misit illum··hic
uerax est etiniustitia inillo nonest (19) nonne moses dedit uobís legem··7

Etnemo exuobís facit legem·(20) quid me queritis interficere··re-
spondit·turba etdixit demonium habes quis te querit interficere···

(21) Respondit·ihesus etdixit eís unum opus feci etomnes miranamini[2]
(22) propterea moyses[3] dedit uobís circumcissionem[4] nonquia exmoses[5] est
sed expatribus etinsabbato circumciditis hominem·

(23) Si circumcisionem accipit homo insabbato vtnonsaluatur[6] léx mosi· Fol. 56 b.
mihi indignamini quia totum hominem sanum feci insabbato··(24) Nolite
iudicare secundum faciem sed iustum iudicium iudicate·(25) dicebant ergo
quidam exhierusolimís[7] nonne híc est quem querunt interficere··(26) Etecce
palam loquitur et nihil ei dicunt numquid uere cognouerunt principes quia
hic est christus (27) sed hunc scimus unde sit··christus autem cum uenerit
nemo scit unde sit··

(28) Clamabat ergo docens intemplo ihesus [8]dicens etnescitis[9] etunde
sim scitis[10] (29) ego scio eum quia abipso sum·etipse me misit··

(30) Querebant ergo eum adprehendere[11] etnemo misit inillum manus
quia nondum uenerat hora eius··(31) deturba autem multi crediderunt ineum
etdicebant christus cum uenerit numquid plura signa faciet quamque hic
fecit[12] (32) audierunt farisei[13] turbam murmurantem deillo háec···7

Etmiserunt principes··etpharisei ministros utadprehenderent[14]·
(33) Dixit ergo ihesus adhúc modicum tempus uobis cum sum··etuado
adeum qui misit me (34) queritis me etnoninuenietis etubi sum ego uos
nonpotestis uenire·(35) Dixerunt ergo iudei adse ipsos quo hic iturus est Fol. 57.
quia noninueniemus eum numquid indispersionem gentium iturus est et-
docturus gentes (36) quis est hic sermo quem dixit queritis me etnon
inuenietis me[15] etubi sumego nonpotestis uenire (37) innouissimo autem dic

[1] Qui.
[2] miramini.
[3] Mosea.
[4] circumcisionem.
[5] Mose.
[6] solvatur.
[7] Hierosolymis.
[8] V. adds et.
[9] et me scitis.
[10] V. adds et a me ipso non veni sed est verus qui misit me, quem vos nescitis.
[11] apprehendere.
[12] facit?
[13] Pharisaei.
[14] Apprehenderent eum.
[15] V om.

mognouit[1] festiuitatis stabat ihesus etclamabat dicens··quis[2] sitit ueniat
adme etbibat (38) qui credit inme sicut dixit scriptura flumina deuentre eius
fluent[3] aque uiuæ··

(39) Hoc autem dixit despiritu[4] accepturi[5] erant credentes ineum nonenim erat spiritus datus quia ihesus nondum fuerat glorificatus··7

(40) Exilla ergo turba cum audisent[6] hos sermones eius dicebant hic[7]
uere propheta (41) alii dicebant hic est christus··

Quidam autem[8] numquid agaliliæ[9] christus uenit (42) nonne
scriptura dicit quia exsemine dauid[10] debethlem[11] castello ubi erat dauid
uenit christus··(43) Desensio[12] itaque facta est inturba propter eum··7

(44) Quidam[13] exipsís uobebant[14] adprehendere[15] eum sednemo misit
super illum manus (45) uenerunt·igitur[16] ministri ad pontifices etfariseos[17]
etdixerunt eís illi quare nonconduxistis[18] eum (46) responderunt ministri·
Fol. 57 b. numquam síc locutus est homo sicut híc homo··(47) Responderunt ergo
eis pharisei··Numquit[19] etuós seducti estis (48) numquid aliquis ex-
principibus credidit ineum aut exfariseis[20] (49) sed turba hec que[21] nouit
legem maledicti sunt (50) dicit nicodimus[22] adeos ille qui uenit adeum
nocte qui unus erat exipsis·

(51) Numquid léx nostra iudicat hominem nisi audierit prius[23] abipso
etcognouerit quid faciat·

(52) Responderunt[10] dixerunt ei numquid ettú galileus es·scrutare etuide quia propheta agalilea nonsurgit··(53) etreuersi sunt unus quisque
indomum suam··7

[Cap. VIII.] (1) Ihesus autem perrexit inmontem olieueti[24]··(2) [25]deluculo[26] iterum
uenit intemplum etomnis populus uenit adeum·etsedens docebat eos··

---

1 magno.
2 Qui.
3 fluent.
4 V. adds quem.
5 accepturi.
6 audissent.
7 V. adds est.
8 V. adds dicebant.
9 Galilaea.
10 V. adds et.
11 Bethleem.
12 dissensio.
13 V. adds autem.
14 volebant.
15 apprehendere.
16 ergo.
17 Pharisaeos.
18 adduxistis.
19 Numquid.
20 Pharisaeis.
21 V. adds non.
22 Nicodemus.
23 Ab ipso prius.
24 Oliveti.
25 V. adds et.
26 diluculo.

(3) Aducunt[1] autem scribæ et pharisei mulierem inadulterio deprehensam etstatuerunt eam inmedio (4) etdixerunt ei magister·Haće mulier modo deprehensa est inadulterio (5) in lege autem moyses[2] mandauit nobís·· Huiusmodi lapidare·tu ergo quid dicis (6) hæc autem dicebant temptantes[3] eum vt possint[4] accussare[5] eum··ihesus autem inclinans sé deorsum digito scribebat interram[6] (7) cum autem perseuerauerant[7] interrogantes eum··7 Erexit sé etdixit eis quis[8] ine peccato est uestrum primus inillam lapidem mittat··(8) et iterum sé inclinans scribebat interram[6] (9) audientes autem unus post unum exibant[9] incipientes asenioribus etremansit solus etmulier inmedio stans·(10) Erigens autem sé ihesus dixit ei mulier ubi sunt qui te accussabant[10] nemo te condemnauit··(11) que dixit nemo domine·dixit autem ihesus nec ego te condemnabo uade··etamplius iam noli peccare· (12) Iterum[11] locutus est eis ihesus dicens···7 Fol. 58.

Ego sum lúx mundi qui sequitur me nonambulauit[12] intenebris sed habebit lumen[13] uite··7

(13) Dixerunt ergo ei farisei[14] tú dete ipso testimonium perhibes testimonium tuum nonest uerum··

(14) Respondit ihesus etdixit eís etsi ego testimonium perhibeo deme ipso uerum est testimonium meum quia scio unde ueni etquo uado·uos autem nescitis unde ueni aut quo uado··(15) uós secundum carnem iudicatis·· Ego noniudicio[15] quemquam (16) etsi iudicio[15] ego iudicium meum uerum est quia solus nonsum··sed ego etqui misit[16] me pater··(17) etinlege uestra scriptum est quia duorum hominum testimonium uerum est·(18) Ego sum qui testimonium perhibeo deme ipso··ettestimonium perhibet deme pater[17]· Fol. 58 b.
qui me[18] misit pater··(19) dicebant ergo ei ubi est pater tuus··

Respondit ihesus··neque me scitis·neque patrem meum sí me sciritis[19] forsitán etpatrem meum sci[19]·

[1] Adducunt.
[2] Moses.
[3] temtantes.
[4] possent.
[5] accusare.
[6] terra.
[7] perseverarent.
[8] Qui sine.
[9] exiebant.
[10] V. om. these three words.
[11] V. adds ergo.
[12] ambulabit.
[13] lucem.
[14] Pharisaei.
[15] iudico.
[16] me misit.
[17] V. om.
[18] misit me.
[19] sciretis.

(20) Haec uerba locutus est ingazofilacio[1] docins[2] docens intemplo ··et- nemo adprehendit[3] eum··quia nec dum uenerit[4] hora eius·····7

(21) Dixit ergo iterum eis[5] ego uado etqueritis me etinpeccato uestro moriemini quo ego uado uós nonpotestis uenire·(22) Dicebant ergo iudei numquid interficiet semet ipsum··quia dicit quo ego uado uós nonpotestis uenire (23) etdicebat eis··uós[6] deorsum estis··Ego desupernís sum··uos demundo hoc estis··Ego nonsum dehóc mundo·(24) dixí ergo uobís quia moriemini inpeccatís uestris sí enim noncrediretis[7]·quia ego sum moriemini inpeccato uestro··(25) dicebant ergo ei et[2] tú quis es dicit[8] eís ihesus principium qui[9] ethæc[2] loquor uobís (26) multa habeo deuobís loqui etiudicare sed qui misit me uerax est et ego que audiui habeo[10] hec loquor inmundo (27) etnoncognouerunt quia patrem eís dicebat····7

(28) Dixit ergo eis ihesus··cum exaltaueritis filium hominis tunc cognoscetis quia ego sum··etame[11] ipso facio nihil sed sicut docuit me pater hec loquor (29) et qui misit[12] me mecum est·

Fol. 59. Nonreliquit me solum quia ego que placita sunt ei facio semper (30) **hec** illo loquente multi crediderunt ineum (31) dicebat ergo ihesus adeos qui crediderunt ei iudeos sí uós permanseritis[13] insermone meo··**uere** discipuli mei··eritis (32) etcognoscetis ueritatem··etueritás liberauit[14] uós· (33) responderunt ei·semen abrache[15] sumus etnemini seruiuimus umquam quomodo tú dicis liberi eritis··(34) respondit eís ihesus··7

Amén amén dico uobís quia omnis qui facit peccatum seruus est peccati··(35) seruus autem nonmanet indomo inæternum filius manet inæternum··7

(36) Si ergo filius uós liberauerit·uere liberieritis·(37) scio quia filii abrache[15] estis··sed queritis me interficere quia sermo meus noncapit inuobís **(38) Ego quod** uidi aput[16] patrem loquor etuos qui[17] uidistis aput[16] patrem **uestrum facitis** (39) responderunt etdixerunt ei pater noster abracham[18] est·

[1] gazophylacio.
[2] V. om.
[3] apprehendit.
[4] **venerat.**
[5] **V. adds Iesus.**
[6] V. adds de.
[7] credideritis.
[8] dixit.
[9] quia.
[10] ab eo.
[11] et a me.
[12] me misit.
[13] manseritis.
[14] liberabit.
[15] Abrahae.
[16] apud.
[17] quae.
[18] Abraham.

dicit[1] eís ihesus sí filii abrache[2] estis·opera abrache[2] facite·(40) Nunc
autem queritis me interficere hominem qui ueritatem locutus sum quam
audiui·adeo hoc abraham nonfecit··(41) Uós autem[3] facias[4] opera patris
uestri dixerunt itaque ei··Nós exfornicatione nonsumus nati···7 Unum Fol. 59 *b*.
patrem habemus deum··(42) Dixit ergo eís ihesus··

Sí deus pater uester[5]··diligeritis me utique[6] ego enim processi[7]
aexdeo etuenio[8] neque enim ame ipso ueni sed ille me misit·(43) quare
loquellam meam noncognoscetis[9] quia nonpotestis audire sermonem meum
(44) uos expatre zabulo[10] estis etdesideria patris uestri uultís facire[11] ille
homicida erat abinitio etinueritate nonstetit quianonest ueritas inco qui[12]
loquitur mendacium expropriis loquitur quia mendax est etpater eius
(45) Ego autem qui[13] ueritatem dico noncreditis mihi (46) quis exuobís
arguit me depeccato sí ueritatem dico quare uós noncreditis mihi (47) qui
exdeo[14] est uerba dei audit propterea uós nonauditis quia exdeo nonestis··
(48) Responderunt igitur iudei et dixerunt ei nonne benedicimus nos quia
samaritanus es tu etdemonium habes··(49) respondit·ihesus ego demonium
nonhabeo sed honorifico patrem meum etuós·inhonorastis[15] me (50) ego
autem nonquero gloriam meam··estqui querit etiudicat··

(51) Amén amén dico uobís siquis sermonem meum seruauerit mortem
nonuidebit inæternum···7

(52) Dixerunt ergo iudei nunc cognouimus quia demonium habes Fol. 60.
abracham mortuus est etprophete··ettu dicis si quis **sermonem** meum
seruauerit mortem[16] nongustauit inæternum (53) numquid tu maior es·
patre nostro abracham qui mortuus est etprofete[17] mortui sunt··quem te
ipsum facis·(54) respondit ihesus sí ergo[18] glorifico me ipsum··gloria mea
nihil est[19] pater meus qui glorificat me quem uos dicitis quia deus noster est
(55) etnoncognouitis[20] eum··Ego autem noui eum··etsí dixero quia nonscio
eum·ero similis uobís mendax **sed scio** eum etsermonem eius seruo

[1] Dixit.
[2] Abrahae.
[3] V. om.
[4] facitis.
[5] V. adds esset.
[6] utique me.
[7] ex deo processi.
[8] veni.
[9] cognoscitis.
[10] diabolo.
[11] facere.
[12] cum.
[13] quia.
[14] est ex deo.
[15] inhonoratis.
[16] non gustabit mortem.
[17] prophetæ.
[18] ego.
[19] V. adds est.
[20] cognovistis.

(56) abracham pater uester exultauit vtuideret diem meum etuidit etgauisus est··

(57) Dixerunt ergo iudei adeum quinquaginta annos nondum habes etabracham uidisti (58) dixit eis ihesus··

Amén amén dico uobis antequam abracham fieret ego sum (59) tulerunt ergo lapides vtiactarent[1] ineum ihesus autem abscondit se etexiuit detemplo··

[CAP. IX.] (1) Et preteriens uidit iohannem[2] cecum·anauitate[3] (2) etinterrogauerunt eum[4] discipuli eius[5] rabbi quis peccauit[6] neque[4] parentes eius vtcecus nasceretur··

Fol. 60 b. (3) Respondit ihesus neque hic peccauit neque parentes[7] sed utmanifestantur[8] opera[9] dei inillo (4) meo[10] por operari opera eiis[11] qui misit me donec dies est··7

Venit nox quando nemo potest operari (5) quandiu[12] inhoc[4] mundo sum lux sum mundi (6) hec cum dixisset et[4]expuit interram etfecit lutum exputo[13] etlinuit[14] lutum super occulos[15] eius·(7) etdixit ei uade et[16]laua **innatatoria** siloæ quod interpretatur misus[17] abiit ergo etlauit etuenit uidens (8) itaque uicini etqui uidebant eum prius quia mendicus erat[18] **dicebant** nonne **hic est qui** sedebat··etmendicabat (9) alii dicebant quia hic est··alii autem nequaquam··sed similis est eius ille dicebat quia ego sum (10) dicebant ergo ei quomodo aperti sunt occuli[19] tibi· (11) Respondit·ille homo quidicitur ihesus lutum fecit etunexit[20] occulos[21] meos··etdixit mihi uade adnatoriam siloæ etlaua etabii etlaui etuidi·(12) dixerunt ei ubi est ille ait··Nescio (13) adducunt eum adfariseos[22] qui cecus fuerat (14) erat autem sabbatum··quando lutum fecit ihesus etaperuit occulos[21] eius· (15) Iterum ergo interrogabant eum farisei[23] quomodo uidisset ille autem dixit

1 iacerent.
2 hominem.
3 natiuitate.
4 V. om.
5 sui.
6 V. adds hic aut.
7 V. **adds** eius.
8 manifestetur.
9 opus.
10 **me** oportet.
11 eius.
12 Quamdiu.
13 ex sputo.
14 levit.
15 oculos.
16 V. om.
17 missus.
18 V. adds et.
19 oculi.
20 unxit.
21 oculos.
22 Pharisaeos.
23 Pharisaei.

eis lutum possuit[1] mihisup er[2] etlaui etuideo··(16) dicebant ergo exfariseis[3] quidam nonest homo hic a deo qui[4] sabbatum noncustodit··

Alii dicebant quomodo potest homo peccator hæc signa facire[5] Fol. 61.
etscisma erat ineis··

(17) Et[6]dicunt ergo ceco iterum tuquid dicis deeo quiaperuit occulos[7] tuos ille autem dixit quia profeta[8] (18) noncrediderunt ergo iudei deillo qui[9] cecus fuisset etuidisset donec uocauerunt parentes eius quiuiderat (19) etinterrogauerunt eos dicentes hic est filius uester quem uos dicitis quia cecus natus est quomodo ergo nunc uidet (20) responderunt eís parentes eius etdixerunt·scimus[10] híc[11] filius noster··Et quia cecus natus est·(21) quomodo autem nunc uidet[12] nescimus aut quis eius **aperuit occulos[7]** [13]nescimus·ipsum interrogate ætatem habet ipse dese loquatur··(22) hǽc dixerunt parentes eius quia timebant iudeos iam enim conspirauerant iudei·· vtsíquis eum confiteretur christum extra sinagogam[14] fieret (23) propteria parentes eius dixerunt qui[15] habet ætatem ipsum interrogate (24) uocauerunt ergo rursum hominum[16] qui fuerat cecus etdixerunt ei··Dá gloriam deo nós scimus quia híchomo peccator est (25) dixit ergo ille sí peccator est nescio unum scio·quia cecus cum essem modo uideo·(26) dixerunt ergo illi quid fecit tibi quomodo aperuit tibi occulos[7]··(27) Respondit eís dixi nobís iam etaudistis quid iterum uultís[17] discipuli eius··

Hieri (28) male dixerunt ei·etdixerunt tú discipulus illius es·· Fol. 61 b.
Nos autem moysi[18] discipuli sumus (29) nos scimus quia[19] mosi locutus est deus hunc autem nescimus unde sit··(30) Respondit·ille homo[20] dixit eís inhoc enim mirabile est·quianós nescitis unde sit etaperuit meos occulos[7] (31) scimus quia peccatores deus nonaudit sed sí quis dei cultor est etuoluntatem eius facit hunc exaudit (32) asseculo nonest auditum quia aparuit[21] quis occulos[7] ceci nati··(33) Nisi esset hic adeo·nonpoterat[22]

---

1 posuit.
2 V. adds oculos.
3 Pharisaeis.
4 quia.
5 facere.
6 V. om.
7 oculos.
8 propheta est.
9 quia.
10 V. adds quia.
11 V. adds est.
12 videat.
13 V. adds nos.
14 synagogam.
15 quia aetatem habet.
16 hominem.
17 V. adds audire? numquid et vos vultis.
18 Mosi.
19 quoniam.
20 V. adds et.
21 aperuit.
22 V. adds facere.

quicquam·(34) responderunt etdixerunt ei inpeccatis natus es totus·cttu
doces nos etæcierunt[1] eum foras (35) audiuit ihesus quia ecierunt[1] eum
foras etcum inuenisset eum dixit[2] et[3]tú dixisset[4] et[3]infilium dei·(36)
respondit·ille etdixit··quisest **domine** vteredam ineum··(37) etdixit ei
ihesus et uidisti eum·etqui loquitur tecum ipseest (38) at ille ait··7

Credo domine etprocedens[5] adorauit eum·(39) et[6] dixit ei ihesus
iniudicium ego inhunc mundum ueni vtqui nonuident uideant etqui uideant[7]
caecifiant (40) etaudierunt exfariseís[8]··7 Quicum ipso erant etdixerunt ei
numquid etnos cæci sumus·(41) dixit eís ihesus si cæci essetis nonhaberetis
Fol. 62. peccatum nunc **vero dicitis** quia uidemus·peccatum uestrum manet···7

[Cap. X.] (1) Amen amen dico uobis qui nonintrat perostium inouile ouium sed
ascendit aliunde ille fúr **est** etlatro (2) qui autem intrat perostialum[9]
postor[10] est ouium···7

(3) Huic ostiarius aperit etoues uocemeius audiunt etproprias oues
uocat nominatim eteducit eas·(4) et cum proprias ouis[11]emiserit··ante eas
uadit **etoues** illum secuntur quia sciunt uocem eius··(5) alienum autem
nonsecuntur[12] **sed** fugiunt[13] abeo quia[14] uoluerunt[15] uocem alienorum (6)
hoc prouerbium··dixit **eis**[16] ihesus illi autem noncognouerunt quid
loqueretur eís·(7) dixit ergo eis iterum ihesus··

Amen amen dico uobis quia ego sum ostium ouium (8) omnes quot
quot uenerunt fures sunt etlatrones sed nonaudierunt eos oues (9) ego sum
ostium··perme síquis introierit saluabitur etingredietur etegredietur
etpascua inueniet··(10) fúr nonuenit nisi vtfuretur etmactet etperdat ego
ueni vtuitam habeant ethabundantius[17] habeant··7

(11) Ego sum pastor bonus··bonus pastoranimam suam dat prouibus[18]···7
Fol. 62 b. (12) Mercenárius etqui nonest pastor·cuius nonsunt oues propriæ uidit[19]
lupum uenientem: etdemittit[20] oues etfugit etlupus rapit etdispergit oues

1 eiecerunt.
2 V. adds ei.
3 V. om.
4 credis.
5 procidens.
6 V. om.
7 vident.
8 Pharisaeis.
9 per ostium.
10 pastor.
11 oves.
12 non sequentur.
13 fugient.
14 V. adds non.
15 noverunt.
16 illis.
17 et abundantius.
18 pro ovibus.
19 videt.
20 dimittet.

(13) mercinarius[1] autem fugit··quia mercinarius[1] est etnonpertinet adeum deouibus (14) ego sum pastor bonus·etcognosco meas etcognoscunt me·[2] (15) Sicut nouit me pater etego cognosco[3] patrem··Et animam meam pono proouibus··

(16) Et alias oues habeo que nonsunt exhoc ouili··etillas oportet me adducere etuocem meam audient etfiet unum ouile··etunus pastor (17) propterea me pater diligit quia ego pono animam meam··vtiterum sumam eam· (18) nemo tollit eam ame·sed ego pono eam ame·ipso potestatem habeo ponendi eam etpotestatem habeo **iterum** sumendi eam·hoc mandatum accipi[4] apatre[5]·

(19) Discensio[6] iterum facta est iter[7] iudeos propter sermones hós· (20) dicebant autem multi exipsis demonium habet[8] insanit quid **cum** auditis··(21) Alii dicebant hæc uerba nonsunt··demonium habentis numquid demonium potest cecorum occulos[9] aperire····7

(22) Facta sunt autem incenia[10] inhierusolimís[11] ethiempserat[12] (23) Fol. 63.
etambulabat ihesus intemplo inportico[13] salomonis·(24) circumdederunt ergo eum iudei etdicebant ei··7

Quo usque animam nostram tollis sítúes christus dic nobis palam·· (25) Respondit·eís ihesus loquor uobis etnoncreditis opera que ego facio innomine patris mei··Hec testimonium perhibent deme··(26) sed uos non creditis quia nonestis[14] ouibus meis (27) oues meæ uocem meam audiunt·etego cognosco eas etsecuntur me··(28) etego uitam eternam dono[15] eís etnonperibunt ineternum··et[16]nonrapiet eas quisquam demanu mea (29) pater meus quod dedit mihi maius omnibus[17] etnemo potest rapere demanu patris mei· (30) Ego etpater unum sumus (31) sustullerunt[18] lapides iudei vtlapidarent eum··(32) Respondit·eís ihesus multa opera bona ostendi uobís expatre meo propterquod eorum opus me lapidatis··(33) Responderunt ei iudei debono opere nonlapidamus te[19] deblasfemia[20] etquia tu homo cum sis··facis te

---

[1] mercennarius.
[2] V. adds meae.
[3] agnosco.
[4] accepi.
[5] V. adds meo
[6] Dissensio.
[7] inter.
[8] V. adds et.
[9] oculos.
[10] encenia.
[11] Hierosolymis.
[12] hiems erat.
[13] porticu.
[14] V. adds ex.
[15] do.
[16] V. om.
[17] V. adds est.
[18] sustulerunt.
[19] V. adds sed.
[20] blasphemia.

ipsum deum··(34) Respondit·eis ihesus nonne scriptum est inlege uestra·
Fol. 63 b. Quia ego dixi dii estis·(35) et[1]illos dixit deos et[2]quos sermo dei factus est
etnonpotest solui scriptura (36) quem ergo[3] pater sanctificauit etmisit
inmundum uós dicitis qui[4] blasphemat[5] quia dixi filius dei sum··

(37) Sí nonfacio opera patris mei nolite credere mihi·(38) sí autem facio
etsí mihi nonuultis credere operibus credite vtcognoscatis etcredatis quia
inme[6] pater etego inpatre···

(39) Querebant ergo eum adprehendere[7] etexiuit demanibus eorum (40)
etabiit iterum trans iordanén ineum locum ubi erat iohannes babtizans
primum etmansit illíc··7

(41) Et multi uenerunt[8] adeum etdicebant quia iohannis[9] quidem signum fecit nullum (42) omnia[10] quecunque[11] dixit iohannis[9]·dehóc uera
erant etmulti crediderunt ineum···7

[Cap. XI.] (1) Erat autem quidam languens lazarus abethania decastello mariæ
etmarthe sororis eius (2) maria autem erat que uncxit[12] dominum ungento
etextersit pedes eius capillís eius[13] cuius frater lazarus infirmabatur (3) misserunt[14] ergo sorores adeum·dicentes domine·ecce quem amas infirmatur
Fol. 64. (4) audiens[15] ihesus dixit eís infirmitas hec nonest admortem··sed progloria
dei vtglorificetur filius dei pereum[16] (5) diligebat autem ihesus martham
etsororem eius mariam etlazarum (6) vtergo vt[17]audiuit quia infirmabatur
tunc quidem mansit ineodem loco duobus diebus (7) deinde post hec dicit
discipulis suis·· Eamus iniudiam[18] iterum (8) discipuli[19] dicunt rabi[20]
nunc querebant te iudei lapidare[21] etiterum uadis illúc··

(9) Respondit ihesus nonne duocem[22] hore sunt dici síquis ambulauerit indie nonoffendit quia lucem huius mundi uidet·(10) si autem
ambulauerit nocte offendit[23] quia lux nonest ineo··7

[1] Si.
[2] ad.
[3] V. om.
[4] quia.
[5] blasphemas.
[6] V. adds est.
[7] prendere.
[8] veniebant.
[9] Iohannes.
[10] V. adds autem.
[11] quaecumque.
[12] unxit.
[13] suis.
[14] miserunt.
[15] V. adds autem.
[16] per eam.
[17] V. om.
[18] in Iudaeam.
[19] Dicunt ei discipuli.
[20] Rabbi.
[21] lapidare Iudaei.
[22] duodecim.
[23] offendet.

(11) Hecait etpost hoc dicit eis··lazarus amicus noster dormit sed uado
vtasumno[1] exsuscitem eum·(12) dixerunt ergo discipuli eius domine sí dor-
mit saluus erit·(13) dixerat autem ihesus demorte eius illi autem putuerunt
quia dedormitione somni[2] diceret··7

(14) Tunc ergo dixit eis ihesus manifeste lazarus mortuus est (15) et-
gaudeo propter uos vteredatis quoniam noneram[3] sed eamus adeum··
(16) dixit ergo thomas qui dicitur dedimus[4] adcondiscipulos suos[5] eamus
etnos utmoriamur cum eo····7··7

(17) Uenit itaque ihesus etinuenit eum quatuor[6] diebus[7] iaminmonu- Fol. 64 b.
mento iacentem[8]··(18) Erat autem bethania iuxta hierusolimam[9] quassi[10]
stadis[11] quindecim (19) multi autem ex iudeis uenerant admartham··et-
mariam vteonsularentur[12] eas defratre suo··7

(20) Martha ergo utaudiuit quia ihesus uenit occurrit illi maria autem
domi sedebat···7

(21) Dixit ergo martha et[13] ihesum domine sí tú[14] fuisses hic frater
meus nonfuisset mortuus (22) sedet nunc·scio quia que cumque poposceris
adeo dabit tibi deus[14]··(23) dicit illi ihesus resurget frater tuus·(24) dicit ei
martha scio quia resurget inresurrectione innouissimo[15] die··(25) dixit ei
ihesus·Ego sum resurrectio etuita qui credit inme etiam sí mortuus fuerit
uiuit[16] (26) etomnis qui uiuit etcredit inme nonmorietur inæternum···7

Credis hoc (27) at[17] illa[18] utique domine·[19]credidi **quia tu es**
christus filius dei qui inmundum uenisti (28) etcum **hec dixisset abiit et-**
uocauit mariam sororem suam sílentio dicens magister **adest ad[14] uocat te**
(29) illa vtaudiuit surgit cito···7

Etuenit adeum (30) nondum enim uenerat ihesus incastellum Fol. 65.
sederat adhuc inillo loco ubi acurrerat[20] ei martha (31) iudei igitur quierant
cum ea[21] indomo etconsulabuntur[22] eam cum uidissent mariam quam[23] cito

[1] somno.
[2] somnii.
[3] V. adds ibi.
[4] Didymus.
[5] V. om.
[6] quattuor.
[7] dies.
[8] habentem.
[9] Hierosolyma.
[10] quasi.
[11] stadiis.
[12] consolarentur.
[13] ad.
[14] V. om.
[15] in novissima.
[16] vivet.
[17] Ait.
[18] illi.
[19] **V. adds** ego.
[20] occurrerat.
[21] illa.
[22] consolabantur.
[23] quia.

surrexit etexit[1] secuti sunt eam dicentes quia uadit admonumentum vtploret ibi (32) maria ergo cum uenisset ubi erat ihesus uidens eum·cecidit adpedes eius··etdixit ei domine si fuisses híc nonesset mortuus frater meus (33) ihesus ergo ui[2] uidit eam plorantem··et iudeos qui uenerant cum ea plorantes·· fremuit spiritu[3] turbant[4] sé ipsum·(34) etdixit ubi possuisti[5] eum dicunt ei domine ueni etuide (35) etlacrimatus est ihesus·(36) dixerunt ergo[6] iudei·· ecce quomodo amabat eum (37) quidam autem dixerunt exipsis nonpoterat híc qui aperuit occulos[7] ceci facire[8] utet hic non morietur[9]··(38) ihesus ergo rursum fremens insemet ipso uenit admonumentum erat autem spelunca etlapis super possitus[10] erat ei·(39) ait ihesus tollite lapidem·dicit ei martha soror eius qui mortuus fuerat····7

Fol. 65 b. Domine iam fœtet quadriduanus enim est·(40) dicit ei ihesus·nonne ego[6] dixi tibi quoniam si credederis[11] uidebis gloriam dei (41) tolle[12] ergo lapidem ihesus autem eleuatis sursum··7 occulis[13] dixit pater gratias ago tibi quoniam audisti me (42) ego autem sciebam quia semper me audis sed propter populum qui circumstant[14]·dixi vtcredant quia tu me misisti (43) hec cum dixisset uoce magna exclamauit[15] lazare ueni foras (44) etstatim prodit[16] qui fuerat mortuu ligatus pedes etmanus institís etfacies illius sudario erat ligata·dicit ihesus eis soluite eum etsinite abire (45) multi ergo exiudeis qui uenerant admariam etuiderant que fecit crediderunt ineum (46) quidam autem exipsis abierunt adfariscos[17] et dixerunt eís que fecit ihesus (47) colligerunt[18] ergo pontifices etpharisci fecerunt[6] concilium·**et** dicebant quid facimus quia híc homo multa signa facit··(48) si dimittimus eum síc omnes credent[19] ineum etuenient romani ettollent nostrum etlocum etgentem (49) unus autem exipsis caiphas[20]····7

Fol. 66. Cum esset pontifex anni illius dixit eís **uos** nescitis quicquam nec cogitatis quia expedit nobís vtunus moriatur homo propopulo etnontota gens pereat··

1 exiit.
2 ut.
3 V. adds et.
4 turbavit.
5 posuistis.
6 V. om.
7 oculos.
8 facere.
9 moreretur.
10 positus.
11 credideris.
12 Tulerunt.
13 oculis.
14 circumstat.
15 clamavit.
16 prodiit.
17 Pharisaeos.
18 collegerunt.
19 credunt.
20 Caiaphas.

(51) Hoc autem asemet ipso nondixit sed cum esset pontifex anni illius prophetauit quia Ihesus moriturus erat progente (52) etnontantum progente sed etut filios dei qui erant dispersi congregaret inunum··7

(53) Abillo ergo die cogitauerunt vtinterficerent eum·(54) Ihesus ergo iam noninpalam ambulabat apud iudeos··sed abiit inregionem iuxta desertum inciuitatem que dicitur effrem[1] et ibi morabatur·cum discipulis suis[2]··7

(55) Proximum autem erat phasca iudeorum·Etascenderunt multi in-[2] hierusolima[3] deregione[4] phasca[5] vtsanctificarent se ipsos (56) querebant ergo ihesum··etconloquebantur adinuicem intemplo stantes quid putatis quia nonuenit[6] addiem festum (57) dederant autem pontifices et farisei[7] mandatum vtsiquis cognouerit ubi sit indicet vtadprehendant[8] eum·

[Cap. XII.] (1) Ihesus ergo antes[9] exdies pasche··7 uenit in[2]bethaniam **ubi** Fol. 66 b. lazurus[10] fuerat mortuus quem sus citauit[11] ihesus···

(2) Fecerunt autem ei cenam ibi etmartha ministrabat lazurus uero unus erat exdiscumbentibus cum eo·(3) maria ergo accipiens[12] libram ungenti nardipistici pretiosi unexit[13] pedes ihesu··etextèrsit capillis suis pedes eius··et domus impleta[14] est adore[15] ungenti (4) dicit ergo unus **ex** discipulis eius iudas scariothís[16]·qui erat cum traditurus **(5)** quare **hoc** ungentum nonuenit[17] tregentis[18] denarís[19]·et datum esset[20] egenís (6) dixit autem hoc nonquia deegenís pertinebat adeum sed quia fúr **erat** etloculos habens ea que mittebantur portabat···7

(7) Dixit ergo ihesus sine illam vtindiem[21] sepulture meæ seruet illud· (8) pauperes enim[22] habebitis[23] uobiscum me autem nonsemper habebitis·[23] (9) cognouit ergo turba multa exiudeis quia **illic est etuenerunt** nonproter

---

1 Efrem.
2 V. om.
3 Hierosolyma.
4 V. adds ante.
5 pascha.
6 veniat.
7 Pharisaei.
8 apprehendant.
9 ante sex dies.
10 fuerat Lazarus.
11 suscitavit.
12 accepit.
13 unxit.
14 impleta.
15 ex odore.
16 Scariotis.
17 venlit.
18 trecentis.
19 denariis.
20 est.
21 in die.
22 V. adds semper.
23 habetis.

ihesum tantum sed vtlazarum uiderent quem suscitauit amortuis·(10)
Cogitauerunt autem principes sacerdotum vt[1]lazarum interficerent· (11)
Fol. 67. quia multi propter illum abibant exiudeís etcredebant inihesum···7

(12) Incrastinum autem turba multa que uenerat addiem festum cum
audissent quia uenit ihesus··hierusolima (13) acceperunt ramós palmarum
etprocesserunt obiam[2] ei·etclamabant ós anna benedictus qui uenit innomine domini réx israhél···7

(14) Etinuenit ihesus asellum[3] sedit super eum sicut scriptum est·(15)
nolii[4] timere filia sión·ecce rex tuus uenit sedens super pullum asinæ··

(16) Haec noncognouerunt discipuli eius primum··sed cando[5] glorificatus
est ihesus tunc recordati sunt··quia hæc scripta[6] erant deeo··ethec fecerunt
ei·(17) testimonium ergo perhibebat turba que erat cum eo quando
lazarum uocauit demonumento etsuscitauit eum amortuís (18) propterea
etouiam[7] uenit ei turba qui[8] audierunt eum fecisse hóc signum (19) farisei[9]
ergo dixerunt ad semet ipsos uidetis·quia nihil proficimus·ecce mundus
totus post eum abiit (20) erant autem gentiles quidam exeis[10]···7

Qui ascenderant vt adorauerunt[11]··indie festo hii[12] ergo acces-
Fol. 67 b. serunt adpilippum[13] qui erat abethsaida galiliæ[14] etrogabant eum dicentes
domine uolumus ihesum uidere··

(22) Uenit pilippus[15] etdicit andrea[16]·andrias[17] **rursus[18]·et** pilippus[15]
dixerunt[19] ihesu··(23) Ihesus autem respondit eis dicens uenit hora·
vtclarificetur[20] filius hominis···7

(24) Amén amén dico uobis quia[21] nisi granum frumenti cadens interram
mortuum fuerit·(25) ipsum solum manet·sí autem mortuum fuerit multum
fructum adfert·qui amat animam suam perdet eam·et qui odit animam
suam·Inhoc mundo ínuitam eternam custodit eam··(26) si quís mihi
ministrat me sequatur·etubi sum ego illíc[22] minister meus erit··si quis

---

[1] V. adds et.
[2] obviam.
[3] V. adds et.
[4] Noli.
[5] quando.
[6] erant scripta.
[7] obviam.
[8] quia.
[9] Pharisaei.
[10] ex his.
[11] adorarent.
[12] hi.
[13] Philippum.
[14] Galilaeae.
[15] Philippus.
[16] Andreae.
[17] Andreas.
[18] rursum.
[19] dicunt.
[20] glorificetur.
[21] V. om.
[22] V. adds et.

mihi ministrauit[1] honorificauit[2] cum pater meus··(27) Nunc anima mea turbata est etquiddicam pater salui fica me exhác[3] hora··

Sed propterea ueni inhoram hanc (28) pater clarificatum[4] nomen uenit ergo uox decelo et clarificaui etiterum clarificabo (29) turba ergo que stabat etaudiebat[5] dicebat[6] tonitruum factum esset[7] alii dicebant Fol. 68.
angelus ei locutus est··7

(30) Respondit ihesus etdixit nonpropter me uóx hec uenit sed propter uos (31) nunc iudicium est mundi nunc princeps mundi[8] huius eicietur foras·

(32) Et ego sí exaltatus fuero aterra omnia traham adme ipsum··(33) hoc autem dicebant[9] significans qua morte esset moriturus··(34) Respondit·ei turba nos audiuimus exlege quiachristus manet inæternum· etquomodo tudicis oportet exaltari filium hominis[10]··7

(35) Dixit ergo eis[11] ihesus adhuc modicum lumen inuobis est ambulate dum lucem habetis vtnon tenebre uós conprehendant··et qui ambulat intenebris nescit quo uadat (36) dum lucem habetis··credite inlucem vtfilii lucis sitis·hæc locutus est[12] ihesus et abiit et abscondit se abeís··(37) Cum autem tanta signa fecisset coram eís noncredebant incum·(38) vtsermo esaiæ prophete inpleretur quem dixit domine quis crededit[13] auditui nostro etbrachium domini·cui reuelatum est··(39) propterea nonpoterant credere quia iterum dixit essaias[14] (40) excecauit deus[15] occulos[16] eorum··et indurauit eorum cor··vtuideant[17] occulís[18] etintellegant corde etconuertantur Fol. 68 b.
et sanem eos··

(41) Hec dixit essaias[14] quando[19] gloriam eius etlocutus est deo[20] (42) uerumtamen[21] ex principibus multi crediderunt ineum sed propter fariseos[22] nonconfitebantur vtdesinagoga[23] nonei[24] querentur (43) dilexerunt enim gloriam hominum magis quam gloriam dei··7

---

1 ministrabit.
2 honorificabit.
3 ex hora hac.
4 clarifica tuum.
5 audierat.
6 dicebant.
7 esse.
8 huius mundi.
9 dicebat.
10 V. adds quis est iste filius hominis.
11 V. om.
12 V. adds eis.
13 credidit.
14 Esaias.
15 V. om.
16 oculos.
17 non videant.
18 oculis.
19 V. adds vidit.
20 de eo.
21 V. adds et.
22 Pharisaeos.
23 synagoga.
24 non eicerentur.

(44) Ihesus autem clamauit etdixit qui credit inme noncredit inme·sed
ineum qui misit me (45) etqui uidet me uidet eum qui missit[1] me··7
(46) Ego lúx inmundum ueni vtomnis qui credit inme intenebrís non-
maneat··(47) etsí quis audierit uerba mea etnoncustodierit ego noniudicio
eum nonenim ueni vtiudicem mundum sed vtsaluificem mundum (48) qui
spernit me··et[2] accipit uerba mea··habet qui iudicet eum sermo quem
locutus sum ille iudicauit[3] eum·innouissimo die (49) quia ego exme **ipso**
nonsum locutus est[4] sed qui misit me pater ipse mihi mandatum dedit **quid**
dicam etquid loquar (50) etscio quia mandatum eius uita eterna est que[5]
Fol. 69. ego loquor·sicut dixit mihi pater síc loquor···7

[Cap. XIII.] (1) Ante diem autem festum pasce[6] sciens ihesus quia uenit eius hora
vttranseat de[7]hoc mundo adpatrem cum dilexisset suos qui erant inmundo
usque[4] infinem dilexit eos·(2) etcena facta est[4] cum zabulus[8] **iam**
missiset[9] incorde vttraderet eum iudas simón scaríothis[10]·(3) Sciens quia
omnia dedit ei pater inmanum[11] etquia adeo exiuit etaddeum uadit··
(4) Surgit acena·etponit uestimenta sua etcum accipisset[12] linteum
precinexit[13] sé (5) deinde mittit aquam inpiluem[14] etcoepit lauare pedes
discipulorum·Et extergere linteo quo erat precinctus·(6) uenit ergo adsimonem petrum·etdicit ei petrus domine tú mihi lauas pedes··7
(7) Respondit ihesus etdicit ei quod ego **facio et[4] tu nescis modo··scies**
autem postea (8) dicit ei petrus nonlauis[15] mihi pedes **inæternum··**
Respondit ei[16]ihesus etsi[17] nonlauero té nonhabebis[18] partem
mecum·(9) dicit ei simón petrus domine nontantum pedes meos sedet manus
etcaput··7
Fol. 69 b. (10) Dicit ei ihesus qui locutus[19] est nonindiget vtlauet[20] sed est
mundus totus etuós mundi estis··sed nonomnes (11) sciebat enim quisnam
esset quitraderet eum propterea dixit nonestis mundi omnes (12) postquam

[1] **misit.**
[2] **V. adds non.**
[3] **iudicabit.**
[4] **V. om.**
[5] **V. adds ergo.**
[6] paschae.
[7] ex.
[8] Diabolus.
[9] misisset.
[10] Simonis Scariotis.
[11] manus.
[12] accepisset.
[13] praecinxit.
[14] pelvem.
[15] lavabis.
[16] Iesus ei.
[17] **si.**
[18] **habes.**
[19] **lotus.**
[20] **nisi** ut pedes lavet.

ergo lauit pedes eorum··etaccipisset[1] uestimenta sua cum recumbuisset[2]
iterum dixit eis·scitis quid fecerim uobis (13) uós uocatis me magister·
etdomine etbenedictis[3] sum etenim
(14) Si ergo[4] laui pedes uestros dominus etmagister etuos debetis alter
alterius lauare pedes·(15) exemplum·enim dedi uobis·vtquemadmodum
ego feci uobis·ita[5] etuós faciatis··
(16) Amén amén dico uobis nonest seruus maior domino suo·neque
apostulus maior eo qui misit illum (17) sí hæc scitis beati eritis sí facieritis[6]
ea··
(18) Nondeomnibus uobís dico ego enim[7] scio quos elegeri[8] sed vtinpleatur scriptura·qui manducat mecum panem leuauit[9] contra me
calcaneum suum··(19) Amodo dico uobís priusquam fiat vtcum factum
fuerit credatis[10] quia ego sum···7
(20) Amén amén dico uobis qui accipit sí quem missero[11] me accipit qui
autem me accipit accipit eum qui me missit[12]····7
(21) Cum hec dixisset ihesus turbatus estspiritu etprotestatus est etdixit··7 Fol. 70.
Amén amén dico uobís quia unus exuobis tradet me··
(22) Aspiciebant ergo adinuicem discipuli hessitantes[13] dequo diceret·
(23) Erat ergo recumbens unus exdiscipulis eius insinu ihesu quem diligebat ihesus (24) innuit ergo huic simón petrus etdicit ei quis est dequo
dicit (25) itaque cum recumbuisset[14] ille supra pectus ihesu dicit ei··
Domine quis est (26) cui·respondit ihesus illeest cui ego intinctum panem
porrexero etcum intinxisset panem··dedit iudæ simoni scariothis[15] (27)
etpost bucellam[16]·tunc introuit inillum·satanas··7
Dicit ei ihesus·quod facis faccitius·(28) hócautem nemo sciuit discumbentium adquid dixerit ei (29) quidam enim putabant quia locolos[17]
habebat iudas quia dicit ei ihesus eme ea que opus sunt nobis addiem

---

1 accepit.
2 recubuisset.
3 dicitis.
4 V. adds ego.
5 V. adds et.
6 feceritis.
7 V. om.
8 elegerim.
9 levabit.
10 ut credatis cum factum fuerit.
11 misero.
12 misit.
13 hesitantes.
14 recubuisset.
15 Simonis Scariotis.
16 buccellam.
17 loculos.

festum aut egenis vtaliquid daret·(30) cum ergo accipisset[1] ille bucellam[2]·
exiuit continuo·erat enim[3] nox···7

Fol. 70 *b*. (31) Cum ergo exisset dicit ihesus nunc clarificatus est filius hominis·
etdeus clarificatus est ineo··(32) sí[4] clarificatus est ineo·etdeus clarificabit eum·insemet ipso··etcontin[5] clarificabit eum··7

(33) Filioli adhúc modicum uobiscum sum queritis me·etsicut dixi
iudeis quo ego uado uos nonpotestis uenire etuobis dico modo (34) mandatum nouum·dó uobís utdiligatis inuicem·sicut dilexi uós vtdet[6] uos
diligatis inuicem (35) inhóc cognoscent omnes·quia mei discipuli estis sí
dilectionem habueritis adinuecem[7]··7

(36) Dicit ei simon petrus domine quo uadis·respondit·ihesus quo ego
uado nonpotes me modo sequi·sequeris autem postea··(37) Dicit ei
petrus quare nonpossum sequi[8] te modo·animam meam prote ponam·
(38) Respondit·ihesus animam tuam prome pones··7

Amén amén dico tibi noncantauit[9] gallus donec ter[10] me neges··7

[Cap. XIV.] (1) Nonturbetur cor uestrum creditis indeum etnonme[11] credite (2) indomo patris mei mansionis[12] multe sunt sí quominus dixissem uobis quia
Fol. 71. uado parare uobís locum (3) et sí abiero·et preparauero uobis locum iterum
uenio etaccipiam uós adme ipsum vtubi sum ego etuos sitis·(4) etquo ego
uado scitis·etuiam scitis·(5) dicit ei thomas domine nescimus quo uadis
etquomodo possumus uiam scire·(6) dicit ei ihesus··

Ego sum uia etueritas etuita nemo uenit adpatrem nisi perme··7

(7) Si cognouistis[13] me etpatrem meum utique cognouissetis utique[14]
amodo cognoscetis[15] eum·etuidistis eum··(8) Dicit ei filippus[16] domine
ostende nobis patrem etsufficit nobis···

(9) Dicit ei ihesus tanto tempore uobiscum sum etnoncognouistis me
filippe[17] quiuidet[18] me uidet etpatrem quomodo tu dicis ostende nobis patrem

---

[1] accepisset.
[2] buccellam.
[3] autem.
[4] V. adds deus.
[5] continuo.
[6] ut et.
[7] invicem.
[8] te sequi.
[9] cantabit.
[10] me ter.
[11] et in me.
[12] mansiones.
[13] cognovissetis.
[14] et.
[15] cognoscitis.
[16] Philippus.
[17] Philippe.
[18] vidit.

(10) noncredis[1] quia ego inpatre etpater inme est·uerbaque ego loquor uobís ame ipso nonloquor pater autem inme manens ipse facit opera (11) noncreditis quia ego inpatre etpater inme est·(12) alioquín propter operam[2] ipsam credite··

Amen amen dico uobis qui credit inme opera que ego facio etipse faciet etmaiora horum faciet·quia ego adpatrem uado··7 Fol. 71 b.

(13) Et quod cumque petieritis innomine meo hoc faciam vtglorificetur pater infilio·(14) Siquit[3] petieritis[4] innomine meo hoc faciam·(15) Si diligitis me mandata mea seruate·(16) et ego rogabo patrem etalium paraclitum[5] dabit uobis vtmaneat uobiscum inæternum (17) spiritum ueritatis quem mundus nonpotest accipere quia nonuidet eum nescit[6] eum·uos autem cognoscetis[7] eum quia aput[8] uós manebit etinuobis erit (18) nonrelinquam uos orfanos[9] et[10]uos (19) adhúc modicum etmundus me iam nonuidet uos autem uidetis me quia bitis[11] ego uiuo etuós uiuetis (20) inillo die uox[12] cognoscetis quia ego sum inpatre meo etuos inme etego inuobis (21) qui habet mandata mea etseruat ea ille·qui diligit me··

Qui autem diligit me diligetur apatre meo·etego diligam eum etmanifestabo et[13] me ipsum··

(22) Dicit ei iudas nonille scariothis[14] domine quid factum est quia nobis manifesturus[15] es te ipsum etnonmundo···7

(23) Respondit·ihesus etdixit ei si quis diligit me sermonem[16] seruabit· Fol. 72.
etpater meus diligit[17] eum·7 Et adeum ueniemus etmansionis[18] aput[8] eum faciemus·(24) qui nondigilit me sermonem meum[19] **aput eum** faciemus· qui nondiligit me sermonem meum[20] nonseruat··7

Etsermo[21] quemaudistis nonest meus sed eius qui missit[22] me patris (25) hæc locutus sum uobis aput[8] uos manens··7

(26) Paraclitus[23] autem inspiritus[24] sanctus quem mittet pater innomine

---

[1] creditis.
[2] opera ipsa.
[3] Si quid.
[4] V. adds me.
[5] paracletum.
[6] nec scit.
[7] cognoscitis.
[8] apud.
[9] V. adds veniam.
[10] ad.
[11] V. om.
[12] Vos.
[13] **ei.**
[14] Scariotis.
[15] manifestaturus.
[16] V. adds meum.
[17] diliget.
[18] mansiones.
[19] sermones meos.
[20] a repetition.
[21] sermonem.
[22] me misit.
[23] paracletus.
[24] spiritus.

meo ille uos docebit omnia etsurgeret[1] uobis omniaquecunque dixero
uobis·(27) pacem meam dó uobis pacem relinquo uobis[2]·Nonquomodo
mundus dat ego do uobis nonturbetur cor uestrum neque formidet (28)
audistis quia ego dixi **uobis uado etuenio et[3] uos** si diligeretis me gaude-
retis utique quia uado adpatrem **quia pater maior me est·**

(29) Etnunc dixi uobis priusquam fiat vtcum factum fuerit credatis (30)
iam nonmulta loquar uobiscum uenit enim princeps mundi huius etinme
nonhabet quicquam (31) sed vtcognoscat mundus quia diligo patrem etsi[4]
[Cap. XV.] mandatum dedit mihi pater síc facio surgite eamus hinc (1) ego sum uitis
uera et pater meus agricula[5] est (2) omnem palmitem·inmé nonferente[6]
Fol. 72 b. fructum tollet eum··etomnem qui fert fructum purgauit[7] eum vtfructum
plus adferat (3) iam uos mundi estis propter sermonem quem loqutus[8] uobís
(4) manete inme etego inuobis si[9] palmes nonpotest facere[10] fructum·
asemet ipso nisi manserit inuite·síc nec uos nisi manseritis[11] INme··7

(5) Ego sum uitis uos autem[12] palmites qui manet inme etego ineo hic
fert fructum multum quodsine me nihil potestis facere (6) si quis inme non-
manserit··mittetur foras sícut palmes etaruit··etcolligent eum[13] etinignem
mittent[14]·7 Et **ardent (7) si manseritis** inme·etuerba mea inuobis man-
serint quod cumque uolueritis petetis et fiet uobis··

(8) Enhoc clarificatus **est pater** meus vtfructum plurimum adferatis et
efficiamini mei discipuli (9) sicut dilexit me pater·etego dilexi uos manete
indilectione mea·(10) si precepta mea seruaueritis manebitis indilectione
mea sicut etego patris mei precepta seruaui etmaneo ineius dilectione·(11)
Fol. 73. Haec locutus **sum** uobis vtgaudium meum ínuobis sit·etgaudium uestrum
inpleatur (12) hoc est preceptum meum vtdiligatis inuicem sicut dilexi uos··

(13) Maiorem hác dilectione[15] némo habet vt animam suam·quis ponat
proamicis suis (14) uos amici mei estis si feceritis que ego precipio uobis

[1] suggeret.
[2] Pacem relinquo vobis, pacem meam do vobis:
[3] ad.
[4] et sicut.
[5] agricola.
[6] ferentem.
[7] purgabit.
[8] locutus sum.
[9] sicut.
[10] ferre.
[11] in me manseritis.
[12] V. om.
[13] eos.
[14] mittunt.
[15] dilectionem.

(15) iam nondico uos seruos quia seruus nescit quid facit dominus eius uos
autem dixi amicos quia omnia que cunque audiui apatre meo nota feci uobis·
(16) Non uos me elegistis sed ego uos[1] elegi etpossui[2] uos vteatis etfructum
adferatis[3] etfructus uester maneat vtquod cunque petieritis patrem innomine
meo dæt[4] uobis··
(17) Hæc mando uobis vtdiligatis inuicem (18) si mundus uos odit scitote
quia me priorem uobis odio habuit.·.(19) si demundo fuissetis mundus
quodsuum erat diligeret quia uero demundo nonestis sed ego elegi uos demundo propteria[5] odit uos mundus··7
(20) Mementote sermonis mei quem ego dixi uobis nonest seruus maior
domino suo··7
Si me persecuti sunt etuos persequentur si sermonem meum serua- Fol. 73 b.
uerunt etuestrum seruabunt··
(21) Sed hec omnia facient uobis propter nomen meum quia nesciunt
eum qui [6]me missit[6]··
(22) Si nonuenisem etlocutus fuissem eis peccatum nonhaberent nunc
autem excussationem[7] nonhabent depeccato suo (23) qui me odit etpatrem
meum odit··
(24) Si opera nonfecissem ineis que nemo alius fecit peccatum nonha-
berent··nunc autem etuiderunt·etoderunt me etpatrem meum (25) sed
vtinpleatur sermo qui inlege eorum scriptus est·qui[8] oderunt[9] me
gratis·(26) cum autem uenerit paraclitus[10] **quem ego mittam** uobis·
apatre spiritum ueritatis qui apatre procedit·ille **testimonium** perhibet[11]
[Cap. XVI.] deme (27) etuos testimonium perhibetis quia abinitio mecum estis (1) hec
locutus sum uobis··vtnon scandalizemini (2) absque sinagogis[12] facient
uos·sed uenit hora vtomnis qui interfecit uos arbitretur obsequium se
prestare deo (3) et hæc facient quia nonnouerunt patrem neque me (4) sed
hæc locutus sum uobis vtcum uenerit hora eorum·reminiscemini[13] quia[14]
dixi uobis··7

---

[1] elegi vos.
[2] posui.
[3] afferatis.
[4] det.
[5] propterea.
[6] misit me.
[7] excusationem.
[8] quia.
[9] odio me habuerunt.
[10] paracletus.
[11] perhibebit.
[12] synagogis.
[13] reminiscamini.
[14] V. adds ego.

Fol. 74. (5) Haec autem uobis abinitio nondixi quia uobiscum eram·at nunc
uado adeum qui me missit[1] etnemo exuobis interrogat me quo uadis (6)
sed quia hæc locutus sum uobis trestitia[2] inpleuit cor uestrum (7) sed ego
ueritatem dico uobis expedit uobis vtego uadam·sienim nonhabiero[3] paraclitus[4] nonuenict aduos·si autem abiero mittam eum aduos··(8) etcum
uenerit ille arguet mundum depeccato·etde iudicio[5]etdeiustitia (9) depeccato quidem quia noncredunt inme (10) deiustitia uero quia ad patrem
uado··etiam nonuidibetis[6] me (11) deiudicio autem quia princeps huius[7]
mundi iudicatus est (12) adhuc multa habeo uobis dicere sed nonpotestis
portare modo (13) cum autem uenerit ille spiritus ueritatis docebit uos
inomnem ueritatem nonenim loquetur·asemet ipso se[8] cumque audiet
loquetur[9] adnuntiabit[10] uobis (14) ille me[11] quia demeo accipiat[12]·etad-
nuntiabit uobis···7
(15) Omnia que cunque habet pater mea sunt·propteria[13] dixi quia
demeo accipiet etadnuntiabit uobis (16) modicum·etiam nonuidebitis
Fol. 74 b. me··etiterum modicum etuidebitis me quia uado adpatrem et[14] (17)
dixerunt ergo exdiscipulis eius adinuicem quid est hoc quod dicit[15] modicum[16] (18) nescimus quid loquitur·(19) cognouit autem ihesus quia
uolebant illum[17] interrogare etdixiteis dehoc queritis inter uos quia dixi
modicum etnonuidebitis me·etiterum modicum etuidebitis me··7
(20) Amen amen dico uobis quia plorabitis etflebitis uos·mundus autem
gaudebit·uos autem contristabemini[18]·sed tristitia uestra uertetur in-
gaudium··(21) mulier cum parit tristitiam habet quia uenit hora eius·
cum autem peperit[19] puerum iam nonmeminit presurae[20] propter gaudium
quia natus est homo inmundum··(22) etuos igitur nunc quidem tristitiam
habebitis·Iterum autem uidebo uos etgaudebit cor uestrum etgaudium

---

[1] misit.
[2] tristitia.
[3] non abiero.
[4] paracletus.
[5] iustitia et de iudicio.
[6] videbitis.
[7] mundi huius.
[8] sed quaecumque.
[9] V. adds et quae ventura sunt.
[10] annuntiabit.
[11] clarificabit.
[12] accipiet.
[13] propterea.
[14] V. om.
[15] V. adds nobis.
[16] V. adds et non videbitis me, et iterum modicum et videbitis me? et quia vado ad patrem? Dicebant ergo Quid est hoc quod dicit modicum?
[17] eum.
[18] contristabimini.
[19] pepererit.
[20] pressurae.

uestrum nemo tollet[1] auobis (23) etillo[2] die me interrogabitis[3] quic-
quam··7

Amen amen dico uobis si quid petieritis patrem innomine meo dabit
uobis (24) usque modo nonpetitis[4] quicquam innomine meo·petite et-
accipietis utgaudium uestrum sit plenum··7

(25) Haec inprouerbis[5] locutus sum uobis uenit hora cum iam nonin- Fol. 75.
prouerbis[5] loquar uobis sed palam depatre adnuntiabo[6] uobis in[7] (26) illo
die innomine meo petitis[8] etnondico uobis quia ego rogabo patrem deuobis
(27) ipse enim pater amat uos quia uos me amatis et credistis[9] quia ego[7]
adeo (28) exiui [10]apatre etueni inmundum·Iterum relinquo mundum etuado
adpatrem (29) dicunt ei discipuli eius ecce nunc palam loqueris etprouer-
bium nullum dicis (30) nunc scimus quia scis omnia etnonopus est tibi
vtquis te interrogat[11] inhoc credimus quia adeo existi··7··

(31) Respondit eis ihesus modo creditis (32) ecce uenit hora[12] uenit
vtdispergamini unus quisque inpropria etme solum relinqua[13] etnonsum
solus relinquatis etnonsum solus[14] quia pater mecum est··7

(33) Hæc locutus sum uobis vtinme pacem habeatis inmundo[15] presuram[16]
[CAP. XVII.] habeatis[17] sed confidite[18] ego uici mundum (1) hæc locutus est ihesus et-
subleuatis occulis[19] incelum dixit pater uenit hora clarifica filium tuum
vtfilius tuus clarificat[20] te (2) sicut dedisti ei·potestatem[21] carnis vtomne Fol. 75 b.
quos[22] dedisti ei det eis uitam æternam··

(3) Hæc est autem uita æterna vtcognoscant te solum deum uerum
etquod[23] misisti ihesum christum (4) et[24] ego te clarificaui super terram opus
consummaui quod dedisti mihi vtfaciem[25] (5) etnunc clarifica me tu pater
aput[26] temet ipsum claritate quam habui priusquam mundus esset aput[26] te
(6) manifestaui nomen tuum hominibus quos dedisti mihi demundo tui
erant et mihi eos dedisti etsermonem tuum seruauerunt (7) nunc cog-

---

1 tollit.
2 et in illo.
3 non rogabitis.
4 petistis.
5 proverbiis.
6 annuntiabo.
7 V. om.
8 petetis.
9 credidistis.
10 V. adds Exivi.
11 interroget.
12 V. adds et jam.
13 relinquatis.
14 repetition.
15 mundum.
16 pressuram.
17 habebitis.
18 confidete.
19 oculis.
20 clarificet.
21 V. adds omnis.
22 quod.
23 quem.
24 V. om.
25 faciam.
26 apud.

nouerunt quia omnia que dedisti mihi abste sunt (8) quia uerba que dedisti mihi dedi eis etipsi acceperunt··etcognouerunt uere quia ate exiui et crediderunt quia tu me misisti·(9) ego procis rogo·nonpromundo rogo sed prohis quos dedisti mihi quia tui sunt (10) etmea omnia tua sunt·ettua **mea sunt** etclarificatus sum incís (11) etiam nonsum inmundo ethi inmundo sunt··7

Et ego ate[1] uenio pater sanctus[2] serua eos innomine tuo **quos** dedisti mihi·utsint in[3] unum sicut etuos (12) cum essem cum **eis ego** seruabam eos innomine tuo quos dedisti mihi custodiui··

Fol. 76. Et nemo exhís periit[4] nisi filius perditionis vtscriptura inpleatur
(13) nunc autem adte uenio ethæc loquor inmundo vthabeant gaudium meum inpletum insemet ipsis·(14) ego dedi eis sermonem tuum etmundus odio **eos habuit quia nonsunt** demundo sicut etego nonsum demundo (15) nonrogo **vttollas eos** demundo sed vtserues eos exmalo (16) demundo·nonsunt sicut etego nonsum demundo (17) sanctifica eos inueritate··

SErmo tuus ueritas est·(18) sicut me misisti inmundum etego missi[5] eos inmundum··7

(19) Etprocis **ego** sanctifico me ipsum vtsint·etipsi sanctificati inueritate··(20) Nonprohis autem tantum[6] rogo **sed** etprocis **qui** credituri sunt·peruerbum eorum·inme (21) vtomnes vtunum sint··sicut tu pater inme etego inte vtipsi[7] innobis[8] ut mundus credat·quia tu me misisti (22) etego claritatem quam dedisti mihi dedi illis ut sint unum sicut et[9] nos unum sumus (23) ego ineis ettu inme vtsint consummati inunum etcognoscat mundus quia tu me missisti[10] etdilexisti eos sicut ad[11] me dilexisti (24) pater quos dedisti mihi uolo vtubi ego sum·etilli sint mecum
Fol. 76 b. vtuidiant[12] claritatem meam quam dedisti mihi quia dilexisti me ante constitutionem mundi··

(25) Pater iuste etmundus te noncognouit ego autem te cognoui··7

Et hii[13] cognouerunt quod tu me misisti (26) etnotum feci eis nomen

---

[1] ad te.
[2] sancte.
[3] V. om.
[4] peribit.
[5] misi.
[6] rogo tantum.
[7] ut et ipsi.
[8] V. adds unum sint.
[9] V. om.
[10] misisti.
[11] et.
[12] videant.
[13] hi.

tuum et notum faciam vtdilectio qua dilexisti me inipsis·sit etego inipsis···

] (1) Haec cum dixisset ihesus egresus[1] est cum discipulis suis transtorrentem cedrón·ubi erat hortus·Inquem introiuit ipse etdiscipuli eius··7

(2) Sciebat autem etiudas qui tradebat eum locum **quod**[2] frequenter conuenerat[3]·ihesus illuc cum discipulis suis··7

(3) IVdas ergo cum accepisset[4] cohortem etapontificibus **etphariscis** ministros·vt[5] uenit illúc cum lanternis etfacibus etarmís··7

(4) IHESUS itaque sciens omnia queuentura erant[6] processit etdicit eis· quid[7] queritis (5) responderunt[8] ihesum natzarenum[9]·dicit eis ihesus ego sum stabat autem etiudas qui tradebat eum cum ipsis·(6) vtergo dixit eis ego sum abierunt retrorsum etceciderunt[10] interram (7) iterum ergo eos interrogauit quem queritis··7 Illi **autem** dixerunt ihesum natzarenum[9] (8) Fol. 77. respondit ihesus dixi uobis quia ego sum si ergo me queritis sinete[11] hos abire (9) vtinpleretur sermo quemdixit quiaquos dedisti mihi nonperdidi exipsis quemquam···

(10) Simon ergo petrus abens[12] gladium eduxit eum etpercussit seruum[13] pontificis etabscidit eius auriculam dextram·Erat autem nomen serno malchus·(11) dicit[14] ergo ihesus petro mitte gladium inuaginam·7

Calicem quem dedit mihi pater nonbibam illam··

(12) Chors[15] ergo ettribunus etministri iudeorum conprehenderunt ihesum etligauerunt eum··7

(13) Et adduxerunt eum adannam primum·erat autem[16] socer caiphe[17] quia erat pontifex anni illius·(14) Erat autem caiphas[18] qui consilium dedit[19] iudeis·quia expedit unum hominem mori propopulo··

(15) Sequebatur autem ihesum simon petrus etalius discipulus·dis-

---

[1] egressus.
[2] quia.
[3] Iesus convenerat.
[4] accepisset.
[5] V. om.
[6] V. adds super eum.
[7] Quem.
[8] V. adds ei.
[9] Nazarenum.
[10] ceciderunt.
[11] sinite.
[12] habens.
[13] pontificis servum.
[14] Dixit.
[15] Cohors.
[16] enim.
[17] Caiaphae.
[18] Caiaphas.
[19] dederat.

cipulus autem ille erat notus pontifici etintroiuit cum ihesu inatrium
pontificis··7
Fol. 77. (16) Petrus autem stabat adhostium[1] foris··7
Exiuit ergo discipulus alius[2] qui erat notus pontifici etdixit ostiarie
etintroduxit petram[3]··
(17) Dicit ergo petro ancilla ostiaria numquid ettu exdiscipulis es
hominis istius·dicit ille nonsum··7
(18) Stabant autem serui etministri adprunas quia frigus erat etcalc-
ficabant[4] erat autem cum eis·etpetrus stans et calefaciens se (19) pontifex
ergo interrogauit ihesum[5] discipulis suis etdedoctrina eius··7
(20) Respondit[6] ihesus ego palam locutus sum mundo·Ego semper
docui insinagoga[7] etintemplo quo omnes iudei conueniunt etinoccultum[8]
loqutus[9] sum nihil (21) quid me interrogas·Interroga eos qui audierunt
quid locutus sum ipsis ecce hii[10] sciunt que dixirim[11] ego (22) hæc autem
cum dixisset unus adsistens ministrorum dedit alapam ihesu dicens·
sicrespem[12] dispontifici·(23) Respondit ei ihesus si male loqutus[9] sum
Fol. 78. testimonium perhibe demalo·si autem bene quid me cedis·(24) et missit[13]
cum annas ligatum·adcaifán[14] pontificem·(25) Erat autem simon petrus
stans etcalefaciens se dixerunt ergo ei·numquid[15] tu exdiscipulis eius es
negauit ille etdixit nonsum·(26) dicit unus exseruis pontificis cognatus
eius·cuius abscidit petrus auriculam·nonne ego te uidi inorto[16] cum illo
(27) iterum ergo negauit petrus·etstatim gallus cantauit·(28) adducunt
ergo ihesum adcaiphán[17] inpretorium·Erat autem mane etipsi nonintroie-
runt inpretorium vtnoncontaminarentur sed manducarent pascha·
(29) Exiuit ergo pilatus adeos foras·etdixitquam accussationem[18]adfertis
aduersus hominem hunc·(30) responderunt[19] ei si nonesset hic malefacter[20]
nontibi tradisemus[21] eum·(31) dixit ergo eis pylatus[22] accipite ergo[23] eum[24]

[1] ad ostium.
[2] ille.
[3] Petrum.
[4] calefiebant.
[5] V. adds de.
[6] V. adds ei.
[7] synagoga.
[8] occulto.
[9] locutus.
[10] hi.
[11] dixerim.
[12] Sic respondis pontifici.
[13] misit.
[14] Caiaphan.
[15] V. adds et.
[16] in horto.
[17] a Caiapha.
[18] accusationem.
[19] V. adds et dixerunt.
[20] malefactor.
[21] tradidissemus.
[22] Pilatus.
[23] V. om.
[24] V. adds vos.

etsecundum legem uestram iudicate eum·dixerunt ergo iudei·nobis nonlicet interficire[1] quemquam (32) vtsermo ihesu inpleretur quem dixit
significans qua morte[2]esset moriturus·(33) Introiuit ergo iterum inpretorium pylatus[3]·etuocauit ihesum etdixit ei tu es rex iudeorum···7
(34) Et respondit ihesus atemet ipso hocdicis án alii tibi dixerunt deme· Fol. 78 b.
(35) respondit eis[4] pylatus[3]·numquid et[4]ego iudeus[5] **gens tua et-**
pontifices tradiderunt te mihi quid fecisti··

(36) Respondit ihesus regnum[6] nonest **de** hoc[7]mundo **si de**[8] hoc
mundo **esset** meum regnum[9] ministri mei utique[4] decartarent[10] vtnon-
tradirer[11] **iudeis·Nunc** autem meum regnum nonest hinc·(37) dixit[12] ei
pylatus[3]·ergo **réx es** tu·respondit ihesus tudicis·quia rex sum ego ego
inhoc **natus** sum·etadhóc ueni in hunc[4] mundum vtthestimonium[13] per-
hibeam ueritati omnis quiest exueritate audit meam[14]·(38) dicit ei pylatus[3]·
quidest ueritas etcumhocdixisset iterum exiuit foras[4] adiudeos etdixit[15]eis
ego nullam inuenio ineo causam·(39) **est** autem consuetudo uobis vtunum
uinctum[4] **dimittam** uobis IN pascha uultis ergo ego[4] dimittam uobis·
regem iudeorum·(40) clamauerunt **rursum** omnes dicentes·Nonhunc sed
barabam[16] erat autem barabas[17] **latro**··

[CAP. XIX.] (1) Nunc **ergo** adprehendit pylatus[3] ihesum etfilagillauit[18] eum[4]·(2) Fol. 79.
[19]milites plectentes choronam[20] despinís·Inpossuerunt[21] capiti eius et
uestem[22]purpuram·circumdederunt eum (3) etueniebant adeum[23] dicebant aue[24] réx iudeorum·etdabant ei palmasset[25]··

(4) Exiuit[26] iterum pylatus[3] foras etdicit eis·ecce adduco[27] eum foras
vtcognoscatis quia ineo nullam causam inuenio·

(5) Exiuit[26] ergo ihesus portans spineam coronam·etpurpuream[28]
uestimentum·etdicit eis ecce homo (6) cum ergo uidissent eum pontifices

[1] interficere.
[2] esset morte.
[3] Pilatus.
[4] V. om.
[5] V. adds sum.
[6] V. adds meum.
[7] mundo hoc.
[8] ex.
[9] regnum meum.
[10] decertarent.
[11] traderer.
[12] V. adds itaque.
[13] testimonium.
[14] V. adds vocem.
[15] dicit.
[16] Barabban.
[17] Barabbas.
[18] flagellavit.
[19] V. adds et.
[20] **coronam.**
[21] **inposuerunt.**
[22] veste purpurea.
[23] **V.** adds et.
[24] **Have.**
[25] alapas.
[26] Exiit.
[27] V adds vobis.
[28] purpuream.

etministri clamabant·dicentes crucifige[1] eum[2]·dicit eis pylatus[3] accipite
eum uos et crucifigite ego enim noninuenio[4] causam·(7) Responderunt ei
iudei etdixerunt[2] nos legem habemus·etsecundum legem debet mori
quia filium dei sé fecit·(8) cum ergo audisset pylatus[3] hunc sermonem·
magis timuit (9) etingresus[5] est pretorium iterum·etdicit ad ihesum unde
es tu·ihesus autem responsum nondedit ei·(10) dicit ei ergo pylatus[3]·
mihi nonloqueris nescis quia potestatem habeo crucifigere te etpotestatem
habeo dimittere te··7

(11) Respondit ihesus nonhaberis[6] potestatem aduersum me ullam··
Fol. 79 b. nisi tibi datum[7] esset desuper propterea qui tradidit me tibi maius peccatum habet (12) exinde querebat pylatus[3] dimittere eum·Iudei autem
clamabant dicentes sihunc dimittis nones amicus cesæris[8]·omnis qui se
regem facit contra dicit[9] (13) pylatus[3] ergo cum audisset hos sermones
adduxit foras ihesum etsedit pro tribunali inloco[10] quidicitur lithostrotus
hebreice autem galbatha[11]·(14) eratautem parascue[12] paschæ hora quasi
sexta·etdicit eis[13] ecce rex uester (15) illi autem clamabant tolle tolle
crucifige eum··7

Dicit eis pylatus[3] regem uestrum crucifigam responderunt ponti-
ficos·nonhabemus regem nisi cæssarem[14]·(16) Tunc[15] tradidit eis illum
vtcrucifigeretur suscipierunt[16] autem ihesum etduxerunt (17) etbaiolans[17]
sibi crucem et[2] exiuit incum locum[2] qui dicitur caluarie[18] hebrece[19] gol-
gotha (18) ibi[20] eum crucifixerunt··Et cum eoalios duos latrones[2]·hinc
ethinc medium autem ihesum·(19) scripsit autem ettitulum pylatus[3]
etpossuit[21] super crucem·erat autem scriptum ihesum natzareus[22]·rex
iudeorum (20) hunc ergo titulum multi legerunt iudeorum qui[23] propeci-
uitatem erat locus ubi crucifixus est ihesus·

Fol. 80. Et erat scriptum hebreice grece[24] latine·(21) dicebant[25] pylato[2]

---

1 V. adds crucifige.
2 V. om.
3 Pilatus.
4 V. adds in eo.
5 ingressus.
6 haberes.
7 esset datum.
8 Caesaris.
9 V. adds Caesari.
10 locum.
11 Gabbatha.
12 parasceve.
13 Iudaeis.
14 Caesarem.
15 V. adds ergo.
16 susceperunt.
17 baiulans.
18 V adds locum.
19 hebraice.
20 ubi.
21 posuit.
22 Iesus Nazarenus.
23 quia.
24 V. adds et.
25 V. adds ergo.

pontifices iudeorum[1]·noli scribere réx iudeorum sedquia ipse dixit rexsum iudeorum·(22) respondit pylatus[2] quod scripsi scripsi·(23) milites ergo cum crucifigessent[3] cum acciperunt[4] uestimenta sua[5] etfecerunt quatuor partes·unicuique militi partem et tunicam·erat autem tunica inconsutilis desuper texa[6] pertotum·

(24) Dixerunt[7] inuicem nonscindamus eam·sed sortiamur deilla cuius sit·vtscribtura[8] inpleatur·dicens partiti sunt uestimenta **mea** sibi etsuper[9] uestem meam misserunt[10] sortem·etmilites quidem hec fecerunt··

(25) Stabant autem iuxta crucem·ihesu mater eius·etsoror **matris eius** maria cleope etmaria magdalenæ (26) cum uidisset ergo **ihesus matrem**· etdiscipulum stantem quem diligebat ihesus[1]·

Dicit matris[11] suæ mulier·ecce filius tuus·(27) deinde dicit discipulo ecce mater tua·Etexilla hora suscipit[12] eam discipulus insuam[13]· (28) postea sciens ihesus quia iam[14]·consummata sunt vtconsummaretur scriptura··7

Dicit sitio (29) uas ergo possitum[15] erat aceto plenum illi autem Fol. 80 b. spungiam[16] plenum[17] aceto hissopo[18] circumponentes obtullerunt[19] ori eius·· (30) Cum ergo accipisset[20] ihesus acetum·dixit consummatum est capite[21] inclinato·tradidit spiritum [22]cum autem exspirasset uelum templi scisum est medium·asonmo usque addeorsum[22]·(31) Iudei ergo quoniam parasciue[23] erat·vtnonremanerent incruce corpora sabbato·erat enim dies[24] magnus illa[25] sabbati·rogauerunt pylatum[26] vtfrangentur[27] eorum crura ettollerentur·(32) uenerunt ergo milites etprimi quidem·fregerunt crura etalterius **qui** simul[1] crucifixus est cum eo·(33) addominum[28] autem cum uenisent[29] vtuiderunt eum iam mortuum nonfrangerunt[30] eius crura (34) sed unus militum lancea latus eius aperuit etcontinuo exiuit sanguis etaqua·

---

1 V. om.
2 Pilatus.
3 crucifixissent.
4 acceperunt.
5 eius.
6 contexta.
7 V. adds ergo ad.
8 scriptura.
9 **in.**
10 **miserunt.**
11 **matri.**
12 **accepit.**
13 **in sua.**
14 **V. adds omnia.**
15 **positum.**
16 **spongiam.**
17 plenam.
18 hysopo.
19 obtulerunt.
20 accepisset.
21 et inclinato capite.
22 V. om. these 12 words.
23 parasceve.
24 magnus dies.
25 ille.
26 Pilatum.
27 frangerentur.
28 ad Iesum.
29 venissent.
30 fregerunt.

(35) Et qui uidit testimonium perhibuit etuerum est eius testimonium·
etille scit quia uera dicit vt[1] uos credatis·(36) facta sunt enim hæc vtscriptura impleatur oss[2] eius[3] noncomminetis[4] exeo·(37) etiterum alia
scribtura dicit [5]inquem transfixerunt uidebunt·(38) post hec autem rogauit
Fol. 81. pylatum[6] ioseph abarimathia eo quod esset discipulus ihesu oculte[7] autem
propter metum iudeorum vttolleret corpus ihesu etpermisit pylatus·uenit
ergo ettollet[8] corpus ihesu (39) uenit autem etnicodimus[9]·qui uenerat ad
ihesum nocte primum·ferens mixturam mirre[10] etoloues[11] quasi libras centum (40) acciperunt[12] ergo corpus ihesu etligauerunt eum linteis·Cum
aromatibus sicut mos iudeis est sepelire·(41) erat autem inloco ubi crucifixus est hortus etin eo[8] orto[13] monumentum nouum inquo nondum quisquam possitus[14] erat (42) ibi ergo propter parasciue[15] iudeorum quia iuxta
erat monomentum possuerunt[16] ihesum····7

[Cap. XX.] (1) Una autem sabbati maria magdalenæ uenit mane cum adhúc
tenebre essent admonomentum[17]·etuidet lapidem sublatum amono-
mento[18]··(2) Cucurrit ergo etuenit adsimonem petrum et[19]alium discipulum
quem amabat ihesus etdicit eis tullerunt[20] dominum demonomento[18] et-
nesci[21] ubi possuerunt[16] eum·

(3) EXiit ergo petrus etille alius discipulus etuenerunt admonomen-
Fol. 81 b. tum[17]·(4) currebant autem duos[22] simul etille alius discipulus·precurrit[23]
citius petro etuenit prius[24]·admonomentum[17] (5) etcum se inclinasset uidit[25]
possita[26] lintiamina[27] nontamen introiuit inmonomentum[8]·(6) Uenit
ergo simón petrus subsequens[28] cum·etintrouit[29] inmonomentum[17]·
etuidit[25] lintiamina[27] possita[26] (7) etsudarium quod fuerat super[30] capud[31]
eius·noncum lintiaminibus[32] possitum sed separatim·inuolutum inunum

[1] V. adds et.
[2] Os.
[3] V. om.
[4] comminuetis.
[5] Videbunt inquem transfixerunt.
[6] Pilatum.
[7] occultus autem.
[8] tulit.
[9] Nicodemus.
[10] murrae.
[11] aloes.
[12] acceperunt.
[13] horto.
[14] positus.
[15] parasceven.
[16] posuerunt.
[17] monumentum.
[18] monumento.
[19] V. adds ad.
[20] Tulerunt.
[21] nescimus.
[22] duo.
[23] praecucurrit.
[24] primus.
[25] videt.
[26] posita.
[27] linteamina.
[28] sequens.
[29] introivit.
[30] supra.
[31] caput.
[32] linteaminibus positum.

locum·(8) Tunc ergo introiuit etille discipulus·qui uenerat prius[1] admonomentum[2] etuidit[3] etcredit[4] (9) nondum enim sciebat scripturam quia [5]amor-
tuis opereret eum resurgere (10) abierunt ergo[6] adsemet ipsosdiscipuli··
(11) Maria autem sedebat[7] admonomentum[2] **foris plorans** dum ergo
fleret inclinauit **sé** etprospexit inmonomentum[2] (12) **etuidit duos** angelos
inalbis sedentes unum adcapud[8] etunum adpedes **ubi possitum[9]** fuerat
corpus ihesu··
(13) Dicunt ei illi mulier quid ploras dicit eís quia **tullerunt[10]** dominum
meum etnescio ubi possuerunt[11] eum·(14) hæc cum dixisset conuersa est
retrorsum etuidit[3] ihesum stantem etnonsciebat quiaihesusest (15) dicit ei
ihesus mulier quid ploras·Quem queris illa existimans quia hortulanus Fol. 82.
est[12] dicit ei domine si tu sustulisti eum dicito mihi ubi possuisti[13] eum et
ego[14] tollam (16) dicit ei ihesus maria conuersa illa dicit[15] rabboni·quod
dicitur magister·(17) **dicit** eis[16] ihesus noli me tangere·nondum **enim**
ascendi adpatrem meum·Uade autem adfratres meos Et díc eis ascendo
adpatrem **meum** etpatrem uestrum etdeum meum etdeum uestrum·(18)
uenit maria **magdalene** etnuntians[17] discipulis quia uidi dominum ethæc
dixit mihi···7
(19) Cum esset ergo sero die[18] sabbatorum etforess[19] essent clausæ ubi erant
discipuli propter metum iudeorum·Uenit ihesus etstetit inmedio etdixit[20]
eis páx uobis·(20) ethoc cum dixisset ostendit eis manus etlatus··7

Gauisi sunt èrgo discipuli uiso domino·(21) dicit[21] eis iterum páx
uobis·sicut **me[22]** missit pater **etego** mitto uos·(22) hoc **cum** dixisset in-
soflauit[23] accipite spiritum[24]··7
(25) Quorum remisieritis[25] **peccata** remitentur[26] eis[27]·quorum retenu-
eritis[28] detenta[29] sunt···7

---

[1] primus.
[2] monumentum.
[3] videt.
[4] credidit.
[5] **oporteret eum a mortuis resurgere.**
[6] **V. adds iterum.**
[7] **stabat.**
[8] caput.
[9] positum.
[10] tulerunt.
[11] posuerunt.
[12] esset.
[13] posuisti.
[14] V. adds eum.
[15] V. adds ei.
[16] ei.
[17] annuntians.
[18] V. adds illo una.
[19] fores.
[20] dicit.
[21] dixit ergo.
[22] misit me.
[23] insuflavit et dicit eis.
[24] V. adds sanctum.
[25] remiseritis.
[26] remittentur.
[27] V. adds et.
[28] retinueritis.
[29] retenta.

Fol. 82 b. (24) Thomas autem unus ex·xii[1]·qui dicitur dedimus[2] nonerat cum
eis quando uenit ihesus (25) dixerunt ergo ei alii discipuli uidimus
dominum ille autem dixit eis·nisi uidero inmanibus eius figuram clauorum
etmittam digitum meum inlocum clauorum·etmittam manum meam inlatus
eius noncredam··7

(26) Post dies octo iterum·erant discipuli eius intus et thomas cum eis·
Uenit ihesus ianuis clausis etstetit inmedio eorum[3]···7

Etdixit páx uobis (27) deinde dicit thomæ infer digitum tuum húc
etuide manus meas et adefer[4] manum tuam etmitte inlatus meum etnolii[5]
esse incredulus sed fidelis·(28) Respondit thomas etdixit ei dominus meus
etdeus meus·(29) Dicit ei ihesus quia uidisti[6] etcredidisti·Beati qui non-
uiderunt etcrediderunt··

(30) Multa quidem etalia **signa fecit**[7] **que** nonsunt scripta inconspectu
discipulorum suorum inhoc libro··

(31) Hec autem scripta sunt·vtcredatis quia ihesus est christus filius dei
etut credentes uitam habeatis innomine eius···7··7

[Cap. XXI.] (1) Postea manifestauit sé iterum ihesus admare tibriadis[8]·Manifest-
Fol. 83. auit autem sic (2) erant [9]simon petrus simul et thomas qui **dicitur**
dedimus[2] etnathanél[10] qui erat ahanna[11] galileæ etfilii zebeidei[12]··7

Et alii exdiscipulis eis[13] duo·(3) dicit eis simon petrus·uado
piscari·dicunt ei uenimus étnos tecum·[14]Exierunt etascenderunt innauem
etilla nocte nihil coeperunt[15]·(4) Mane autem iam facto stetit ihesus
inlitore nontamen cognouerunt discipuli quia ihesus est·(5) dicit ergo eís
ihesus **pueri** numquid palmentarium[16] habetis responderunt[17] non·(6)
Dixit[18] **cis** mittite indexteram partem[3] nauim[19] rete etinuinictis·[20]Dixerunt
autem pertotam noctem laborantes nihil coepimus··INuerbo autem tuo

1 duodecim.
2 Didymus.
3 V. om.
4 adfer.
5 noli.
6 V. adds me.
7 V. has, Iesus, in conspectu discipulorum suorum, quæ non sunt scripta.
8 Tiberiadis.
9 **simul** Simon Petrus.
10 Nathanahel.
11 a Cana.
12 Zebedaei.
13 eius.
14 V. adds et.
15 prendiderunt.
16 pulmentarium.
17 V. adds ei.
18 dicit.
19 navigii.
20 V. om. these 12 words.

mittimus·Misserunt[1] ergo etiam nonualaerunt[2] illud trahere amultitudine
piscivm···7
(7) Dicit ergo discipulus ille quem dilegebat[3] ihesus petro dominus est
simon petrus cum audisset quia dominus est·tonicam[4] precinxit[5] se erat
enim nudus etmisit sé inmare·
(8) Alii autem discipuli nauigio uenerunt non enim longe erant aterra Fol. 83 b.
sed quassi[6] cubitis·cctis[7]·trahentes rete piscivm·
(9) Ut ergo discenderunt[8] interram·uiderant[9] prunas possitas[10]·et-
piscem super possitum[11]·et panem·(10) Dicit eis ihesus adferte depis-
cibus quos preendidistis[12] nunc···7
(11) Ascendit simon petrus ettrahit[13] rete interra[14] plenum maignis[15]
piscibus quassi[16]·cl[17]·et[16] tribus etcum tanti essent nonest piscium[18] rete··
(12) Dixit[19] eis ihesus uenite prandite[20]
Et nemo audiebat[21] exdiscipulis[16] [22]interrogare eum tu quis es
scientes quia dominus esset·
(13) Et uenit ihesus etaccepit panem etdat eis etpiscem similiter··
(14) Hoc iam tertio manifestatus est ihesus disciplis cum surrexisset[23]
amortuis (15) cum ergo prandisset[24]·
Dicit simoni petro ihesus simon iohannis diligis me plus hís dicit ei
etiam domine [25]scís quiaamote dicit ei pasce agnos meos··7
(16) Dicit ei iterum simon iohannis diligis me·ait eilli[26] etiam domine
tu scís quiaamo te dicit ei pasce agnos meos···7
(17) Dicit ei tertio simon ioannis[27] amas me contristatus est petrus quia Fol. 84.
dixit[28] amas me et[16] dicit ei·domine tu omnia scis[29] quia amo te···
Dicit ei pasce oues meas·(18) amen amen dico tibi cum esses

---

1 miserunt.
2 non valebant.
3 diligebat.
4 tunicam.
5 succinxit.
6 quasi.
7 ducentia.
8 descenderunt.
9 viderunt.
10 positas.
11 positum.
12 prendistis.
13 traxit.
14 terram.
15 magnis.
16 V. om.
17 centum quinquaginta.
18 sciesum.
19 Dicit.
20 prandete.
21 audebat.
22 V. adds discumbentium.
23 resurrexisset.
24 prandissent.
25 V. adds tu.
26 ille.
27 Iohannis.
28 V. adds ei tertio.
29 V. adds tu scis.

iunior cingebas te·etambulabas ubi uolebas cum autem senueris extendis[1] manus tuas etalius·te cinget et ducit[2] quod[3] nonuis quo nonuis[4]·(19) hoc autem dixit significans qua morte clarificaturus esset deum ethoc·cum dixiset[5]·dicit ei sequere me (20) conuersus petrus·uidit illum discipulum quem diligebat ihesus sequentem quietrecubuit incena super pectus eius· et dicit[6] domine quis est qui tradet[7] te (21) hunc ergo cum uidisset petrus· Dixit[8] ihesu domine hic autem quid (22) dicit[9] ihesus sic eum uolo manere donec ueniam·Quid adte tu me sequere·

(23) Exiuit ergo sermo iste infratres quia discipulus ille nonmoritur[10] nondixit ei ihesus nonmoritur sed sic eum uolo manere donec uenio·quid
Fol. 84 b. adte (24) hic est discipulus qui testimonium perhibet dehís etscribsit hæc etscimus qui[11] uerum est testimonium eius·(25) sunt autem etalia multa que fecit ihesus quae si scribantur[12] singula nec ipsum arbitror mundum· capere eos qui scribendi sunt libros[13]····7··7

Explicit·[4]euangelium secundum iohannem[4]····7

---

[1] extendes.
[2] ducet.
[3] quo.
[4] V. om.
[5] dixisset.
[6] dixit.
[7] tradit.
[8] dicit.
[9] V. adds ei.
[10] V. adds et.
[11] quia.
[12] V. adds per.
[13] V. adds Amen.

qui testimonium perhibet de his
et scribsit haec et scimus quia uerum
est testimonium eius · sunt autem
et alia multa quae fecit iesus quae
si scribantur singula nec ipsum
arbitror mundum · capere eos
qui scribendi sunt libros

Explicit euangelium secundum iohannem

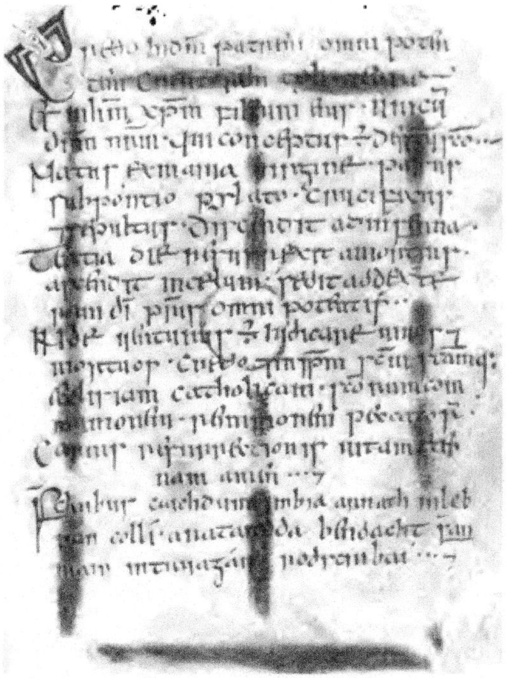

Credo in deum patrem omnipoten
tem creatorem caeli et terrae
Et in ihesum christum filium eius unicum
dominum nostrum qui conceptus est de spiritu sancto
Natus ex maria femina uirgine passus
sub pontio pilato crucifixus
et sepultus discendit ad inferna
Tertia die resurrexit a mortuis
ascendit in caelum sedit ad dexteram
patris dei patris omnipotentis
Inde uenturus est iudicare uiuos et
mortuos Credo et in spiritum sanctum sanctam
ecclesiam catholicam sanctorum com
munionem remissionem peccatorum
Carnis resurrectionis uitam aeter
nam amen

Benibuis cach duine [illegible] annach in leb
ran [illegible] bendacht [illegible]
[illegible] podrambai

Plate XI

Credo indeum patrem omni potentem·Creatorem caeli etterre – Fol. 85.

Et inihesum christum filium eius·unicum dominum nostrum·Qui conceptus est despiritu sancto··–

Natus exmaria uirgine·passus subpontio pylato·Crucifixus etsepultus·Discendit adinferna·

Tertia die resurrexit amortuis·ascendit incelum·sedit addexteram dei patris omni potentis··

Inde uenturus est iudicare uiuos etmortuos·Credo etinspiritum sanctum sanctamque æclisiam catholicam·sanctorum communionem·remisionem peccatorum·

Carnis resurrectionis uitam eternam amen···7

Forchubus caichduini imbia arrath inlebrán collí·aratardda bendacht foranmain intruagáin rodscribai···

"(Be it) on (the) conscience of every one in whom shall be for grace the booklet with splendour: that he give a blessing on (the) soul of the wretchock who wrote it."

Item oratio ante dominicam orationem Fol. 28 b.

Creator naturarum omnium deus etparens uniuersarum incelo etinterra originum hás trementis populi tui relegiosas preces exillo inaccessibilcis lucis trono tuo suscipe etinterhiruphín etzaraphin indefessas circumstantium laudes exaudi spei nonambigue precationes · Pater noster quies · usque infinem

Libera nós Domine amálo Domine christe íhesu custodi nos semper inomni opere bona fons etauctor omnium bonorum deus euacua nos uitiis · et reple nos uirtutibus bonis · perte christe ihesu : · —

Hisund dubei sacorfaice dau · 7

Here give the sacrifice to him.

Corpus cum sangine domini nostri ihesu christi sanitas sit tibi inuitam perpetua et salutem

Reffecti christi corpore et sanguine tibi semper dicamus domine alleluia alleluia

Qui satiauit animam inanem et animam esurientem satiauit bonis alleluia alleluia

Et sacrificent sacrificium laudis et usque exultatione · alleluia alleluia

Calicem salútaris accipiam et nomen domini inuocabo · alleluia alleluia

Reffecti christi corpore · alleluia alleluia ·

Omnes igitur generationes ab ab
racham usque ad david genera
tiones xiiii. et a david usque ad
transmigrationem babilonis ge
nerationes xiiii. et a transmig
ratione babilonis usque ad christum
generationes xiiii.

Finit prologus. Item incipit nunc
euangelium secundum matheum.

Columcille ⁊ drostan mac cosgreg a dalta
tangator a hi mar ro fhoillsig dia doib go
nic abbordoboir ⁊ bede cruthnec robo mor
maer buchan ar a ginn ⁊ is se ro thidnaig doib
in cathraig sain in saere go brath o mormaer
⁊ o thosec. tangator as a athle sen in cathraig
ele ⁊ do ratha si ri colucille iar fallan do rath
de ⁊ do rodlog ar in mormaer .i. bede gonda
tabrad do ⁊ ni thabrad ⁊ ro gab mac do galar
iar n-diultad na cleric ⁊ robo marb acht mad bec
iar sen do chuid in mor d'attac na cleric gondenda[s]

bennacte lis in mac gondiad plante do 7 dorat
ard in mordair uacloic in tiprat gonice cloic pette
mic garnait · doronsat in edbairt 7 tanic
slante do · iarsen dorat collumcille do dros
tan in chadraig sen 7 rosbennact 7 foracaib in brei
thir gebe tisad ris na bad blienec buadacc tan
gator déara drostan ar scarthain fri collumcille
rolaboir columcille bedear anim ohunn imacc;
Comgeall mc éda dorat uaorti nice púréne
docolumcille 7 do drostan · Moridac mc morcunn
dorat pett mc garnait 7 achad toche temni
7 bahé robomormair 7 robothosec · Matain
mc cairill dorat cuit mormoir i nalteri 7 culí mc
batin dorat cuit toisig · Domnall mc giric
7 malbrigte mc chathail dorat pett in mulenn
do drostan · Cathal mc morcunt dorat achad
naglerec do drostan · Domnall mc ruadri 7
malcolum mc culeon doratsat bidbin do dia 7 do
drostan · Malcoloum mc cinatha dorat cuit
ríg ibbidbin 7 ipett mc gobroig 7 da dabeg
uactair rosabard · Malcolum mc moilbrigte
dorat indelerc · Malsnecte mc luloig dorat

Laudate dominum omnes gentes alleluia alleluia
Gloria··reffecti christi·alleluia alleluia
et nunc·Et semper·Reffecti
Sacrificate sacrificium iustitiæ etsperate indomino

Deus tibi gratias agimus perquem misteria sancta celebrauimus et ate sanctitatis dona deposcimus miserere nobis domine saluator mundi·Qui regnas insecula seculorum amen·finit

Columcille acusdrostán mac cósgreg adálta tangator áhí marroalseg Fol. 3.
día doíb goníc abbordobóir acusbéde cruthnec robomormér búchan aragínn acusessé rothídnaíg dóib ingathráig sáin insaere gobraíth ómormaer acus-óthóséc·tangator asááthle sen incathraig ele acusdoráten ricolumcille sí iarfallán dórath dé acusdorodloeg arinmormér·i·bédó gondas tabrád dó acusníthárat acusrogab mac dó galár iarnéré naglerec acusrobomaréb act mádbec iarsén dochuíd inmōr dattác naglerec góndendæs ernacde les inmac Fol 3 b.
gondisád slánté dó acusdórat inedbairt doíb uácloic intiprat goníce chlóic pette mic garnáit doronsat innernacde acustanic slante dó; Iarsén dorat collumcille dódrostán inchadráig sén acusrosbenact acusforacaib imbrether gebe tisad ris nabad blienec buadacc tangator deara drostán arscartháin fri collumcille rolaboir columcille bedcár ánim óhúnñ ímácé;

Columcille and Drostán son of Cosgrach his pupil came from I as God had shown to them unto Abbordoboir and Bede the Pict was mormaer of Buchan before them, and it was he that gave them that town in freedom for ever from mormaer and tosech. They came after that to the other town, and it was pleasing to Columcille, because it was full of God's grace, and he asked of the mormaer to wit Bede that he should give it to him; and he did not give it; and a son of his took an illness after [or in consequence of] refusing the clerics, and he was nearly dead [lit. he was dead but if it were a little]. After this the mormaer went to intreat the clerics that they should make prayer for the son that health should come to him, and he gave in offering to them from Cloch in tiprat to Cloch pette mic Garnait. They made the prayer, and health came to him. After that Columcille gave to Drostán that town and blessed it and left as (his) word "Whosoever should come against it, let him not be many-yeared [or] victorious." Drostán's tears (deara) came on parting with Columcille·Said Columcille "Let Dear be its name henceforward."—

Cómgeall mac éda dórat úaorti níce fúrené docolumcille acusdodrostán . Moridac mac morcunn dorat pett mic garnaít acusáchád toche temní·acusbahé robomormaír acusrobothosec·Mataín mac caerill dorat cuit mormoir inálteri acusculíí mac batín dorat cuít toíség·Domnall mac gíric acusmalbrigte mac chathail dorat pett inmulenn·dodrostán·Cathal mac morcunt dorat áchad naglerec dodrostán·Domnall mac ruádri acusmalcolum mac culeón doratsat bidbín dó diá acusdódrostán·Malcoloum mac cinathá dorat cúit ríig íbbidbín acusinpett mic gobróig acusdádabég uactaír rósábard·Malcolum mac moilbrigte dorat indelerc·Málsnecte mac

Fol. 4. lulóig dorat pett maldúib dó drostán ; Domnall mac meic dubbacín robaíth nahúle edbarta rodrostán arthabárt áhule dó·Robáith cathál árachóir chetna acuitíd thoisíg acusdorat próinń chét cecnolloce acusceccasc dó día acusdó drostán·Cainnéch mac meic dobarcon acuscathal doratsat alterín alla úcthé na camone gonice in béíth edarda álterin ; Dorat domnall acuscathál étdanin dó dia acusdó drostán·Robaíth cainnec acusdomnall acus cathál nahúle edbarta ri dia acusrí drostan othósach ·goderad issáere omor·acus othosech culaithi bratha··[1]

"Comgeall son of Ed gave from Orti to Furene to Columcille and to Drostán. Moridach son of Morcunn gave Pett meic Garnait and Achad toche temni; and it was he that was mormaer and was tosech·Matáin son of Caerell gave the mormaer's share in Altere and Culi son of Baten gave (the) toisech's share·Domnall son of Girec and Maelbrigte son of Cathal, gave Pett in Mulenn to Drostán·Cathal son of Morcunt gave Achad

[1] The words between asterisks are written in ink of a different colour from the others. See Preface, pp. xxiv. xxvi.

pett maldub do drostan. Domnall mac meic
dubbacin robaith na huile edbarta ro dros
tan ar a thabart a huile do. Robaith cathal
ar a chomallain cetna ar a chuit toisig 7 dorat
proinn chet cecnolloce 7 cecasca do dia
7 do drostan. Cainnech mac meic dobarcon
7 cathal dorat altrin alla uethe
na camone gonice in beith edarda alterin.
Dorat domnall 7 cathal etdanin
do dia 7 do drostan. Robaith cainnech
7 domnall 7 cathal na huile edbarta ri
dia 7 ri drostan othosach [illegible]

Gartnait mac cannech 7 ete ingen gillemichel
dorat pett ipuir fri coisecrad eclasi
crist 7 petir abstoil 7 do colum cille 7 do drostan
sér onna huilib dolodib conna andsore do cormac
escob dunicallenn in ochtmad bliadin rigi dauid.
Testibus istis nectan escob abb dein 7 leot ab brecini
7 malcoluim mac molini 7 algune mac arcill 7 ruadri
mormar marr 7 matadin brithem 7 gillecrist
mac cormaic 7 malpetir mac domnaill 7 domongart
ferleginn turbruad 7 gillecolaim mac muredig 7 dub
ni mac malcolaim [illegible]

[illegible]

naglérech ("the clerics' field") to Drostán. Domnall son of Ruadri and Maelcoluim son of Culéon, gave Bidbin to God and to Drostán. Maelcoluim son of Cinaed, gave (the) king's share in Bidbin and in Pett meic Gobroig and two davochs of Upper Rosabard·Maelcoluim, son of Maelbrigte, gave the Delerc. Maelsnechte, son of Lúlóg, gave Pett Maelduib to Drostán· Domnall, son of Mac Dubbacín, immolated all the offering to Drostán, giving the whole of it to him·Cathal immolated in (the) same way his toisech's share, and gave a dinner of a hundred every Christmas and every Easter to God and to Drostán·Cainnech son of Mac Dobarcon (otter's son) gave Alterin alla bhethe (birch-cliff) na camone as far as the birch-tree between (the) two Alterins. Domnall and Cathal gave Etdanin to God and to Drostán·Cainnech and Domnall and Cathal immolated all these offerings to God and to Drostán from beginning · to end in freedom from mormaer and from toisech to (the) day of judgment." ·

Gartnait mac cannech acuséte ingengillemíchel dóratsat petmeccóbrig ricosecrad éclasi críst acuspetir abstoil acusdocolumcille acusdodrostan sér ónáhulib dolodib cónánascad dócórmac éscob dunicallenn·inócmad bliádi· rigi·dá Testibus istis·néctan·escop abberdeon·acusléot áb brécini acusmáledouni mac mic bead·acusálgune mac árcill·acusrúadri mórmar márr acusmatadin bríthem·acusgillecríst mac córmaic·acusmalpetir mac domnaill·acusdomongart ferleginn turbruad·acusgillecolaim mac muredig· acusdubni mac mál colaim

Dorat gartnait acusingengillemicel báll dómin ipet ipáir docrist acusdocolimcilli acusdodrostan Teste·gillecalline sacart·acusferadac mac málbrícin·acus malgirc mac tralin

"Gartnait son of Cainnech and Ete daughter of Gille Michel gave Pet-mec-Cobrig for (the) consecration of a Church of Christ and Peter (the) apostle both to Columcille and to Drostán free from all the exactions (?) With the gift (?) of them to Cormac Bishop of Dunkeld in the eighth year of David's reign. *Testibus istis* Nectán Bishop of Aberdeen, and Leot Abbot of Brechin, and Maledoun son of Mac Be[th]ad, and

Algune son of Arcell, and Ruadri mormaer of Mar and Matadin (the Brehon and Gille Christ son of Cormac, and Mael-petir son of Domnall, and Domongart ferleginn (reader) of Turbruad and Gillecolaim son of Muredach, and Dubni son of Maelcolaim·

Gartnait and the daughter of Gillemichel gave *Ball Domin* in Pet Ipuir to Christ and to Columcille and to Drostan.

Teste Gillecalline, Priest, and Feradach son of Maelbhricin, and Maelgire son of Tralin."

Fol. 4 b. ACUSBENNACT INCHOMDED ARCECMORMAR ACUSARCECTOSECH CHOMALLFAS ACUSDANSIL DANEIS.

"AND THE LORD'S BLESSING ON EVERY MORMAER AND ON EVERY TOISECH WHO SHALL FULFIL (THIS) AND TO THEIR SEED AFTER THEM."

Donchad mac mec bead mec hídid dorat acchad madchór docrist acusdodrostan acusdocholuimcille insóre gobrád malechí acuscómgell acusgillecrist mac fingúni innáienasi intestes·acus malcoluim mac molíní·Cormac mac cennedig dorat goñige scáli merlec·Comgell mac cáennaig táesec clande canan dórat docrist acusdodrostán acusdócholuim cille gonige ingort lie mór igginn infius isnesu daldín alenn ódubúci gólurchárí etarsliab acusachad·• issaeri othesseach cubráth acusabennacht arcachhén chomallfas araer cubrath acusamallact arcachén ticfa ris ;•

Donchad son of Mac Bethad son of Ided gave Achad Madchor to Christ and to Drostán and to Columcille in freedom for ever: Malechi and Comgell and Gille-Christ son of Fingune in witness whereof in testimony, and Maelcoluim son of Molíne·Cormac son of Cennedig gave as far as Scale Merlech·Comgell son of Caennech, chief of Clan Canan, gave to Christ and to Drostán and to Columcille as far as the Gort-lie-Mór at (the) hither (?) End which is nearest to Aldin Alenn from Dobaci to Lurchari both mountain and field • in freedom from chief for ever; and his blessing on every one who shall fulfil (this) and his curse on every one who shall go against it."•

Robaid colbain mormær buchan acuseua ingen gartnait abenphústa Fol. 5.
acusdonnachac mac sithig tœsech clenni morgainn nahuli edbarta ri día acusridrostán acus riacolumcilli acusrípetar apstal onahulib dolaidib archuit cetri dabach do nithíssad ardmandaidib alban cucotchenn acusarhardchellaib·Testibus his broccin acuscormac abb turbruaid acusmorgunn mac donnchid acusgilli petair mac donnchaid acusmalæchín acusda mac matni acusmathe buchan huli naiaidnaisse in helaín ;–

Colbain mormaer of Buchan, and Eva daughter of Garnait, his wedded wife, and Donnachac, son of Sithech, chief of Clann Morgainn, immolated all the offerings to God and to Drostán and to Columcille and to Peter the apostle from all the burthens for a share of four davochs of what would come on the chief residences of Scotland generally and on chief churches, *Testibus his* Broccín and Cormac Abbot of Turbrúaid and Morgunn, son of Donchad, and Gille-Petair son of Donnchad, and Malaechin, and Matne's two sons, and (the) nobles of Buchan, all in witness hereof in Elan.

Dauid·rex scottorum omnibus probis hominibus suis·salutes Fol. 40.
Sciatis quod clerici·dedér·sunt quieti etimmunes abomni laicorum officio·etexactione indebita sicut inlibro eorum scribtum est·etdirationauerunt apud·bánb·etiurauerunt apud abberdeon·quapropter firmiter precipio·utnullus eis·aut eorum catellis·aliquam iniuriam inferre presumat·Teste·gregorio episcopo·deduncallden·Teste·andrea episcopo·decat'·Teste·samsone episcopo·debrechin·Teste·doncado comite·deffb·etmalmori·dathótla·etggillebrite·comite·déngus·etghgillcomded·mac æd·etbrocin·etcormac·deturbrud·etadam·mac·ferdomnac·etgillendrias·mac·mátni·apud·abberdeon·